PROPHETIC COUNSEL *for* AMERICA

Daily Sermons & Inspired Thoughts

MARY JANE WOODGER

CFI
An imprint of Cedar Fort, Inc.
Springville, Utah

Paperback ISBN 13: 978-1-4621-4995-7
Ebook ISBN 13: 978-1-4621-4996-4

Published by CFI, an imprint of Cedar Fort, Inc.
2373 W. 700 S., Suite 100 Springville, UT 84663
Distributed by Cedar Fort, Inc., www.cedarfort.com

Library of Congress Registration Number: 2025945541

Cover design by Shawnda Craig

Printed in the United States of America

10 9 8 7 6 5 4 3 2 1

Printed on acid-free paper

PROPHETIC COUNSEL *for* AMERICA

Daily Sermons & Inspired Thoughts

Acknowledgments

Any book is collaboration and an unconscious recipient of indebtedness to others such as these great supporters and so many others. I am grateful to Tony Sweat, my department chair (Church History and Doctrine Department, Brigham Young University) for providing a CORE Grant and an Experiential Learning Grant that greatly enhanced the learning of a team of students who helped create this volume.

I appreciate my student assistants who were always cheerful, dependable, and intelligent. Katelynn Barton, Donovan Blackham, Mia Watson Blackham, Madeline Briggs, Derek Charlton, Andrew Cheney, Ian Eliason, Eli Gurney, Maylan Kunkel, Elizabeth Long, Annie Meek, Anna Pomares, Madison Searle, Tanner Stott, and Zoey Slaughter participated in varying degrees over the last three years in the large task of researching, finding, selecting, typing, and analyzing the material in this manuscript. I also acknowledge the assistance received from a variety of "This Day in History" websites.

I am indebted to Kyle Lund, editor-in-chief, Cedar Fort Publishing & Media for supporting my vision by bringing *Prophetic Counsel for America—Daily Sermons & Inspired Thoughts* to publication.

Introduction

This book is being published in honor of the 250th anniversary of the writing and signing of the Declaration of Independence. I hope that the profound thoughts and admonitions included in these pages will be read and pondered for many years to come.

This 250th anniversary is worth noting. Whereas 100 years is a centennial and one 150 years is a sesquicentennial, there are several terms that can refer to a 250th anniversary. Here are some of them:

Sestercentennial: a word derived from Latin, meaning "two and a half centuries."
Semiquincentennial: another Latin-based term, meaning "half of 500 years."
Quarter Millennium: a straightforward term emphasizing a 250-year milestone.
Bisesquicentennial: a less common term, also rooted in Latin.

From the earliest days of The Church of Jesus Christ of Latter-day Saints, there has been a deep connection between the United States of America and the prophets of God. In July 1840, Martha Jane Knowlton Coray recorded Joseph Smith's teaching that "even this Nation will be on the very verge of crumbling to pieces and tumbling to the ground and when the constitution is upon the brink of ruin this people will be the Staff up[on] which the nation shall lean and they shall bear away the constitution away from the very verge of destruction."[1]

Historian Donald Q. Cannon's 1991 volume *Latter-day Saint Prophets and the United States Constitution* observed that eight prophets quoted Joseph Smith's comments about the Constitution one day hanging by a thread. Twelve additional prophets prophesied that the Constitution would be in future jeopardy and then rescued by the elders of Israel.[2]

You might ask, Why is it necessary to have a book of quotations from Church leaders about America?[*] My purpose is to help readers understand more fully the counsel General Authorities of The Church of Jesus Christ of Latter-day Saints have given to American citizens.

In October 1987, President Ezra Taft Benson made us aware of the importance of this topic when he asked, "Do we know what the prophets have said about the Constitution and the threats to it?"[3] It is my hope that this volume

* Spelling, capitalization, and punctuation have been standardized.

will help you increase your knowledge of what prophets, apostles, and general authorities have taught about this nation and the responsibility Latter-day Saints have in supporting it.

The timing of this volume is especially important. As Thomas Griffith, a former United States federal judge, observed, "Right now, we live in a moment where there are people who are trying to drain all trust from the system. There has never been such fundamental distrust of our fundamental institutions or in our being able to follow the Constitution."[4]

I feel an urgency and a timeliness to share this important prophetic counsel. Current events transpiring in our national discourse necessitate studying what Church leaders have taught. Never has there been such a need to have their words in our minds. In publishing this collection, I hope to "awaken a sleeping and apathetic people to the alarming conditions that are rapidly advancing about us."[5]

Readers will find that these sources teach important truths. These quotes can help you reflect on the importance of the American nation, increase your desire to defend and preserve the Constitution, and help you rededicate yourself to the lofty principles in that divinely inspired document. I hope that by gaining increased familiarity with this counsel, you will seek to protect, defend, and uphold the Constitution of the United States—the instrument that enabled the restoration of The Church of Jesus Christ of Latter-day Saints.

This book is an invitation to reflect on both the Declaration of Independence and the Constitution of the United States that God "suffered to be established . . . for the rights and protection of all flesh, according to just and holy principles" (Doctrine and Covenants 101:77). It is my hope that these prophetic words will bring an increased sense of understanding to members of The Church of Jesus Christ of Latter-day Saints regarding our opportunity to teach these principles and, as President Russell M. Nelson counseled, to "choose to be a peacemaker, now and always."[6]

—*Mary Jane Woodger*

We Shall Build the Zion of the Lord

We shall build the Zion of the Lord in peace until the servants of that Lord shall begin to lay the foundation of a great and high watchtower, and then shall they begin to say within themselves what need hath my Lord of this tower seeing this is a time of peace.

Then the enemy shall come as a thief in the night and scatter the servants abroad. When the seed of these twelve olive trees are scattered abroad, they will wake up the nations of the whole earth. Even this nation will be on the very verge of crumbling to pieces and tumbling to the ground, and when the Constitution is upon the brink of ruin, this people will be the staff up[on] which the nation shall lean and they shall bear the Constitution away from the very verge of destruction.

Then shall the Lord say, "Go tell all my servants who are the strength of mine house my young men and middle aged. Come to the land of my vineyard and fight the battle of the Lord. Then the kings and queens shall come. Then the rulers of the earth shall come. Then shall all Saints come; yea, the foreign Saints shall come to fight for the land of my vineyard, for in this thing shall be their safety and they will have no power to choose but will come as a man fleeeth from a sudden destruction. . . . You say among yourselves as did them of old time, is it I, and is it I? But I know these things by the visions of the Almighty.[7]

—*Joseph Smith, Jr.*

THIS DAY IN AMERICAN HISTORY (1863)

Abraham Lincoln issues the Emancipation Proclamation.

JANUARY 2

The Present Hostility in Public Dialogues Is Alarming

Anger never persuades. Hostility builds no one. Contention never leads to inspired solutions.

True charity towards all men is the hallmark of peacemakers! It is imperative that we have charity in our discourse, both public and private. I thank those of you who took my previous counsel to heart. But we can still do better.

The present hostility in public dialogue and on social media is alarming. Hateful words are deadly weapons. Contention prevents the Holy Ghost from being our constant companion.

As followers of Jesus Christ, we should lead the way as peacemakers. As charity becomes part of our nature, we will lose the impulse to demean others. We will stop judging others. We will have charity for those from all walks of life. Charity towards all men is essential to our progress. Charity is the foundation of a godly character.

Let us plead with our Heavenly Father to fill our hearts with greater charity—especially for those who are difficult to love—for charity is a gift from our Heavenly Father for true followers of Jesus Christ. The Savior is the Prince of Peace. We are to be His instruments for peace.[8]

—Russell M. Nelson

THIS DAY IN AMERICAN HISTORY (1788)

Georgia ratifies U.S. Constitution 26–0 and receives statehood as the 4th state.

Obedience to the Unenforceable

So it is that whenever we talk about patriotism, the risks are that we will define it too narrowly. It is not that any particular dimension of patriotism is unworthy. Rather, no one portion of patriotism comprises the whole of patriotism. For instance, we would all quickly agree that patriotism is more than paying taxes. It is likewise more than voting. Yet it includes these along with all the other unglamorous chores of citizenship. Patriotism requires public perspiration as well as an educated public who truly can see beyond the years.

Besides, the perspective of patriotism is vital because democracy and memory are not automatic partners. Tocqueville observed of America, "Not only does democracy make every man forget his ancestors, but it hides his descendants and separates his contemporaries from him. It throws him back forever upon himself alone and threatens in the end to confine him entirely within the solitude of his own heart." Such loneliness, ladies and gentlemen, increases selfishness. . . .

How are we doing with those years wherein we are set? As we sing the words "Confirm thy soul in self-control," what of our society's increasing lack of impulse control? So many people act out their impulses in so many inappropriate and destructive ways, including the neglect of families and children.

More than we realize, our whole society really rests on the capacity of its citizens to give what is called obedience to the unenforceable. We do this by complying willingly with the law and behaving voluntarily according to time-tested standards. Such citizenship expresses a high form of volunteerism.[9]

—Neal A. Maxwell

THIS DAY IN AMERICAN HISTORY (1861)

Delaware legislature rejects proposal to join the Confederacy.

This Church's Great Efforts to Promote Religious Freedom

Most are aware of this Church's great efforts to promote religious freedom. These efforts are in furtherance of our Heavenly Father's plan. We seek to help *all* of His children—not just our own members—enjoy the precious freedom to choose.

Similarly, we are sometimes asked why we send missionaries to so many nations, even among Christian populations. We are also asked why we give enormous humanitarian aid to persons who are not members of our Church without linking this to our missionary efforts. We do this because the Lord has taught us to esteem all of His children as our brothers and sisters, and we want to share our spiritual and temporal abundance with everyone.

Eternal doctrine also provides a distinctive perspective on children. Through this perspective we see the bearing and nurturing of children as part of the divine plan. It is a joyful and sacred duty of those given the power to participate in it. Therefore, we are commanded to teach and contend for principles and practices that provide the best conditions for the development and happiness of children under God's plan.[10]

—*Dallin H. Oaks*

THIS DAY IN AMERICAN HISTORY (1777)

Utah receives statehood as the 45th state.

We Need the Constitution and Its Guarantees in Freedom

The first Congress of the United States, when it began to consider the operations of the government under the Constitution, became impressed that there was not in that document, as originally drawn, any so-called Bill of Rights; there were in the document no provisions which should keep the people free, which should protect them in their daily lives, nor guarantee to them the great liberties which the Declaration of Independence declared were the heritage of men. Accordingly, this Congress proposed to the original states the first ten amendments to the Constitution, and it is significant, I am sure, of the influence which the Lord was at that time bringing to bear upon the minds of men, that the very first clause of the very first amendment declared:

"Congress shall make no law respecting an establishment of religion or prohibiting the free exercise thereof."

Thus, the very first thing which our fathers sought to secure for themselves and for their posterity was freedom to worship as they wished. I do not need to call to your minds the trials and persecution which this people have suffered in the past, in order to bring home to you the conviction that nothing else in the great document, the Constitution, is so important to this people as is this guarantee of religious freedom, because underneath and behind all that lies in our lives, all that we do in our lives, is our religion, our worship, our belief and faith in God. We need the Constitution and its guarantees of liberty and freedom more than any other people in the world, for, few and weak as we are, we stand naked and helpless except when clothed with its benign provisions.[11]

—J. Reuben Clark Jr.

THIS DAY IN AMERICAN HISTORY (1788)

The Connecticut Constitution Ratifying Convention begins.

God Raised Up America, with a Definite Purpose in Mind

As Latter-day Saints in America we are both citizens of the kingdom of God and of the nation which He founded.

God raised up America, with a definite purpose in mind. And He raised up the Founding Fathers to write an inspired document which has served us well as our national Constitution. He has seen us through war after war when our liberties have been challenged. He literally both "made and preserved us a nation."

Many of our great leaders of the past have told us that our nation will never be conquered from without, but they have warned that it might easily disintegrate from within. They have said further that such disintegration would begin, if ever it should come, with our failure to recognize the Almighty as our Founder, and to serve Him and uphold His precepts.

If America is to save itself, this is one of the points on which she must act, and now. America cannot survive in immorality. It must return to the chastity taught in the scriptures.

And neither can America survive in the "new freedom" which would promote anarchy and a breakdown of law and order. There can be no immunity from the law for anyone. Political expediency cannot justify it. Constitutional law was established "for the rights and protection of all flesh, according to just and holy principles," the Lord declared.[12]

—Mark E. Peterson

THIS DAY IN AMERICAN HISTORY (1959)

Alaska receives statehood as the 49th state.

The Constitution of the United States Was Inspired by God

Every faithful Latter-day Saint believes that the Constitution of the United States was inspired of God, and that this choice land and this nation have been preserved until now in the principles of liberty under the protection of God. . . .

These principles are fundamental to our belief, fundamental to our protection. And in the providences of the Lord, the safeguards which have been incorporated into the basic structure of this nation are, if we preserve them, the guarantee of all men who dwell here against abuses, tyrannies, and usurpations. From my childhood days I have understood that we believe absolutely that the Constitution of our country is an inspired instrument, and that God directed those who created it and those who defended the independence of this nation. . . .

And such the Constitution of the United States must be to every faithful Latter-day Saint who lives under its protection. That the Lord may help him to think straight, and to pursue a straight course regardless of personal advantage, factional interest, or political persuasion, should be the daily prayer of every Latter-day Saint. I counsel you, I urge you, I plead with you, never, so far as you have voice or influence, permit any departure from the principles of government on which this nation was founded, or any disregard of the freedoms which, by the inspiration of God our Father, were written into the Constitution of the United States.[13]

—*Heber J. Grant*

THIS DAY IN AMERICAN HISTORY (1953)

President Harry Truman announces the American development of the hydrogen bomb.

Civility Is What Gives Savor to Our Lives

Much closer to home, civility appears to be fading. Witness the recent growth of gangs in this country. Their members show no respect for their enemies and little respect for life. They mar beautiful walls and buildings with ugly graffiti, and they evidently think only in terms of self. Crime is essentially an absence of civility. . . . All of this speaks of anything but refinement. It speaks of anything but courtesy. It speaks of anything but civility and tolerance. Rather, it speaks of rudeness and crudeness and an utter insensitivity to the feelings and rights of others. . . .

Civility, I submit, is what gives savor to our lives. It is the salt that speaks of good taste, good manners, good breeding. It becomes an expression of the Golden Rule: "Therefore all things whatsoever ye would that men should do to you, do ye even so to them" (Matthew 7:12). Civility covers a host of matters in how one human being relates to another with basic human kindness and goodness. Civility requires us to restrain and control ourselves, and at the same time to act with respect towards others.[14]

—Gordon B. Hinckley

THIS DAY IN AMERICAN HISTORY (1790)

President Washington delivers the First State of the Union address.

A Patriotism Born of an Understanding of the Ultimate Destiny of This Land

A pronouncement of the faith and understanding of the Latter-day Saints concerning the destiny of this land of America comes at a time when it may not be easy for those without this understanding to have full faith and confidence in the future of our democracy. We in America have viewed great depressions; we remember the armies of the unemployed and restless who have frequently raised strange flags of sedition above fearful masses of people.

[These] and other similar conditions indicate to the thinking person a day of reckoning that may result in near-chaotic conditions that God in His mercy may not turn aside from us. Indeed, it has been said by a prophet in our generation that the time would come when the destiny of this nation would hang as by a single thread, but that it would be saved by the people who possessed faith in America and in her destiny.

And what is to be that destiny? It is the patriotism possessed by this people and an expression of their faith in the promises of the Lord concerning the place that this great country and its people may occupy in the moving drama of God's dealings with men and nations. We Latter-day Saints believe that we have come to a time when we need to do more to demonstrate our patriotism than merely wave the flag and doff our hats at its passing and join lustily in singing the strains of patriotic songs. We believe that the American people must subscribe to a patriotism born of an understanding of the ultimate destiny of this land. . . .

To the pioneers of 1847, this land of America was to be a choice land above all other lands as an inheritance to the faithful of the Lord. It was to be a land of liberty upon which no king should ever rule. It would be so fortified against all other nations that whosoever would raise up a king or would fight against this nation should perish, because the Lord, the king of heaven, was to be their king. (See 2 Nephi 10:10–14.) To them, this was the land of Zion, a land of peace, a city of refuge, a place of safety.[15]

—*Harold B. Lee*

THIS DAY IN AMERICAN HISTORY (1777)

Washington and the American Army winters in Morristown, New Jersey.

The Strength of Democracy Rests in the Ordinary Family

Some years ago, President Boyd K. Packer published a book entitled *Let Not Your Heart Be Troubled.* In one of the chapters in that book he made reference to Joseph Smith's prophecies about the Constitution. He then added some great counsel for those of us who are living in the days when his prophecies are being fulfilled:[16]

"It has been prophesied that the Constitution of the United States will hang by a thread and that the elders of Israel will step forth to save it. In my mind that does not require a few heroes in public office steering some saving legislation through the halls of Congress, neither some brilliant military leaders rallying our defense against an invading army. In my mind, it could well be brought about by the rank and file of men and women of faith who revere the Constitution and believe that the strength of democracy rests in the ordinary family and in each member of it."[17]

—Gerald N. Lund

THIS DAY IN AMERICAN HISTORY (1878)

The U.S. Senate first proposes female suffrage.

Build Even More Securely on the Foundations Laid by the Faith and Devotion of Your Pioneer Fathers

Someone has said, "He who carries the lamp will not despair no matter how dark the night. That lamp I call faith" (Myron C. Taylor). I have faith in the future of this promised land of America and in its institutions of representative government, but more than that, I have faith in you, the youth of America, to build even more securely on the foundations laid by the faith and devotion of your pioneer fathers. That you as the youth of the Church would have an important part to play in preserving the ideals of this great country as quoted by one who was very close to him. I quote the words of Eliza R. Snow: "I heard the Prophet Joseph Smith say 'that the time would come when this nation would so far depart from its original purity, its glory, and its love of freedom and the protection of civil and religious rights, that the Constitution of our country would hang, as it were, by a thread.' He also said that this people, the sons of Zion, would rise up and save the Constitution and bear it off triumphantly" (Eliza R. Snow, 1870, *Women of Mormondom* by Tullidge).

So today is no time for youth to whimper the refrain of the defeated and retire to the fancied security of the regimented state. Today is the day for youth to gird themselves with the armor of peace, having as their weapons "the shield of faith: and the sword of the Spirit, which is the word of God" (Ephesians 6:16–17).[18]

—Harold B. Lee

THIS DAY IN AMERICAN HISTORY (1916)

New Mexico receives statehood as the 47th state.

The Bill of Rights Are Divinely Inspired

President Clark was fully aware of the way in which the Bill of Rights had entered the Constitution. Yet, it was his firm belief that the Bill of Rights, no less than the body of the Constitution, fell within the definition of being divinely inspired. He bore his testimony in April Conference of 1957 that the "Constitution of the United States as it came from the hands of the framers, with its coterminous Bill of Rights," was an integral part of his religious faith. "It is," he said, "a revelation from the Lord. I believe and reverence its God-inspired provisions." Since for President Clark the whole concept of limited government was a divinely inspired idea, it is only logical that he should believe that the Bill of Rights, which is the concrete manifestation of that tradition, should warrant the title of "inspired."

Central to the concept of limited government, and in President Clark's eyes, no less important than the separation of powers, was the doctrine represented by the Bill of Rights that there are some areas of human life in which the government has no right to interfere. This concept assumes that the individual is morally supreme and that his moral life can never be invaded by the state. This moral life finds its expression in the exchange of ideas and in the exercise of religion. Therefore, it is in these realms of human existence that the conflict between the state and the individual is the sharpest. Moreover, it is precisely in his moral life that the state seeks to restrict the individual, because it is the individual's claim to moral supremacy which undermines the state's demands that its existence is a transcendent end to which the rights of the individual must be subordinated. In the mid-thirties, President Clark put the matter squarely when he observed that, "the greatest struggle which now rocks the whole earth more and more takes on the character of a struggle of the individual versus the state." He went on to ask: "Does the individual exist for the benefit of the state or does the state exist for the benefit of the individual?" There is no doubt, of course, where President Clark stood on the matter, since the whole of his political and religious philosophy rested on the notion of the moral supremacy of the individual.[19]

—J. Reuben Clark Jr.

THIS DAY IN AMERICAN HISTORY (1906)

The first time the Dow Jones industrial average closes above 100.

The Weed of Tyranny and the Wheat of Democracy

I do not believe that God ever planted the plant of tyranny or kingly despotism. That is a weed that He has permitted to grow up, and you know how careful He is not to prematurely root up, as evinced by His own teaching to the people in that wonderful parable of the wheat and the tares. The impetuous disciples would have rushed into the field to pluck up the tares, but He forbade them, saying, "Let both grow together until the harvest" and explained to them that any forceful extirpation of the tares would have imperiled the wheat.

Never before, since the days of the Son of Man in the flesh, has the earth been prepared for the kind of government that shall be established abroad as it has been established here. Fifty years ago, twenty years ago, ten years ago, to have attempted forcibly to extirpate the weeds of autocracy would have imperiled the wheat of real democracy. There is a wonderful element of timeliness in all the doings of God, and He doeth all things well, and in the right season.

The gospel of Jesus Christ is given of God; it is eternal. Have you ever found a single passage in holy writ that indicates in the least degree any revision or alteration of the fundamental laws and principles of the gospel? Have you ever found it necessary for God to amend Himself and His words? Men make constitutions and enact laws, and then have to repeal and alter them, but the fundamental laws of truth are eternal; they will never be amended, they will never be changed.[20]

—James E. Talmage

THIS DAY IN AMERICAN HISTORY (1789)

First presidential electors chosen.

The Constitution Was Dictated by the Spirit of Wisdom

I will express my ideas, or rather a few of them, in regard to the Constitution of our own country, and its political principles, of their effects, and of the results of the movements which gave rise to that Constitution. The longer I live, and the more acquainted I am with men and things, the more I realize that these movements, and particularly that instrument called the Constitution of American Liberty, was certainly dictated by the spirit of wisdom, by a spirit of unparalleled liberality, and by a spirit of political utility. And if that Constitution be carried out by a just and wise administration, it is calculated to benefit not only all the people that are born under its particular jurisdiction, but all the people of the earth, of whatever nation, kindred, tongue, religion, or tradition, that may seek to take a shelter under its banner. It seems broad enough, and large enough, to receive and protect all that may be in any way deprived of the common rights of man. It was doubtless dictated by the spirit of eternal wisdom, and has thus far proved itself adequate to the wants of the nation, and to the wants of all mankind that have seen fit to attach themselves to it, to come under its protection, and share in its blessings.

The great question, as has been before observed today more than once, is, not the operations of the instruments, the beauty of the writing, the formation of the language, or the principle of liberty guaranteed therein, but the administration of those principles. For instance, paper itself cannot enforce its own precepts; and unhallowed principles in the people, or in the rulers which they choose, may pervert any form of government, however sacred, true, and liberal. They may overthrow and destroy the practical working of those very principles, which are so true, and so dear to us, and in which we so rejoice. It is the living administration, after all, that is the government, although a good form opens the way for good results, if carried out; but if not carried out, the form becomes a dead letter. Much depends on the feeling and action of the people in their choice of men and measures, and much depends on the administration of those they may choose.[21]

—Parley P. Pratt

THIS DAY IN AMERICAN HISTORY (1783)

U.S. Congress of the Confederation ratifies the Treaty of Paris, ending the Revolutionary War.

We Must Protect This American Base

How will we protect this base of operations [the United States of America]? We must protect this base of operations from every threat—from sin, from unrighteousness, immorality, from desecration of the Sabbath day, from lawlessness, from parental and juvenile delinquency.

We must protect this American base from the brain-washing, increasingly administered to our youth in many educational institutions across the land, by some misinformed instructors and some wolves in sheep's clothing. Their false indoctrination, often perpetrated behind the front of so-called academic freedom, is leaving behind many faithless students, socialist-oriented, who are easy subjects for state tyranny. [22]

—Ezra Taft Benson

THIS DAY IN AMERICAN HISTORY (1943)

The Pentagon, the world's largest office building is completed.

We Will Never Permit the Enslavement of the Human Race

What will be the outcome of the awful strife now raging? Will the world be "made safe for democracy," or will it be ground under the iron heel of an autocratic military despotism? I cannot believe that such a calamity is in store. He who died to make man free, and whose gospel is "the perfect law of liberty," will never permit the enslavement of the human race. He who in the beginning instituted laws for man's advancement will never tolerate such a turning back of the wheels of eternal progress. Having decreed the world's emancipation from every form of misrule, he will never allow the enthronement of universal tyranny. . . . Nevertheless, He will accomplish in his own way the work that he has set his hand to do, and will use this people and all peoples in the process. . . .

A greater warfare is in progress than now shakes the shores of Europe—a warfare whose beginning was coeval with the foundation of the world. Far greater than any strife between man and man, is the world-old controversy between God and Satan, between freedom and oppression, between right and wrong. And right will triumph, and God will be glorified. The world will be made safe for democracy—safe for all righteous institutions. Israel will be gathered, Zion redeemed, and the way prepared for the King of kings and the Millennial reign of universal freedom and peace.[23]

—*Orson F. Whitney*

THIS DAY IN AMERICAN HISTORY (1788)

Connecticut ratifies the U.S Constitution and receives statehood as the 5th state.

The Constitution as Written by the Inspiration of Heaven Must Be Preserved

Oh, that all men who are citizens of this favored land could learn the lessons taught by their noble ancestors and could understand that our inheritance in this land of liberty is not merely liberty and freedom that are bequeathed to us without effort on our part, even as the air we breathe. The only true inheritance we have from our pioneer heritage is the knowledge and understanding that the basic principles of courage, honesty, integrity, virtue, and charity are the verities that have made men free. In our veins runs the blood of a virile ancestry, and in our sinews their strength that gives to us, as their descendants, the will to do and the capacity to achieve, even as they have achieved.

We believe that no American citizen who has the same faith as those early pioneers can be true to the teachings handed down to them without having a love for this country and its institutions. In this land, we, together with all those who form the citizenship of this country, are dwelling "in the secret place of the most High" and in "the shadow of the Almighty." (Psalm 91:1.)

May I voice a plea for all Americans to love this country with a fervor that will inspire each to so live as to merit the favor of the Almighty during this time of grave uncertainties, as well as in times to come. I would that all men could believe in the destiny of America as did the early pioneers: that it is the land of Zion; that the founders of this nation were men of inspired vision; that the Constitution as written by the inspiration of heaven must be preserved at all costs. I make a further plea that the citizens of this favored land live righteously that they might enjoy the fruits of their righteousness in this land of promise.

Love the Lord thy God with all thy heart, with all thy might, mind, and strength, and in the name of Jesus Christ, serve Him.[24]

—Harold B. Lee

THIS DAY IN AMERICAN HISTORY (1920)

The prohibition of alcohol takes effect as a result of the U.S. Constitution's 18th Amendment.

God Grant Us Wisdom

I ask each of you now to consider with me for a few moments one of our most precious possessions—our citizenship in the United States of America, this nation under God.

A very fine man who came to the United States a few years ago from a foreign country and who now has his citizenship papers remarked to me that next to God and his loved ones, he considered his citizenship in the United States as his most precious and priceless possession. Yes, his most precious and priceless possession! He said he loved the United States and was grateful for the freedom that it afforded him, because, you see, he had lived in a country where he did not know that freedom. When he said that he loved the United States and that he thanked God for his citizenship in this country, he said it with every fiber of his soul. He said he would fight for this country and this freedom, even if it meant his own life. He said that every citizen of the United States ought to feel that way; and if he did feel that way, talked that way, and loved that way, we would have no problem from within and no fear from without. Yes, this nation under God means exactly what it says.

Let me quote from the Doctrine and Covenants:

"Let no man break the laws of the land, for he that keepeth the laws of God hath no need to break the laws of the land" (D&C 58:21). . . .

We believe in the United States of America without reservations. This nation under God is my home, my country, my hope, and my concern. Here I work and rest and pray, and here I build and dream. Here my toil is rewarded by an unmatched abundance for my wellbeing. Here I have freedom to live, to think, to worship. That freedom is mine yet, guaranteed by the law in this nation under God. Here I am a part of the government, able to vote, to serve, and to carry my share of the common load.

God grant us wisdom and strength to safeguard our country's welfare and to develop a devotion to measure up to this country's greatness.

God bless America. May we live in such a way that next to God and our loved ones, as my good friend said to me, this country, this nation under God, will be nearer and dearer to us.[25]

—*Thorpe B. Isaacson*

THIS DAY IN AMERICAN HISTORY (1861)

Mississippi votes to secede.

God Recognizes the Right of the People to Govern Themselves

The Constitution of the United States inspired of God: Joseph Smith taught that the Constitution of the United States was a God-inspired instrument. "It is not right," he represents the Lord as saying, "that one man should be in bondage to another;" and hence the Constitution should be maintained for the preservation of the rights, and the protection of all flesh, "according to just and holy principles, that every man may act in doctrine and principle, pertaining to futurity, according to the moral agency which I [the Lord] have given unto him, that every man may be accountable for his own sins in the day of judgment. And for this purpose have I established the Constitution of this land by the hands of wise men whom I raised up unto this very purpose."

So Joseph Smith's disciples hold the Constitution of the United States to be inspired of God. I think sometimes, however, that we do not realize all that this truth means. We are apt to think of things en masse, and do not take the time to analyze them. What does it mean to say that the Constitution of the United States is an inspired instrument? Undoubtedly, it means primarily that God recognizes the right of the people, in their political capacity, to govern themselves. It expresses the divine belief, so to speak, in the capacity of man for self-government. It means that the people in their political affairs are sovereign; for this is the chief thing which distinguishes the American government from other political systems of government.[26]

B. H. Roberts

THIS DAY IN AMERICAN HISTORY (1861)

Florida votes to secede from the Union.

No Government Was Ever Framed So Well Adapted to Happiness

This land is a blessed land unto all the inhabitants of the earth who will act righteously but is and will be cursed to those who will not. There is a curse and a blessing upon the land. No nation can prosper in this land that works unrighteousness, and it is a painful thing to say that our own nation, unless it repents, will meet with disasters sooner or later. It pains us to say this, but it is true. God has said it. It will be true about us. This land can only be blessed to us if we work righteously. Let us turn round and oppress the weak and do wrong, and God will curse the land to us. There will be trouble in the land among the inhabitants of the earth as long as they work wickedness, just as sure as God has spoken. There has been no nation prospered as our nation has. No government was ever framed by man that is so strong and so good and well adapted to the happiness of human beings as our government is. There never was a better instrument framed for the happiness of man than the Constitution of the United States. The men who framed it were inspired of God. The men who fought the battles of the Revolution were the same. Washington was inspired of God; he was sustained by the almighty arm of God; and the defeats that the mother country received were in accordance with the plan of God. This land was kept for this purpose.[27]

—George Q. Cannon

THIS DAY IN AMERICAN HISTORY (1861)

Alabama votes to secede.

It Is a Commandment to Elect Good and Wise Leaders

We have a responsibility as Latter-day Saints to use our influence so honest men and wise men and good men will be elected to public office in the community, in the county, in the state, and in the nation. To me this commandment of God is just as binding upon the Latter-day Saints as is the law of tithing, or the Word of Wisdom, or any other commandment which the God of heaven has given us.

As I read that for the first time some years ago I thought, "What an indictment of corrupt would-be political leaders in many parts of the world—demagogues who deal in half-truths, innuendos, and falsehoods! Here the God of heaven has pointed out the type of men he wants elected to public office among his people." It is not enough, my brethren and sisters, just to stand on the sidelines and criticize what is taking place, and to point the finger of scorn at some political leader. It is our job, our duty, and our responsibility to take an active interest in these matters, and carry out the admonition and the commandment which God has given us to see to it that men of character—good men, as measured by the standards of the gospel—are elected to public office.

So, today, I would like to throw out a challenge to the elders of Israel, my brethren of the priesthood, that we put forth an effort to prepare ourselves for statesmanlike work. The Prophet Joseph, as you will recall, had something to say regarding the important part which the elders of Israel would play in the safeguarding, if not the saving, of the Constitution of this land.[28]

—*Ezra Taft Benson*

THIS DAY IN AMERICAN HISTORY (1954)

The USS *Nautilus*, the first nuclear-powered submarine, is launched in Connecticut.

Do Not Underestimate the Profound Influence of the Restored Gospel

The religious freedom established in America made possible the coming forth of the plain and precious truths of the Book of Mormon "to the convincing of the Jew and Gentile that Jesus is the Christ, the Eternal God, manifesting himself unto all nations" (preface to the Book of Mormon). These writings are to come unto the Gentiles that they may "know the decrees of God" and repent (Ether 2:11).

It is incumbent upon the members of the Church who have had the gift of religious freedom to share this knowledge and testimony with the peoples of the world. Do not underestimate the profound influence—politically and socially—of the principles of the restored gospel upon all of mankind.

The opportunity for meaningful service to others is expanding rapidly. To some of us, it's just across the street; to others, across the ocean. The destiny of many nations is now being decided. Every generation is crucial. We may not be responsible for past generations, but we cannot escape the responsibility for this present one. It is beyond our comprehension to imagine the billions of souls who depend upon us to bring them—someway, somehow—this glorious message of the gospel. Of course all people will not respond, but all must be given the opportunity to hear and respond after being taught by the Spirit of Christ.[29]

—David B. Haight

THIS DAY IN AMERICAN HISTORY (1944)

Allied Forces begin World War II, landing at Anzio, Italy.

I Invite You to Champion the Cause of Religious Freedom

Freedom of religion acts as a unifying and rallying force for shaping values and morality.

In the New Testament we read of many turning away from Jesus Christ, murmuring of His doctrine, "This is an hard saying; who can hear it?" (John 6:60).

That cry is still being heard today from those who seek to expel religion from discourse and influence. If religion is not there to help with shaping character and mediating hard times, who will be? Who will teach honesty, gratitude, forgiveness, and patience? Who will exhibit charity, compassion, and kindness for the forgotten and the downtrodden? Who will embrace those who are different yet deserving, as are all of God's children? Who will open their arms to those in need and seek no recompense? Who will reverence peace and obedience to laws greater than the trends of the day? Who will respond to the Savior's plea "Go, and do thou likewise"?

We will! Yes, brothers and sisters, we will.

I invite you to champion the cause of religious freedom. It is an expression of the God-given principle of agency.

Religious freedom brings balance to competing philosophies. The good of religion, its reach, and the daily acts of love which religion inspires only multiply when we protect the freedom to express and act on core beliefs.[30]

—*Ronald A. Rasband*

THIS DAY IN AMERICAN HISTORY (1812)

A 7.8 earthquake shakes New Madrid, Missouri.

The Constitution Paved the Way for the Restoration

If the Restoration was to happen so that the kingdom of God could spread across the world like a stone cut from the mountain without hands, as Daniel foresaw, then something had to happen first. Absolutely essential to the Restoration was a nation that guaranteed the right of its citizens to free speech, the rights of property, and especially, freedom of religion. Had the Church been restored even in the more enlightened countries of Europe at that time, it would have been quickly crushed by state-sponsored religions, which vigorously opposed the rights of other religions.

When the Founding Fathers created the Constitution in 1787 and added the Bill of Rights in 1879, the separation of church and state was firmly established in the land. Though the Founding Fathers did not realize what would come of their vision, Heavenly Father did. The Constitution, with its first ten amendments, was in place about thirty years before the young Joseph Smith went into a grove of trees and took the first step in opening a new dispensation.[31]

—Gerald N. Lund

THIS DAY IN AMERICAN HISTORY (1776)

Thomas Paine publishes his *Common Sense* pamphlet.

God's Plan of Salvation Is Only Possible Under the Free Exercise of Religion

In this country we have a history of tolerant diversity—not perfect but mostly effective at allowing persons with competing visions to live together in peace. Most of us want effective ways to resolve differences without anger and with mutual understanding and accommodation. We all lose when an atmosphere of anger or hostility or contention prevails. We all lose when we cannot debate public policies without resorting to epithets, boycotts, firings, and other intimidation of one's adversaries. We need to promote and practice the virtue of civility.

Latter-day Saints are committed to the free exercise of religion because the fulfillment of God's plan of salvation is only possible under the free exercise of religion guaranteed in our God-inspired Constitution. Thus, for us, the free exercise of religion is not just a basic and cherished principle of our Constitution; it is essential to God's plan of salvation. In pursuit of that plan, all of the children of God must be free to act upon their choices. The free exercise of religion allows all men and women to choose to develop faith in God, to worship Him, and to act on their beliefs and choices. All of this permits the children of God to become what He wants them to become.

We maintain that all citizens should be supportive of religious freedom because religion is uniquely valuable to society. Persons of faith therefore maintain that religious freedom is not just a concern of religious persons. Nonbelievers have a strong interest in religious freedom because it is a strong force for peace and stability in our pluralistic world. As one atheist observed in a recent book, "One does not have to be a religious believer to grasp that the core values of Western Civilization are grounded in religion, and to be concerned that erosion of religious observance therefore undermines these values."[32]

—*Dallin H. Oaks*

THIS DAY IN AMERICAN HISTORY (1961)

President John F. Kennedy holds the first nationally televised live presidential news conference.

JANUARY 26

The Equality of Mankind in the Gospel and Government

It was something more than a coincidence, when the Church of Christ was organized in these days, that the same principles which underlie the structure of the American government were embodied in the foundations of the work of God. I have cited two great principles to which I wish to call your attention—the equality of man and the doctrine of common consent. Thomas Jefferson affirmed, when he wrote the Declaration of Independence, that all men are created equal. We are not to understand from this that all men are alike. All men are not six feet high; all men do not weigh two hundred pounds; all are not rich; all are not poor. All men are not leaders—there are mountains and foot-hills and plains among humanity; there will always be great men and great women to be the leaders and instructors of the rest. Yes, even in a democracy, where all men are declared to be equal.

What is meant, then, by equality, as referred to in the Declaration? It is equality before the law; it means that all men are equally entitled to life, to liberty, and to the pursuit of happiness. It means that the avenues of promotion and advancement should be open to all, as God intended them to be when He sent from Heaven the gospel of salvation, which is no more nor less than a code of laws, a system of principles having in view the eternal progress of man.[33]

—*Orson F. Whitney*

THIS DAY IN AMERICAN HISTORY (1781)

American military victory at Cowpens, South Carolina.

The Creation of the Constitution Was Nothing Short of a Miracle

When the time came to sign the new Constitution, all waited to see what Washington and Franklin would do.

As they took the lead, discarded all thoughts of sectionalism, and signed the document, then and only then did the others follow.

Franklin himself regarded the creation of the Constitution as nothing short of a miracle in view of the nature of the debates. He saw in it the hand of the Almighty, despite the refusal of many of his colleagues even to join him in prayer.

It is a fact—God did raise up strong men to write the Constitution despite the antagonism of many of their colleagues. And this is all the more reason why we who live today should preserve it with equal diligence.[34]

—*Mark E. Peterson*

THIS DAY IN AMERICAN HISTORY (1926)

The U.S. Senate agrees to join the World Court.

Public Opinion Is Uneven

Public opinion is often uneven and episodic in its influence. Thomas Jefferson assumed the American people would be informed and attentive. So often we are uninformed and/or inattentive. The music democracy makes is analogous to a piano keyboard—you and I respond only when our particular key is struck; we resonate and contribute only when the issues affect us. Some keys seem persistently silent, and, thus, what we hear is a cacophony or the "chopsticks" of a few recurring keys, not Chopin—for only occasionally do we experience a chord that cuts across the keyboard and brings us together in human harmony. . . .

While representative government cannot be effective unless it does provide representation, one of the limitations of democracy that some critics have difficulty accepting is the fact that representative government is often just that—representative! The people have spoken, and some don't like what the people have said.[35]

—*Neal A. Maxwell*

THIS DAY IN AMERICAN HISTORY (1915)

The United States Coast Guard is created.

There Are No More Loyal People To Their Country On God's Earth Today Than Are The Latter-day Saints

This great American nation the Almighty raised up by the power of his omnipotent hand, that it might be possible in the latter days for the kingdom of God to be established in the earth. If the Lord had not prepared the way by laying the foundations of this glorious nation, it would have been impossible (under the stringent laws and bigotry of the monarchical governments of the world) to have laid the foundations for the coming of his great kingdom. The Lord has done this. His hand has been over this nation, and it is His purpose and design to enlarge it, make it glorious above all others, and to give it dominion, and power over the earth, to the end that those who are kept in bondage and serfdom may be brought to the enjoyment of the fullest freedom and liberty of conscience possible for intelligent men to exercise in the earth. The Church of Jesus Christ of Latter-day Saints will be a strong supporter of the nation of which we are a part, in the accomplishment of this grand purpose. There are no more loyal people to their country on God's earth today than are the Latter-day Saints to this country. There are no better, purer, or more honorable citizens of the United States to be found than are found within the pale of The Church of Jesus Christ of Latter-day Saints. I testify to this, and I know whereof I speak. We never have been enemies to our nation. We have always been true to it. But let us do right, keep the laws of God, and the laws of man, honor our membership in the kingdom of God, our citizenship in the state of Utah, and our broader citizenship in the nation of which we are a part, and then God will sustain and preserve us, and we will continue to grow as we have done from the beginning, only our future growth will be accelerated and be far greater than it has been in the past. . . . This is the Lord's work, it is not man's, and he will make it triumphant. He is spreading it abroad, and giving it deep root in the earth, that its branches may grow and spread, and its fruit be seen throughout the length and breadth of the land. [36]

—*Joseph Fielding Smith*

THIS DAY IN AMERICAN HISTORY (1991)

The Gulf War begins.

Everyone Is Accountable

The people are sovereign, and the people alone our rulers, and they appoint or elect their servants. Moreover, this Constitution provides for the freedom of the press; for freedom of speech; for freedom and independence of the individual. They guarantee religious liberty, hence a free church, as well as a free state, each independent of and separate from the other. The government is an indestructible union, composed of indestructible states. To hold that the Constitution, which provides for these things, is inspired of God, is to hold that each of these separate things, as well as a thing in mass, is ordained of God by the hands of wise men whom he raised up to establish the system of government; and denied to the people the enjoyment of the several rights, to undertake, by any means whatsoever, to sort the realization of government by the people, to attempt to defeat the expression of their will, or make it result are different from what they're untrammeled judgment would have it, is to make an infraction upon the things that have been ordained of God.

In the above quotation concerning the system of government established by the Constitution of the United States being inspired of God, we made a certain the purpose of God and the establishment of such a government. That purpose is that every man may become directly and personally responsible to God for his actions and matters relating to civil government—"that every man may be accountable for his own sins and the day of judgment."[37]

—*B. H. Roberts*

THIS DAY IN AMERICAN HISTORY (1777)

Congress sends copies of the Declaration of Independence to the States.

Be Loyal

I hope with all my soul that the members of The Church of Jesus Christ of Latter-day Saints will be loyal in their very hearts and souls, to the principles of the Constitution of our country. From them we have derived the liberty that we enjoy. They have been the means of guaranteeing to the foreigner that has come within our gates, and to the native born, and to all the citizens of this country, the freedom and liberty that we possess. We cannot go back upon such principles as these. We may go back upon those who fail to execute the law as they should. We may be dissatisfied with the decision of judges, and may desire to have them removed out of their places. But the law provides ways and means for all these things to be done under the Constitution of our country, and it is better for us to abide the evils that we have than to fly to greater evils that we know not what the results will be....

These principles that I propose to read to you are the foundation and basic principles of the Constitution of our country, and are eternal, enduring forevermore, and cannot be changed or ignored with impunity:

"And God spake all these words, saying, I am the Lord thy God which hath brought thee out of the land of Egypt, out of the house of bondage. Thou shalt have no other gods before me." . . . "Thou shalt not make unto thee any graven image of any likeness of anything that is in heaven above or that is in the earth beneath, or that is in the water under the earth."

"Thou shalt not bow down thyself to them nor serve them." . . . "Thou shalt not take the name of the Lord thy God in vain." . . . "Six days shall thou labor and do all thy work." . . . "Honor thy father and thy mother." . . . "Thou shalt not kill." . . . "Thou shalt not commit adultery." . . . "Thou shalt not steal." "Thou shalt not bear false witness against thy neighbor." "Thou shalt not covet thy neighbor's house, thou shalt not covet thy neighbor's wife, nor his man-servant, nor his maidservant, nor his ox, nor anything that is thy neighbor's" (Exodus 20:1–6).

Now, these are the commandments of God, the principles contained in these commandments of the great Eternal are the principles that underlie the Constitution of our country and all just laws.[38]

—*Joseph F. Smith*

THIS DAY IN AMERICAN HISTORY (1865)

Congress passes the 13th Amendment of the U.S. Constitution, abolishing slavery.

First Written Constitution in the World

The United States Constitution was the first written constitution in the world. It has served Americans well, enhancing freedom and prosperity during the changed conditions of more than two hundred years. Frequently copied, it has become the United States' most important export. After two centuries, every nation in the world except six have adopted written constitutions, and the U.S. Constitution was a model for all of them. No wonder modern revelation says that God established the U.S. Constitution and that it "should be maintained for the rights and protection of all flesh, according to just and holy principles" (D&C 101:77).

George Washington was perhaps the first to use the word *miracle* in describing the drafting of the U.S. Constitution. . . . It was a miracle. Consider the setting.

It was nine months before nine states had ratified, and the last of the key states was not included until a month later, when the New York convention ratified by a vote of thirty to twenty-seven. To the "miracle of Philadelphia" one must therefore add "the miracle of ratification." . . .

That the Constitution was ratified is largely attributable to the fact that the principal leaders in the states were willing to vote for a document that failed to embody every one of their preferences. . . .

One should not expect perfection—one certainly should not expect all of his personal preferences—in a document that must represent a consensus. One should not sulk over a representative body's failure to attain perfection. Americans are well advised to support the best that can be obtained in the circumstances that prevail. That is sound advice not only for the drafting of a constitution but also for the adoption and administration of laws under it.[39]

—*Dallin H. Oaks*

THIS DAY IN AMERICAN HISTORY (1779)

Delaware ratifies the Articles of Confederation.

All Good Laws Emanate from God

All good principles and laws have emanated from the Almighty, and have come to man by inspiration from Him. For instance, the government of the United States, or the Constitution, came from Him; it was given, we believe, by inspiration, and there are many things connected with the various institutions of men that are very good. There are many good laws and good institutions in the government of the United States, as well as among many other governments, but the government of the United States is one of the best that has been organized among men upon the face of the earth for many generations.

"Did the Lord have a hand in the organization of the United States government?" asks the enquirer. Yes, the Lord had a hand in framing its Constitution. Why did not the Lord at that time, introduce a perfect government—a theocracy? It was simply because the people were not prepared for it—they were too corrupt and although they had more integrity, more virtue, more honesty, and more sympathy and feeling for that which is just and upright and good, than any other portion of the inhabitants of the earth, and probably more than a great many now have, yet they were far from being prepared for the government of God, which is a government of union.

They were far from that, consequently the Lord inspired them to introduce a government that He knew would be just suited to their capacity, and hence it was that He inspired Jefferson, Washington, Franklin, and others to introduce those measures which they did, and to carry them out, and they were such as were just suited to the conditions and circumstances of the people; hence the government of the United States we, as a people, venerate and defend.[40]

—*Orson Pratt*

THIS DAY IN AMERICAN HISTORY (1848)

The Mexican War ends (Treaty of Guadalupe Hidalgo).

Types or Shadows of Things That Are to Happen in Our Day

We still reap the blessings of the U.S. Constitution more than two hundred years later. But other prophets gave warning about the land of promise (all of North and South America), which would also be applicable to the United States. For example, as the brother of Jared was being prepared to take his people to a new land, the Lord promised him that it would be "a land of promise; and whatsoever nation shall possess it shall serve God, or they shall be swept off when the fullness of his wrath shall come upon them. And the fulness of his wrath cometh upon them when they are ripened in iniquity. . . . This is a choice land, and whatsoever nation shall possess it shall be free from bondage, and from captivity, and from all other nations under heaven, if they will but serve the God of the land, who is Jesus Christ (Ether 2:9, 12)."

As we know from the Book of Mormon, when the Nephites implemented [a] new form of government they prospered greatly. But, as it often does, prosperity led to pride, and the righteousness of the people began to decline. This eventually brought them into various political crises as well as creating serious problems for the Church. Think of the king-men versus the freemen, the Gadianton robbers versus the elected government, and finally the total collapse of the government when the Gadianton robbers seized full power. These examples may serve as types or shadows of things that are to happen in our day.[41]

—Gerald N. Lund

THIS DAY IN AMERICAN HISTORY (1870, 1913)

The 15th (1870) and 16th (1913) Amendments to the U.S. Constitution are ratified.

We, Can Be and Should Be the Leaven in the Loaf for Freedom

Every Latter-day Saint has spiritual obligations in four basic areas: his home, his church, his job, and his citizenship responsibility. Each of these areas should receive consistent attention although not necessarily equal time. Are we doing our duty in these important fields? What about our citizenship responsibility—our obligation to safeguard our freedom and preserve the Constitution?

The Prophet Joseph Smith said the time would come when the Constitution would hang as it were by a thread. Modern-day prophets for the last thirty years have been warning us that we have been rapidly moving in that direction. Fortunately, the Prophet Joseph saw the part the elders of Israel would play in this crisis. Will there be some of us who won't care about saving the Constitution—others who will be blinded by the craftiness of men—and some who will knowingly be working to destroy it? He that has ears to hear and eyes to see can discern by the spirit, and through the words of God's mouthpiece, that our liberties are being taken. The enemy is amongst and upon us. Zion must awake and arouse herself.

We, the elders of Israel, can be and should be the leaven in the loaf for freedom. . . . May we as a people face courageously the challenging responsibility which faces us. "All that is necessary for the triumph of evil is that good men do nothing" (Edmund Burke). We are not here to sit by complacently while our birthright of freedom is exchanged for a mess of socialist-communist pottage.[42]

—Ezra Taft Benson

THIS DAY IN AMERICAN HISTORY (1787)

Shay's Rebellion ends.

We Are a People Who Uphold the Constitution

What about the government under which we live? Why, it is one of the very best, as to its form, that the human family have ever devised. It was founded by excellent, honorable, upright, liberal and high-minded men who, in framing the constitution, were measurably inspired by that Holy Spirit which our Father in the heavens bestows upon whom He will.

That is the view that we, as Latter-day Saints, have in regard to the fundamental or basic instrument of the government of the United States termed the Constitution; and however much we may be misrepresented, maligned, or lied about in regard to that matter, as a people we are loyal to that constitution to the minutest principle therein contained. We understand that constitution—its spirit as well as its letter—and, so far as it is observed, it is a very excellent instrument for the conducting of human affairs.

We are a people that uphold that constitution, and we ever have done so, and take great pleasure in doing so, and so also with every constitutional law; and I am at the defiance of the wide world to truthfully controvert the statement that we, as Latter-day Saints, have ever transgressed one single particle of constitutional law, or have ever had any occasion to do so, or ever will have in obeying the principles of the Gospel and laboring to build up and establish the kingdom of God on the earth.

What do you think of that? The world will tell you that we are a terrible set, that we are disloyal, ignorant, stupid, fanatical, bigoted, deceivers and deceived, and in all these statements and as many more about the Latter-day Saints, the world will lie like the devil. Now, you heard me say constitutional law. Mark it well. I understand, as a general thing, somewhat of what I am saying when I speak, and I made use of the expression understandingly. The constitutional laws of this government, what are they? They are laws enacted in pursuance of the principles couched in that constitution under the authority given the Congress of our nation to enact laws for the whole United States, and to make treaties for our government. All that is beyond that one hair's breadth is just that far usurpation, tyranny and wrong.[43]

—*Albert Carrington*

THIS DAY IN AMERICAN HISTORY (1778)

South Carolina ratifies the Articles of Confederation.

Men Are Being Made Statesmen in Spite of Themselves

As God lives the day will come that constitutional government and the rights of man will have to be maintained by the Latter-day Saints, and that at a time when there will be no other power upon this land that will be able to make headway against the tide of evil that will flood the country. And it will be due to our organization that is magnificent as our enemies freely admit. We are a consolidated power. And when anarchy reigns, as it will do, for it is coming, and every man that opens his eyes to see the evils that abound—if he does not persistently resist the truth—must have a secret dread of it in his heart, when that comes, there will be no power upon this continent that will be able to stem it, except the organization which God has given to us.

We are gaining experience day by day. God is training us in this way. We are receiving a training such as no other people receive. Men are being made statesmen in spite of themselves. . . . The day will come when we will exercise this authority in a far wider sphere than in the limited territory. The same wisdom that has maintained the organization of this people, and that enables us to withstand attacks that would swamp any other people, will enable us to act in a far more extended sphere.

There will be trouble. You may look for it. God has said it, and it will come; and the day will come, just as sure as God has spoken it, when the Latter-day Saints will be the only people upon this North American continent that will have the power to uphold constitutional government.[44]

—*George Q. Cannon*

THIS DAY IN AMERICAN HISTORY (1788)

Massachusetts ratifies the Constitution 187–168 and receives statehood.

Keep Your Ancestors in Memory

Some time ago there appeared in a local newspaper an account of an interview with an elderly statesman who wielded great influence in American politics. This elderly statesman, in explaining the reason for his determination and zeal, told of a statement his own father—now long since dead—had made to his four sons just before he died. This is what the father said: "America, with its government and constitution, is the greatest institution invented by the mind of man. If you let them touch a stick or stone of it, I will come back and haunt you."

As I thought of that statement, my mind went back to our ancestors who pioneered in this dispensation an even greater constitution than that of the American nation, even the constitution of the kingdom of God, which might be said to be another definition of the gospel of Jesus Christ. As I thought of our pioneers, I was reminded of their virtues and their accomplishments and of the underlying principles that made them willing to leave all that they possessed and even willing to sacrifice their lives, if need be, to uphold and to maintain their beliefs. As I remembered that and thought of the statement of this aged American patriot, I wondered if we might not say: "The Lord help us to keep in memory our ancestors that we might be willing to uphold and sustain, by our lives and all that we possess, that for which they gave so much."[45]

—Harold B. Lee

THIS DAY IN AMERICAN HISTORY (1795)

The 11th Amendment is ratified, affirming the power of the states.

The Power of a Righteous Minority

I once heard a man say, "Democracy is not what is written on a piece of paper. It is the expression of what is within the heart of men." Our country came into existence just that way, in that the power is resident in the people and that every right and every privilege that is given to our officers is a concession from the people

I remember reading about when in the Magna Charta, the right of kings was circumscribed in Great Britain, the voice of the people determined that certain things only could be exercised, even by men who claimed that they presided by divine right, the divine right of kings. That voice, brethren and sisters, has come down to us. It was the voice which produced the Constitution of the United States of America, the grandest country in the world, and with all its shortcomings, and with all the evil that there is in it, I believe that it comes the nearest to being a civil government that is in harmony with the principles that govern in The Church of Jesus Christ of Latter-day Saints. . . .

I fear, brethren and sisters, that we approach these topics with too much apathy. We hardly realize the power that there is in the organization which we have. Even though it be small in numbers compared to the total population of the United States, it could exercise a tremendous influence, and does, as a matter of fact, for righteousness throughout the country.[46]

Antoine R. Ivins

THIS DAY IN AMERICAN HISTORY (1779)

Delaware ratifies the Articles of Confederation.

FEBRUARY 9

There Are a Great Many More Afflictions Yet Awaiting This Nation

The gospel reveals many things to us which others are unacquainted with. I knew of those terrible events which were coming upon this nation previous to the breaking out of our great fratricidal war, just as well as I now know that they transpired, and I have spoken of them to many. What of that? Do I not know that a nation like that in which we live, a nation which is blessed with, the freest, the most enlightened and magnificent government in the world today, with privileges which would exalt people to heaven if lived up to—do I not know that if they do not live up to them, but violate them and trample them under their feet, and discard the sacred principles of liberty by which we ought to be governed—do I not know that their punishment will be commensurate with the enlightenment which they possess? I do. And I know—I cannot help but know—that there are a great many more afflictions yet awaiting this nation.

But would I put forth my hand to help bring them on? God forbid! And you, you Latter-day Saints, would you exercise your influence to the accomplishment of an object of that kind? God forbid! But we cannot help but know these things. But our foreknowledge of these matters does not make us the agents in bringing them to pass. We are told that the wicked will slay the wicked. We are told in sacred writ, "that vengeance is mine, saith the Lord, and I will repay." And in speaking of ourselves we need not be under any apprehensions pertaining to the acts of men, for the Lord has said, "It is my business to take care of my Saints;" but it is our business to be Saints.[47]

—*John Taylor*

THIS DAY IN AMERICAN HISTORY (1778)

Rhode Island ratifies the Articles of Confederation.

The Warning of This House Should Resound Through the Corridors of Every American Institution

Now I would say that in a great free country like ours, if these men advocate these suicidal and often treasonable doctrines, shouldn't every patriotic American be free to speak out against them?

At this particular moment in history the United States Constitution is definitely threatened, and every citizen should know about it. The warning of this hour should resound through the corridors of every American Institution—schools, churches, the halls of Congress, press, radio, and TV, and so far, as I am concerned it will resound—with God's help.

Wherever possible I have tried to speak out. It is for this very reason that certain people in Washington have bitterly criticized me. They don't want people to hear the message. It embarrasses them. The things which are destroying the Constitution are the things they have been voting for. They are afraid of their political careers if these facts are pointed out. They therefore try to silence any who carry the message—anyone who will stand up and be counted.

But these liberal politicians are not the only ones who are trying to silence the warning voice of American patriots. Moscow is equally alarmed. It was in 1960 when the communist leaders first decided to do something drastic about the rising tide of patriotism in the United States. . . . The more they studied the more they realized how fast communism was advancing on all fronts. They also learned to their amazement that Washington politicians were doing practically nothing about it. In fact, in many cases, they were doing things to promote communism. So, the protests began to pour into the national capital from every state in the union. All over America there was an awakening. [48]

—*Ezra Taft Benson*

THIS DAY IN AMERICAN HISTORY (1967)

The 25th Amendment to the U.S. Constitution is ratified.

FEBRUARY 11

A Peculiar People

We are a peculiar people in many ways, and in this particularly are we peculiar, in that we believe that the Constitution of the United States was inspired by our Heavenly Father, and he has told us that he raised up the very men who framed the Constitution of the United States. . . .

There is only one way whereby we may enjoy peace and happiness, and that is by observing the law of our land, and by sustaining the principles embodied in the Constitution which was inspired by our Heavenly Father at the inception of this great government. . . .

This nation was established under divine guidance, as part of our Father's plan whereby men may enjoy freedom, and where all faiths and beliefs and doctrines may enjoy liberty and be amenable to the law of the land; and where no group of individuals may array themselves against the rights and privileges of their fellows. . . .

I say to you: Sustain the Constitution of the United States, and let not our voices be heard among those that deride or would violate the Constitution that is so important for us and for all men.

I am grateful to my Heavenly Father for his advice to us that we support the Constitution of the United States and maintain the liberty that we enjoy under it.[49]

—*George Albert Smith*

THIS DAY IN AMERICAN HISTORY (1766)

The Stamp Act is declared unconstitutional in Virginia.

Because Some Americans Have Not Kept Faith with Our Founding Fathers, the Constitution Faces Severe Challenges

We encourage Latter-day Saints throughout the nation to familiarize themselves with the Constitution. They should focus attention on it by reading and studying it. They should ponder the blessings that come through it. They should recommit themselves to its principles and be prepared to defend it and the freedom it provides.

Because some Americans have not kept faith with our Founding Fathers, the Constitution faces severe challenges. Those who do not prize individual freedom are trying to erode its great principles. We believe the Constitution will stand, but it will take the efforts of patriotic and dedicated Americans to uphold it. . . . We, as Latter-day Saints, must be vigilant in doing our part to preserve the Constitution and safeguard the way of life it makes possible.

This Bicentennial year affords us renewed opportunities to learn more about this divinely inspired charter of our liberty, to speak in its defense, and to preserve and protect it against evil or destruction.

May we be worthy of the freedoms that have been provided us in our Constitution, and equal to the trials and tests that shall surely come. We truly have special and individual responsibilities to befriend and to defend that "glorious standard," our Constitution.

Our Heavenly Father raised up the men who founded this government (see D&C 101:80), thereby fulfilling the prophecy of His Beloved Son that the people "should be established in this land and be set up as a free people by the power of the Father" (3 Nephi 21:4).[50]

—Ezra Taft Benson, Gordon B. Hinckley, Thomas S. Monson

THIS DAY IN AMERICAN HISTORY (1778)

Connecticut ratifies the Articles of Confederation.

Begin Now to Reflect More Intently on the Meaning and Importance of the Constitution

On this, the 186th anniversary of the signing of the divinely inspired Constitution of the United States, we are pleased to announce the appointment of a general committee to initiate and correlate Church activities and observances in connection with the Bicentennial in 1976 of the birth of our nation.

We urge members of the Church and all Americans to begin now to reflect more intently on the meaning and importance of the Constitution, and of adherence to its principles, in giving strength not only to this country but to the entire family of nations.

In these challenging days, when there are so many influences which would divert us, there is a need to rededicate ourselves to the lofty principles and practices of our Founding Fathers. While we must never permit an erosion of the freedoms the Constitution guarantees, we cannot let permissiveness replace responsibility.[51]

—Harold B. Lee, N. Eldon Tanner, Marion G. Romney

THIS DAY IN AMERICAN HISTORY (1795)

The University of North Carolina, the first state university, opens.

Constitutional Truths Are Timeless

Nearly two hundred years ago some inspired men walked this land. Not perfect men—but men raised up by the perfect Man to perform great work. Foreordained were they to lay the foundation of this Republic. Blessed by the Almighty in their struggle for liberty and independence, the power of heaven rested on these Founders as they drafted that great document for governing men—the Constitution of the United States. Like the Ten Commandments, the truths on which the Constitution were based were timeless; and also as with the Decalogue—the hand of the Lord was in it. They filled their mission well. From them we were endowed with a legacy of liberty—a Constitutional Republic.

But today the Christian constitutionalist mourns for his country. He sees the spiritual and political faith of his fathers betrayed by wolves in sheep's clothing. He sees the forces of evil increasing in strength and momentum under the leadership of Satan, the archenemy of freedom. He sees the wicked honored and the valiant abused. He sense that his own generation faces Gethsemanes and Valley Forges that may yet rival or surpass the trials of the early apostles and the men of '76. And this gives him cause to reflect on the most basic of fundamentals –the reason for our existence. Once we understand that fundamental, the purpose for mortality, we may more easily chart a correct course in the perilous seas that are engulfing our nation.[52]

—*Ezra Taft Benson*

THIS DAY IN AMERICAN HISTORY (1859, 1916)

Oregon (1859) and Arizona (1916) receive statehood as the 33rd and 48th states, respectively.

God Has Blessed and Prospered This Nation

Neither in mental attitude nor in conduct have we been disloyal to the government under whose guarantee of religious freedom our Church was founded. The Book of Mormon proclaims America to be the land of Zion; a land dedicated to righteousness and liberty; a land of promise to certain branches of the house of Israel, and also to the Gentiles. It declares that God will fortify this land against all other nations; and "he that fighteth against Zion shall perish." By revelation to Joseph Smith the Prophet, the Lord declared that he had established the Constitution of the United States through "wise men raised up unto this very purpose."

It is also our belief that God has blessed and prospered this nation, and given unto it power to enforce the divine decrees concerning the land of Zion that free institutions might not perish from the earth. Cherishing such convictions, we have no place in our hearts for disloyal sentiments, nor is there likelihood of treason in our conduct. Were we evil-disposed toward American institutions, or disloyal to the United States, we would be recreant to those principles to which by interest and education we are attached, and would repudiate the revelations of God concerning this land.

In reaffirming our belief in the high destiny of America, our attachment to American institutions, and our loyalty to the United States, we declare that these sentiments, this loyalty, have outlived the memory of all the wrongs inflicted upon our fathers and ourselves.[53]

—*Joseph F. Smith, John R. Winder, Anthon H. Lund*

THIS DAY IN AMERICAN HISTORY (1799)

The first American printed ballots are authorized in Pennsylvania.

There Is Too Much Fruitless Carping and Criticism of America

We live in an intriguing age, a curious age in many respects, an age in which the ability and power to communicate, and therefore to influence and persuade, reign supreme. With the proliferation of technology, and the various forms of media clamoring to take advantage of it, has come an interesting side effect. It seems today that we are subjected to a constant barrage of character assassination that has nearly obscured national discussion of vital issues—issues that truly could and would improve the daily lives of men and women, boys and girls. A large factor in all of this is the media. . . . It is impossible to read the columns or listen to the commentaries without sensing that there is a terrible ailment of gloom in this land. We are constantly fed a steady and sour diet of pessimism, faultfinding, second-guessing, and evil speaking one of another. The pathetic fact is: Negativism sells. . . .

It will do us no good to be naive about the challenges we face in this country. We do have problems, and they are not a few. There are issues that demand our earnest, inspired attention. But there is too much fruitless carping and criticism of America. What might become of this land if we spoke less of its weaknesses and more of its goodness and strength, its capacity and potential? Without doubt, we shall have days of trial. So long as we have more politicians than statesmen, we shall have problems. But if we will turn our time and talents away from vituperative criticism, away from constantly looking for evil, and will emphasize instead the greater good, America will continue to go forward with the blessing of the Almighty and stand as an ensign of strength and peace and generosity to all the world. This is a great land, a choice land, a chosen land.[54]

—*Gordon B. Hinckley*

THIS DAY IN AMERICAN HISTORY (1861)

Abraham Lincoln stops his train at Westfield, New York, on his way to Washington to thank 11-year-old Grace Bedell in person for her advice to grow a beard.

We Can Dwell in Peace and Harmony

The Constitution was an instrument devised by the highest human wisdom, and was admirably adapted for the purpose for which it was designed. No better instrument was ever framed by human intellect. Under its wise provisions and guarantees, the people of every section and of every creed on this great land could dwell in peace and harmony, and enjoy the most extensive rights consistent with good order. And its benefits need not have been confined to this continent; but the people of every nation and of every land could become part of the blessings which are guaranteed, and dwell in peace and security under its aegis.

But that government which we have guaranteed to us, under our Constitution, has never been exceeded, if indeed it has ever been equal, in the liberality of its provisions for the rights and enjoyment of its citizens. Under its benign working, when properly administered, man can enjoy the most perfect liberty compatible with his well-being, and progress to the highest point of excellence and greatness attainable in a state of mortality. There are no checks, no limits to his progress. His path is unobstructed by any obstacle which perseverance and energy cannot overcome.[55]

—*George Q. Cannon*

THIS DAY IN AMERICAN HISTORY (1780)

The U. S. House of Representatives breaks an electoral college tie by electing Thomas Jefferson president over Aaron Burr.

How to Survive as a Civilized Nation

Faith, courage, and freedom represent the life elements of growth—either in man or a nation. Spiritual faith and courage were the bone and sinew of the first freedom our people enjoyed on this continent. Then, as free hard-working Americans, our growth to abundance was only a matter of time. It is most significant that during this uphill struggle by Americans to create a civilization with an abundance for all, they gave no thought to the word "ease" as it might apply to their won way of life. People who are imbued with a strong spiritual faith which, in turn, endows them with the courage to fight and win their battles for freedom and abundance, would view with contempt any person seeking an easy way through life.

It was William Penn who said that "If we will not be governed by God, we must be governed by tyrants" (*Great Quotations*, 45).

Do we dare ask ourselves if the United States, though cast in the role of a leader to preserve and strengthen world civilization, isn't itself tottering internally because too many of its citizens have abandoned the virtues that comprised the basic format of its own civilization? For instance, if spiritual faith, courage, and the willingness of our forbears to work hard were the sustaining virtues, and if, solely because of them, they were able to create our own civilization, can we now in the United States substitute for these virtues the human weaknesses of selfishness, complacency, apathy, and fear—and still hope to survive as a civilized nation?[56]

—*Ezra Taft Benson*

THIS DAY IN AMERICAN HISTORY (1887)

The Edmunds–Tucker Act becomes law.

This People Will Be the Staff upon Which the Nation Shall Lean

Even this nation will be on the very verge of crumbling to pieces and tumbling to the ground, and when the Constitution is upon the brink of ruin, this people will be the staff upon which the nation shall lean, and they shall bear the Constitution away from the very verge of destruction.

Then shall the Lord say, "Go tell all my servants who are the strength of mine house, my young men and middle aged, etc. Come to the land of my vineyard and fight the battle of the Lord." Then the kings and queens shall come. Then the rulers of the earth shall come. Then shall ail Saints come; yea, the foreign Saints shall come to fight for the land of my vineyard, for in this thing shall be their safety and they will have no power to choose but will come as a man fleeth from a sudden destruction.

But before this the time shall be these who are now my friends shall become my enemies and shall seek to take my life and there are those now before me who will more furiously pursue me and the more diligently seek my life and be more bloodthirsty upon my track than ever were the Missouri Mobbers. You say among yourselves as did them of old time, Is it I and is it I; but I know these things by the visions of the Almighty.[57]

—*Joseph Smith, Jr.*

THIS DAY IN AMERICAN HISTORY (1942)

President Franklin D. Roosevelt orders the detention and incarceration of West-Coast Japanese–Americans.

Members Are Under Divine Commandment to Revere the Constitution

We declare that no bishops or other court in this Church claims or exercises the right to supersede, annul, or modify a judgment of any civil court. Such courts, while established to regulate Christian conduct, are purely ecclesiastical, and their punitive powers go no further than the suspension or excommunication of members from Church fellowship.

That this Church, while offering advice for the welfare of its members in all conditions of life, does not claim or exercise the right to interfere with citizens in the free exercise of social or political rights and privileges. The ballot in this territory is absolutely untrammeled and secret. No man's business or other secular affairs are invaded by the Church or any of its officers. Free agency and direct individual accountability to God are among the essentials of our Church doctrine. All things in the Church must be done by common consent, and no officer is appointed without the vote of the body.

We declare that there is nothing in the ceremony of the Endowment, or in any doctrine, tenet, obligation or injunction of this Church, either private or public, which is hostile or intended to be hostile to the government of the United States.

On the contrary, its members are under divine commandment to revere the Constitution as a heaven-inspired instrument.[58]

—Wilford Woodruff

THIS DAY IN AMERICAN HISTORY (1933)

The 21st Amendment to the U.S. Constitution is proposed for ratification.

Fortify the Moral Principles upon Which This Government Was Built

The Founding Fathers clearly believed in God and His powerful influence for good upon this nation. They knew the need for a moral nation in order for the Constitution to be effective, and that morality was depended upon religion. Therefore, they supported religion in general, both in the private and public sectors, as a means to reemphasize and fortify the moral principles upon which this government was built. It was that simple and straightforward, and accordingly, it was clearly understood for the first two hundred plus years of our nation's history. Nonetheless, in recent times, some have engaged in revisionist history and unwarranted interpretations of the Constitution and have thus supplanted the original intent of our Founding Fathers with secular views that would make this a "nation without God" rather than a "nation under God." This brings to mind the warning of Isaiah: "The nations and kingdoms that will not serve thee [God] shall perish; yea, those nations shall be utterly wasted" (Isaiah 60:12; see also Psalm 127:1). Fortunately, it also brings to mind the converse promise as uttered by the Psalmist: "Blessed is the nation whose God is the Lord" (Psalm 33:12).[59]

—*Tad R. Callister*

THIS DAY IN AMERICAN HISTORY (1792)

Congress passes the Presidential Succession Act.

Religious Freedom Is Supremely Important

The guarantee of the free exercise of religion, which I will call religious freedom, is one of the supremely important founding principles in the United States Constitution, and it is reflected in the constitutions of all of our 50 states. It is the first expression in the First Amendment to the United States Constitution. As noted by many, this "pre-eminent place" identifies freedom of religion as "a cornerstone of American democracy."[1] I maintain that in our nation's founding and in our constitutional order, religious freedom, and the freedoms of speech and press associated with it in the First Amendment, are the motivating and dominating civil liberties and civil rights.

The free "exercise" of religion obviously involves both the right to choose religious beliefs and affiliations and the right to "exercise" or practice those beliefs. But in a nation with citizens of many different religious beliefs the right of some to act upon their religious principles must be qualified by the government's responsibility to protect the health and safety of all. Otherwise, for example, the government could not protect its citizens' person or property from neighbors whose religious principles compelled or justified stealing or taking human life. . . .

Religious *belief* and preaching must be protected against government action, even while the *practice* of that belief must have some limits, as I suggested earlier. But unless the guarantee of free exercise of religion gives a religious actor *greater* protection against government prohibitions than are already guaranteed to all actors by other provisions of the Constitution (like freedom of speech), what is the special value of *religious* freedom? Surely the First Amendment guarantee of free exercise of *religion* was intended to grant more freedom to religious preaching and action than to other kinds of speech and action. Treating actions based on religious belief the same as actions based on other systems of belief should not be enough to satisfy the special place of religion in the United States Constitution.[60]

—*Dallin H. Oaks*

THIS DAY IN AMERICAN HISTORY (1819)

The Adams-Onis Treaty, giving Florida to the U.S., is signed between Spain and the United States.

May We Have Sufficient Common Sense

I ask you, how do we lose the savor that followers of the Lord should have? We lose it as we cease to serve Him, or even by becoming casual in our obedience.

For example, if we become careless about attending our meetings, do we not lose some of the savor that good salt should have?

If we neglect our prayers, our tithes and offerings, what becomes of our savor? . . .

If we are dishonest, unkind, or vengeful, do we not offend the Deity? . . .

When speaking of the preservation of our place in the kingdom of God, President Heber J. Grant said:

"I have seen men, no matter how high the position . . . they have reached, neglect their duties and turn away, and become enemies of the Church" because they did not keep the commandments of God. "My most earnest prayer," President Grant continued, "is that every man and every woman will get it into his or her heart that they are in very deed the architects of their lives. . . . There are two spirits striving with all of us. There is no labor in which we engage but that there is a spirit telling us, 'Oh, you do not need to do that; it is a waste of time, and you ought to be engaged in something else.'

"On the other hand," President Grant continued, "there is a still small voice telling us what is right, and if we listen to that still small voice we shall grow and increase in strength and power, in testimony and in ability not only to live the gospel but to inspire others to do so."[61]

And again Lincoln said: "Remember to call upon and confide in our great and good and merciful Maker, Who will not turn away from [us] in any extremity. He notes the fall of the sparrow, and numbers the hairs of our heads. He will not forget the dying man who puts his trust in Him."[62]

May we have sufficient common sense to trust and obey the Lord our God! It is the only way to security, both for nations and for individuals.[63]

—Mark E. Petersen

THIS DAY IN AMERICAN HISTORY (1870)

Mississippi is readmitted into the Union after the Civil War.

Dangers of Apathy

With regard to the domestic dimensions of American democracy, we are almost over-aspiring, given the limitations that apathy, finite funding, etc., place upon our capacity to deliver. . . .

Democracy requires certain originating or initial conditions to bring it into being. Fortunately, democracy tends to reproduce and reinforce those same necessary conditions—except that it also produces two other consequences, mass bureaucracy and political apathy, that are like a virus threatening to kill the host. Mass bureaucracy is an enemy of pluralism on which our Founding Fathers counted to produce true majorities, to checkrein interest groups, and to filter public opinion.

We may not know if political apathy increases as a democracy ages, but bureaucracy clearly does, and insofar as bureaucracy disenchants individuals, it reinforces apathy, and apathy often reaches plague proportions at the very time the people need to make decisions of immense consequences.[64]

—*Neal A. Maxwell*

THIS DAY IN AMERICAN HISTORY (1868)

The U.S. House of Representatives impeaches President Andrew Johnson.

The Constitution Is an Integral Part of My Faith

I declare that the divine sanction thus repeatedly given by the Lord Himself to the Constitution of the United States, as it came from the hands of the Framers with its coterminous Bill of Rights, makes of the principles of that document an integral part of my religious faith. It is a revelation from the Lord. I believe and reverence its God-inspired provisions. My faith, my knowledge, my testimony of the restored gospel, based on the divine principle of continuous revelation, compel me so to believe. Thus has the Lord approved of our political system, an approval, so far as I know, such as He has given to no other political system of any other people in the world since the time of Jesus.

The Constitution, as approved by the Lord, is still the same great vanguard of liberty and freedom in human government that it was the day it was written. No other human system of government, affording equal protection for human life, liberty, and the pursuit of happiness, has yet been devised or vouchsafed to man. Its great principles are as applicable, efficient, and sufficient to bring today the greatest good to the greatest number, as they were the day the Constitution was signed. Our Constitution, and our government under it, were designed by God as an instrumentality for righteousness through peace, not war.[65]

—*J. Reuben Clark, Jr.*

THIS DAY IN AMERICAN HISTORY (1862)

The Legal Tender Act of 1862 is passed by the U.S. Congress, authorizing the first paper money backed by the U.S. government.

Freedom Is God-Given

I say to you that American heritage of freedom is a plan of God. It was indeed no accident. One of the first considerations given after my appointment to serve as Secretary of Agriculture was to formulate with my closes associates and other interested parties a basic statement on agriculture policy. Among the fundamental concepts stated were the following:

Freedom is a God-given, eternal principle vouchsafed to us under the Constitution. It must be guarded continually as something more precious than life itself. Our guiding purpose will be to strengthen the individual integrity, freedom, and the very moral fiber of each citizen. The supreme test of any government policy, agricultural or other, should be: 'How will this affect the character, morale, and well-being of our people?' In the providence of God, governments were intended to be the servants, not he matters of the people. This eternal truth needs to be emphasized and re-emphasized.

Thomas Jefferson, while President of the United States, expressed what I hope is the conviction of all of us. Mark carefully his wise declaration. "If we can prevent the government from wasting the labors of the people under pretense of caring for them, they will be happy." I subscribe to those words—I hope you do too, and will use your energies to get other to accept these basic truths. . . . "The government is best which governs the least." So taught the courageous founders of this nation. This simple declaration is diametrically opposed to the all too common philosophy that the government should protect one from the cradle to the grave. The policy of the Founding Fathers has made our people and our nation strong. The opposite philosophy leads to moral and spiritual decay. And we must never forget that our greatest weapon is spiritual strength.[66]

—*Ezra Taft Benson*

THIS DAY IN AMERICAN HISTORY (1863)

Abraham Lincoln signs the National Currency Act that establishes a single national currency.

FEBRUARY 27

Religion to Be Forever Encouraged in Public Education

The Northwest Ordinance, which regulated the western expansion of the United States, was adopted by the Confederation Congress in 1787 and two years later adopted by the first United States Congress. It stated, "Religion, morality, and knowledge being necessary to good government and the happiness of mankind, schools and the means of education shall forever be encouraged." None that the government was not to discourage religion or even be neutral in this regard. Rather, it was a powerful endorsement for religion to be forever encouraged by the government in public education! One should keep in mind that this endorsement was given by the same Congress that adopted the Constitution; hence it clearly understood the desired role of religion in the public sector.

This sentiment toward encouragement of religion in education was expressed by a number of the Founding Fathers. Benjamin Rush wrote, "The only foundation for useful education in a republic is to be laid in Religion." He also understood the consequences of removing the Bible and religion from schools: "The great enemy of the salvation of man, my opinion, never invented a more effectual means of extirpating Christianity from the world than by persuading mankind that it was improper to read the Bible at schools." And Gouverneur Morris, one of the signers of the Constitution, added, "Religion is the only solid basis of good morals; therefore education should teach the precepts of religion and the duties of man towards God."[67]

—*Tad R. Callister*

THIS DAY IN AMERICAN HISTORY (1951)

The 22nd Amendment to the U.S. Constitution is ratified.

Dictated by the Invisible Operations of the Almighty

It was observed this morning that the government of the United States was the best or most wholesome one on the earth, and the best adapted to our condition. That is very true.

To accuse us of being unfriendly to the government is to accuse us of hostility to our religion, for no item of inspiration is held more sacred with us than the Constitution under which she acts. As a religious society, we, in common with all other denominations, claim its protection.

The signers of the Declaration of Independence and the Framers of the Constitution were inspired from on High to do that work. But was that which was given to them perfect, not admitting of any addition whatever? No; for if men know anything, they must know that the Almighty has never yet found a man in mortality that was capable, at the first intimation, at the first impulse, to receive anything in a state of entire perfection. They laid the foundation, and it was for after generations to rear the superstructure upon it. It is a progressive—a gradual work.

The general Constitution of our country is good, and a wholesome government could be framed upon it, for it was dictated by the invisible operations of the Almighty; He moved upon Columbus to launch forth upon the trackless deep to discover the American Continent; He moved upon the signers of the Declaration of Independence; and He moved upon Washington to fight and conquer, in the same way as he moved upon ancient and modern prophets, each being inspired to accomplish the particular work he was called to perform in the times, seasons, and dispensations of the Almighty.

God's purposes, in raising up these men and inspiring them with daring sufficient to surmount every opposing power, was to prepare the way for the formation of a true republican government. They laid its foundation; but when others came to build upon it, they reared a superstructure far short of their privileges, if they had walked up-rightly as they should have done.[68]

—Brigham Young

THIS DAY IN AMERICAN HISTORY (1787)

New York selects three delegates for the Constitutional Convention.

It Is Comforting to Me

It is comforting to me that the early founders of this country had the same conviction of the powers of the Almighty. Thomas Paine said, "What is it we want to know? Does not the creation, the universe we behold, preach to us the existence of an Almighty power, that governs and regulates the whole? And is not the evidence that this creation holds out to our senses infinitely stronger than anything we can read in a book that any imposter might make or call the word of God? As for morality, the knowledge of it exists in every man's conscience."[69]

And so today, I sound the same words of warning as Paul the Apostle of old: "For the time will come when they will not endure sound doctrine; but after their own lusts shall they heap to themselves teachers, having itching ears;

"And they shall turn away their ears from the truth, and shall be turned unto fables" (2 Timothy 4:3–4).

I leave you my witness that there is a consistency in the laws of God that will not change. When we conform our lives to his laws we will find a rewarding joy, a fulfillment, and a peace as we live here on earth. When we would pervert or change his laws or disregard them, we must stand the judgments of God, and as surely as that occurs, misery, sorrow, and heartache will be the result.

Let us catch the spirit of the Psalmist who wrote, "The earth is the Lord's, and the fulness thereof; the world, and they that dwell therein" (Psalm 24:1).[70]

—L. Tom Perry

THIS DAY IN AMERICAN HISTORY (1803, 1867)

Ohio (1803) and Nebraska (1867) receive statehood as the 17th and 37th states, respectively.

Will We Be Prepared?

Will we be prepared? Will we be among those who will "bear the Constitution away from the very verge of destruction?" If we desire to be numbered among those who will, here are some things we must do: . . .

We must learn the principles of the Constitution and then abide by its precepts. We have been instructed again and again to reflect more intently on the meaning and importance of the Constitution and to adhere to its principles. What have we done about this instruction? Have we read the Constitution and pondered it? Are we aware of its principles? Could we defend it? Can we recognize when a law is constitutionally unsound? The Church will not tell us how to do this, but we are admonished to do it. I quote Abraham Lincoln: "Let [the Constitution] be taught in schools, in seminaries, and in colleges, let it be written in primers, in spelling books and in almanacs, let it be preached from the pulpit, proclaimed in legislative halls, and enforced in courts of justice. And, in short, let it become the political religion of the nation." . . .

We must make our influence felt by our vote, our letters, and our advice. We must be wisely informed and let others know how we feel. We must take part in local precinct meetings and select delegates who will truly represent our feelings.

I have faith that the Constitution will be saved as prophesied by Joseph Smith. But it will not be saved in Washington. It will be saved by the citizens of this nation who love and cherish freedom. It will be saved by enlightened members of this Church—men and women who will subscribe to and abide the principles of the Constitution.[71]

—*Ezra Taft Benson*

THIS DAY IN AMERICAN HISTORY (1781)

Articles of Confederation adopted.

MARCH 3

Strong Citizens to Maintain Freedom

Our American Constitution places heavy duties on the individual citizen—just as the gospel does. The Constitution depends on a sufficient number of strong citizens for its very establishment; it will depend, likewise, on a crucial mass of strong and able citizens for its preservation. Thus, that the Constitution will one day be "upon the brink of ruin" and on "the very verge of destruction" should not surprise us. Societies composed of strong citizens willing and able to maintain freedom and to cope with its frustrations are not common. Consider, for instance, those situations such as obtained in Sodom which were self-terminating: a doomed people who because of their unrighteousness simply became extinct, save for three survivors.[72]

—*Neal A. Maxwell*

THIS DAY IN AMERICAN HISTORY (1791)

Congress establishes a U. S. mint.

We Need to Work for a Better Way

I love this country, which I believe was established with the blessings of God. I love its Constitution, whose *principles* I believe were divinely inspired. I am, therefore, distressed at the way we are handling the national issues that divide us. We have always had to work through serious political conflicts, but today too many approach that task as if their preferred outcome must entirely prevail over all others, even in our pluralistic society. We need to work for a better way—a way to resolve differences without compromising core values. We need to live together in peace and mutual respect, within our defined constitutional rights. . . .

I begin with a proposition I hope all will share. As a practical basis for coexistence, we should accept the reality that we are fellow citizens who need each other. This requires us to accept some laws we dislike, and to live peacefully with some persons whose values differ from our own. Amid such inevitable differences, we should make every effort to understand the experiences and concerns of others, especially when they differ from our own.

We can only succeed in this effort to the extent that we acknowledge and respect each other's highest ideals and human experiences. We must not be part of what Professor Arthur C. Brooks of Harvard's Kennedy School describes as "a culture of contempt—a habit of seeing people who disagree with us not as merely incorrect or misguided but as worthless." A basic step is to avoid labeling our adversaries with epithets such as "godless" or "bigots." When some advocates voice insults or practice other minor provocations, both sides should ignore them. Our society already has too many ugly confrontations.[73]

—*Dallin H. Oaks*

THIS DAY IN AMERICAN HISTORY (1789)

The first U.S. Congress meets and declares that the Constitution is now in effect to govern the nation.

Mormonism Is Truth

Mormonism is truth, and every man who embraced it felt himself at liberty to embrace every truth. Consequently the shackles of superstition, bigotry, ignorance, and priestcraft fall at once from his neck, and his eyes are opened to see the truth, and truth greatly prevails over priestcraft; hence the priests are alarmed, and they raise a hue and cry: "Down with these men! heresy! heresy! fanaticism! false prophet! false teachers! away with these men! crucify them! crucify them!" And now, sir, this is the sole cause of the persecution against the Mormon people. And now if they had been Mahomedans [Muslims], Hottentots [Khoikhoi of southwestern Africa], or Pagans, or in fine, sir, if their religion was as false as hell, what right would men have to drive them from their homes, and their country, or to exterminate them so long as their religion did not interfere with the civil rights of men, according to the laws of our country? None at all. . . .

Be assured, sir, that I have the most liberal sentiments and feelings of charity towards all sects, parties, and denominations, and the rights and liberties of conscience I hold most sacred and dear, and despise no man for differing with me in matters of opinion.[74]

—Joseph Smith, Jr.

THIS DAY IN AMERICAN HISTORY (1770)

The Boston Massacre occurs in downtown Boston.

The Most Important Thing We Can Do for the Church

Thus the very first thing which our fathers sought to secure for themselves and for their posterity was freedom to worship as they wished. I do not need to call to your minds the trials and persecution which this people have suffered in the past, in order to bring home to you the conviction that nothing else in the great document, the Constitution, is so important to this people as is this guarantee of religious freedom, because underneath and behind all that lies in our lives, all that we do in our lives, is our religion, our worship, our belief and faith in God. . . . One of the most important things that we can do for the Church is to stand behind the Constitution of the United States. That does not mean, and no reasoning person would suppose that it meant, that that Constitution may not from time to time be changed as the needs of the people would seem to require. But it does mean that that Constitution should be changed only under the urge of great necessity, and then only in accordance with its great underlying concepts. It does mean that the great fundamental elements of the Constitution are God-given, for he said so. It does mean to me as an individual that the Constitution of the United States and my adherence to it and support of it is a part of my religion.[75]

—*J. Reuben Clark, Jr.*

THIS DAY IN AMERICAN HISTORY (1857)

The U.S. Supreme Court issues the Dred Scott Decision.

Negotiation Over Litigation: A Better Path to Resolution

Litigation should not be the first recourse in resolving our differences. Courts are constitutionally limited to resolving the specific cases before them. They are ill-suited to the overarching, complex, and comprehensive policy-making that is required in a circumstance like the current conflict between two great values. Notwithstanding my years of working with judicial opinions, I prefer the initial route of legislative law-making on big questions like the ones now before us. I find wisdom in the observation of Professor (later Dean) Martha Minow of the Harvard Law School. In her influential article on this subject, she concluded that "accommodation and negotiation can identify practical solutions where abstract principles sometimes cannot." Professor Minow further observed that problem-solving by negotiation "is highly relevant to *sustaining and replenishing* both American pluralism and constitutional protections for minority groups."

Successful negotiation requires that neither side be unduly influenced by the extreme voices that often drive litigation, especially litigation sponsored by ideological groups. Extreme voices influence popular opinion, but they polarize and sow resentment as they seek to dominate their opponents and achieve absolute victory. Such outcomes are rarely sustainable or even attainable, and they are never preferable to living together in mutual understanding and peace.

Good faith negotiation invites that seldom-appreciated virtue so necessary to democracy: tolerance, free of bigotry toward those whose opinions or practices differ from our own. But learning to live with significant differences requires much more than tolerance. . . .

Far from being a weakness, reconciling adverse positions through respectful negotiation is a virtue. As Jesus taught, "Blessed are the peacemakers: for they shall be called the children of God." The Apostle Paul followed this by teaching Christians to "follow after the things which make for peace," and "[i]f it be possible . . . live peaceably with all men." Similarly, the Book of Mormon teaches that it is a "peaceable walk with the children of men" that distinguishes a true follower of Jesus Christ.[76]

—*Dallin H. Oaks*

THIS DAY IN AMERICAN HISTORY (1876)

Alexander Graham Bell receives a U.S. patent for the telephone.

Oh, God, Give Us Men with a Mandate Higher than the Ballot Box

It is not, however, enough to be acquainted with the grave dangers facing these United States. We must also instruct ourselves, and others, in the great spiritual values underlying our divinely inspired Constitution and our American free-enterprise system. One of the many sure ways of defeating our enemy is to instruct the people about the eternal verities of our own country. A mind, so enlightened, will reject Marxian socialism whether it be in the form of communism, Nazism, fascism, welfare-statism or some other man-made monstrosity.

In this time of deadly peril, we must choose men and women to represent us in our government who have attained an inner attunement of mind, heart and soul with God. Only these people have anchors firmly rooted and strong enough to withstand the slings and arrows of outrageous fortune. They, only, have the inner sense of direction, stability of spirit and firmness of character essential to our survival.

We must not place in positions of trust, cheap opportunists who will sell their souls for a mess of pottage. Rather we should place in public office men and women who place the love of God first in their lives and who, as a consequence, can serve their fellow men with true wisdom.

Not cheap politicians but statemen are needed today. Not opportunists but men and women of principle must be demanded by the people. In this time of great stress and danger we must place only those dedicated to the preservation of our Constitution, our American Republic, and responsible freedom under God. "Oh, God, give us men with a mandate higher than the ballot box."[77]

—*Ezra Taft Benson*

THIS DAY IN AMERICAN HISTORY (1965)

The first American combat forces arrive in Vietnam at Da Nang.

MARCH 9

Until the Kingdoms of This World Become the Kingdom of Our God

Until He rules whose right it is and subdues all enemies under his feet; until he makes a full end of all nations in the day of his coming; until the kingdoms of this world become the kingdom of our God and of his Christ—there will be conflicts between church and state that defy solutions. Neither the Saints nor Lucifer will yield on the issues involved, and a resolution will be found only after the wicked are destroyed by the brightness of His coming.

In every nation the Saints will use their influence in the cause of righteousness, in the cause of truth, the cause of freedom, the gospel cause. In those same nations, Lucifer will seek to enforce his will. Whenever and wherever he can use either a church or a state as an instrument of damnation, he will do it. We may expect greater opposition and a more definite polarization of the people as the great and dreadful day of the Lord draws nearer. Religious influences will cause political kingdoms to engage in the battle of Armageddon, and there will be martyrdom and destruction on all sides as the gospel is preached in those concluding days of the earth's temporal continuance.[78]

—*Bruce R. McConkie*

THIS DAY IN AMERICAN HISTORY (1864)

Ulyssess S. Grant is named Commanding General of the Union Army.

Our Wisely Designed Constitution

Being worthy, therefore, of America's past and deserving God's blessings in the future are vital, but not only for America. More hinges on what happens in America than we realize. It was so in the beginning, as the Declaration of Independence became one of the special acts in all of human history. It affected not only the people of America, but it spurred much of mankind.

America, with all of its problems, is still a beacon. This beacon needs to shine more brightly today for the sake of all mankind in order to continue to give, in Lincoln's words, hope to all the world. Whatever the dimension of patriotism, therefore, it requires that America have and maintain a spiritual core in order that our hopes are not in vain. Without this spiritual core, our liberties, our cities, our fiscal policies, and our brotherhood will finally fail and falter. You must, therefore, reside in the people as well as in the leaders. John Adams so cautioned, saying, "Our Constitution was made only for a moral and religious people. It is wholly inadequate to the government of any other."

Unexciting as a prescription, nevertheless, the best single way to improve the quality of life in America is to improve the quality of our own individual lives and our own neighborhoods. . . . Our inspired Constitution is wisely designed to protect us from excesses of political power, but it can do little to protect us from the excesses of appetite or from individual indifference to great principles or institutions. Any significant unraveling of the moral fiber of the American people, therefore, finally imperils the Constitution. The moral fabric of this society can become dangerously and relentlessly frayed as too few strands strain to hold us together. Hence, having a shared patriotic, spiritual, and moral commitment within this nation's borders is as vital as defending those borders. Therefore, while great leaders are needed, so also are informed and wise followers.[79]

—*Neal A. Maxwell*

THIS DAY IN AMERICAN HISTORY (1778)

Massachusetts ratifies the Articles of Confederation.

Glorious to Think of the Liberties That We Enjoy as Citizens of This Great Republic

Happiness is the end and design of life, for man is that he might have joy; but I repeat, it does not come from without.

The second factor I name as contributing to happiness is a sense of freedom. It is sweet to contemplate that word. It is glorious to think of the liberties that we enjoy as citizens of this great republic. We love to look back to the heroes who offered their lives, their fortunes, and their sacred honor in defense of individual liberty.

"God is endeavoring to make men like himself. To do this he must first make them free." The philosopher who wrote those words got a glimpse of an eternal gospel truth. Man can choose the highest good or choose the lower good and fall short of what he was intended to be.

I leave this fundamental to happiness with the admonition to you to be true to the Constitution of the United States, to the Bill of Rights. Do not let any theories of misguided politicians induce you to do anything that will deprive us of our liberties as vouchsafed by that immortal document.[80]

—David O. McKay

THIS DAY IN AMERICAN HISTORY (1861)

The Confederate States of America Constitution is ratified.

The Lord Uses Imperfect People to Build Strong Societies

Many of our forebears and those who built the foundations of this land were imperfect. They were human. They doubtless made mistakes and fell short from time to time. But the mistakes were minor when compared with the marvelous work they accomplished. To highlight the mistakes of a person and gloss over the greater good is to draw a caricature. Caricatures are amusing, but they are often ugly and dishonest. A man may have a wart on his cheek and still have a face of beauty and strength, but if the wart is emphasized unduly in relation to his other features, the portrait is lacking in integrity.

There was only one perfect man who ever walked the earth. The Lord uses imperfect people—you and me—to build strong societies. If some of us occasionally stumble, or if our characters may have been slightly flawed in one way or another, the wonder is the greater that we accomplish so much.[81]

—*Gordon B. Hinckley*

THIS DAY IN AMERICAN HISTORY (1933)

Franklin D. Roosevelt holds his presidential "fireside chat."

No People Can Maintain Freedom Unless Their Political Institutions Are Founded upon Faith in God

America was built upon a firm foundation and created over many years from the bottom up. Other nations, impatient to acquire equal abundance, security and pursuit of happiness, rush headlong into that final phase of construction without building adequate foundations or supporting pillars. Their efforts are futile. And, even in our country, there are those who think that, because we now have the good things in life, we can afford to dispense with the foundations which have made them possible. They want to remove any recognition of God from government which will undermine and erode our economic and personal freedoms. . . .

As an independent American for constitutional government, I declare that: I believe that no people can maintain freedom unless their political institutions are founded upon faith in God and belief in the existence of moral law. I believe that God has endowed men with certain unalienable rights as set forth in the Declaration of Independence and that no legislature and no majority, however great, may morally limit or destroy these; that the sole function of government is to protect life, liberty, and property, and anything more than this is usurpation and oppression. I believe that the Constitution of the United States was prepared and adopted by men acting under inspiration from Almighty God; that it is a solemn compact between the peoples of the states of this nation which all officers of government are under duty to obey; that the eternal moral laws expressed therein must be adhered to or individual liberty will perish.[82]

—*Ezra Taft Benson*

THIS DAY IN AMERICAN HISTORY (1868)

The U.S. Senate begins the impeachment trial of President Andrew Johnson.

Rededicate Ourselves to Understanding

I believe that we should think seriously about the Constitution and rededicate ourselves to understanding and living by the principles it stands for. As the Savior raised up wise men to establish this tremendous ideal of government, only wise men and women can maintain it. If we do not practice the ideals of the Constitution, we can become anonymous and ineffective.

Our forefathers believed that we should always know what is going on in government and should do our best to keep it relatively small and dedicated to protecting each of us in the enjoyment of life, liberty, and property. We must insist that our government refrain from running our individual lives, so long as we are law-abiding. We must not permit government to take responsibilities that we should bear for ourselves.

Our obligation as citizens is to help retain the liberty granted to us in the Constitution. I encourage each of us to think about government, to participate seriously in every phase of it, and to do our part in blocking its tendency to monopolize our lives. If we will do so, we will please the founders of the Constitution. In short, if we earn again what we have inherited, we will never fail.[83]

—Joseph B. Wirthlin

THIS DAY IN AMERICAN HISTORY (1812)

The U.S. Congress authorizes the sale of war bonds to finance the War of 1812.

That the Lord May Help Him Think Straight

We believe that governments were instituted of God for the benefit of man, and that he holds men accountable for their acts in relation to them, both in making laws and administering them for the good and safety of society.

We believe that no government can exist in peace, except such laws are framed and held inviolate as will secure to each individual the free exercise of conscience, the right and control of property, and the protection of life.

These principles are fundamental to our belief, fundamental to our protection. And in the providences of the Lord, the safeguards which have been incorporated into the basic structure of this nation are, if we preserve them, the guarantee of all men who dwell here against abuses, tyrannies, and usurpations. From my childhood days I have understood that we believe absolutely that the constitution of our country is an inspired instrument and that God directed those who created it and those who defended the independence of this nation.

And such the Constitution of the United States must be to every faithful Latter-day Saint who lives under its protection. That the Lord may help him to think straight, and to pursue a straight course regardless of personal advantage, factional interest, or political persuasion, should be the daily prayer of every Latter-day Saint. I counsel you, I urge you, I plead with you, ne'er, so far as you have voice or influence, permit any departure from the principles of government on which this nation was founded, or any disregard of the freedoms which, by the inspiration of God our Father, were written into the Constitution of the United States.[84]

—*Heber J. Grant*

THIS DAY IN AMERICAN HISTORY (1820)

Maine receives statehood as the 23rd state.

We Are Battling Against Apathy, Blindness, Opportunism, and Propaganda

I have great faith in the American people. When fully informed, they will make wise decisions. They will stand up and be counted for what is right. This I know. I recognize that it is not popular in some circles to be called an anti-communist, but I consider communism a political and economic disease. I do not believe an American citizen can be patriotic and loyal to his own country and its God-inspired Constitution of freedom without being anti-communist—anti-socialist.

Now I know that Moscow has ordered that all anti-communists are to be attacked and discredited in every way possible. I know the Communist Party of the United States has issued a similar mandate. This does not disturb me at all. It should be expected. Meanwhile, we should pursue a calm and steady course. The path of education to alert and inform our people "about the methods, purposes and progress of the conspiracy is the right path. . . . We must be carefully certain that all we say is the truth, and as restrained as circumstances will permit in how we say it. But to spread the simple childlike truth, about the monstrous fabrication and falsehoods which make up the very environment of our lives, is a duty to God and country and family which each of us must assume." (J.B.S. Bulletin, September 1963.) We are battling against apathy, blindness, opportunism, and propaganda directed brilliantly by masters of deceit.[85]

—Ezra Taft Benson

THIS DAY IN AMERICAN HISTORY (1802)

The United States Military Academy at West Point is established by Congress.

Submit Ourselves to the Lord

Now, for the first time since this Church was organized, we are in a position for defending those rights common to all American citizens; and our true and lawful course to abide by the Constitution of the United States in the defense of those rights will probably give the wicked a pretext for complaint; so that in measuring out oppression to us, our enemies will have a new set of pretexts, instead of feasting on infernal lies so much as they have hitherto done....

You will recollect that this is the first time that this Church can say, "We are free." Do we wish to be free from the United States Constitution? No. There is not a word in it but what we can subscribe to with all our hearts. Do we wish to be free from the laws of the United States? No. They are as good laws as we can ask for. It is not the laws and the Constitution of our country that we wish to be free from, but it is from the power of those who profess to be lawmakers and law-executors, but who trample every wholesome law under their feet....

It is said that if we do right we shall overcome. I will tell you one mark you have got to come to, in order to do right. If you can bring yourselves, in your affections, your feelings, your passions, your desires, and all that you have in your organization, to submit to the hand of the Lord, to His providences, and acknowledge His hand in all things, and always be willing that He should dictate, though it should take your houses, your property, your wives and children, your parents, your lives, or anything else you have upon the earth, then you will be exactly right; and until you come to that point, you cannot be entirely right. That is what we have to come to; we have to learn to submit ourselves to the Lord with all our hearts, with all our affections, wishes, desires, passions, and let him reign and rule over us and within us, the God of every motion: then he will lead us to victory and glory; otherwise he will not.[86]

—*Brigham Young*

THIS DAY IN AMERICAN HISTORY (1776)

The British evacuate Boston.

The Future of Religious Freedom Will Depend a Great Deal on What Our Children Are Taught

Study the principles of the American founding and teach them in your families. Teach your families to cherish America's heritage of freedom. Teach them the importance of religion to our nation and society. Teach them to respect the faith of all people, even those with very different beliefs. And teach them that respecting religious freedom means tolerating religious beliefs, speech, and practices we disagree with. That is the price of asking others to respect our own freedoms.

The crisis of religious freedom is as much a cultural crisis as a political or legal one. So get involved in the cultural and civic organizations around you so that you can influence them to respect religious freedom. Be active in the PTA and express your views to the school board; the future of religious freedom will depend a great deal on what our children are taught. If you are a professional or run a business, be involved with your professional association or the chamber of commerce; the lack of business and professional support for religious freedom is a real concern. You can make a difference. Participate in your political party and help guide it toward sound principles. Write to your representatives. Make it a family tradition to vote regularly. There are numerous opportunities to get involved right in your own community.

Finally, and above all, as the Apostle Paul wrote, "Be . . . an example of the believers, in word, in conversation, in charity, in spirit, in faith, in purity" (1 Timothy 4:12). Whatever your religion, live your faith so that others will see your good works, experience your genuine love and friendship, and feel God working through you. Americans tend to respect and protect what they believe is good. So let us show them the highest and best in our faiths—our willingness to love and serve others, to build strong families, to live honorable lives, and to be good citizens.[87]

—*D. Todd Christofferson*

THIS DAY IN AMERICAN HISTORY (1870)

Lake Merritt in Oakland, California, becomes the first U.S. national wildlife refuge.

We Believe in Constitutional Principles

I expect to see the day when the Latter-day Saints will be the people to maintain constitutional government on this land. Men everywhere should know that we believe in constitutional principles, and that we expect that it will be our destiny to maintain them. That the prediction will be fulfilled that was made forty-four years ago the seventh of last March, wherein God said to Joseph Smith—"Ye hear of wars in foreign lands; but behold I say unto you, they are nigh, even at your doors, and not many years hence ye shall hear of wars in your own lands;" but the revelation goes on to say that the day will come among the wicked, that every man that will not take his sword against his neighbor, must needs flee unto Zion for safety.

A portion of that revelation has been fulfilled, the remainder will be. The causes are in operation to bring it about. We are not along in the thought that the republic is drifting steadily I that direction; that we are leaving the old constitutional landmarks, and that the time is not far distant when there will be trouble in consequence of it, when there will be civil broils and strife; and, to despised as they are now.[88]

—George Q. Cannon

THIS DAY IN AMERICAN HISTORY (1920)

The U. S. Senate refuses to ratify the Treaty of Versailles and rejects the League of Nations' covenant.

The Ten Commandments and the Constitution

The work has gone on and under the Constitution of the United States we have been permitted to carry on in this great land. We have been permitted to teach the gospel of Jesus Christ. Our missionaries of course have gone all over the world, but I am speaking now of the United States of America. However, there are many people, many men and women in this land, some of whom may be friends or relatives who are misguided by the idea that the Constitution of the United States isn't as fine a system of government as they have in Russia or Germany or Italy or some other part of the world, notwithstanding the fact that the Lord Himself said that he raised up the very men who framed the Constitution of the United States and directed that the membership of this Church should pray for and sustain those who represented the Constitution of this land. I hold in my hand the Bible and can read the Ten Commandments that were given to Moses for the guidance of the people wherein the Lord told Moses what the people should live for and do. If those Ten Commandments had been lived up to by the people of the world down to the present time, this earth could long ago have been celestialized. But the people refused.

You know, and I know, that the Ten Commandments contain the will of our Heavenly Father, and I am grateful, not only for the civil laws but also for the laws God has given to us. I feel bound to conform my life to the teachings of the Ten Commandments. I feel equally bound to sustain the Constitution of the United States which came from the same source as the Ten Commandments. Unless the people of this great nation can realize these things and repent, they may forfeit the liberty that they now enjoy, and the blessings that are so multiplied among us.[89]

—*George Albert Smith*

THIS DAY IN AMERICAN HISTORY (1816)

The U.S. Supreme Court affirms its right to review state court decisions.

MARCH 21

This Is a Great Land, a Choice Land, a Chosen Land

We live in an intriguing age, a curious age in many respects, an age in which the ability and power to communicate, and therefore to influence and persuade, reign supreme. With the proliferation of technology, and the various forms of media clamoring to take advantage of it, has come an interesting side effect. It seems today that we are subjected to a constant barrage of character assassination that has nearly obscured national discussion of vital issues—issues that truly could and would improve the daily lives of men and women, boys and girls. A large factor in all of this is the media. . . . It is impossible to read the columns or listen to the commentaries without sensing that there is a terrible ailment of gloom in this land. We are constantly fed a steady and sour diet of pessimism, faultfinding, second-guessing, and evil speaking one of another. The pathetic fact is: Negativism sells. . . .

It will do us no good to be naive about the challenges we face in this country. We do have problems, and they are not a few. There are issues that demand our earnest, inspired attention. But there is too much fruitless carping and criticism of America. What might become of this land if we spoke less of its weaknesses and more of its goodness and strength, its capacity and potential? Without doubt, we shall have days of trial. So long as we have more politicians than statesmen, we shall have problems. But if we will turn our time and talents away from vituperative criticism, away from constantly looking for evil, and will emphasize instead the greater good, America will continue to go forward with the blessing of the Almighty and stand as an ensign of strength and peace and generosity to all the world. This is a great land, a choice land, a chosen land.[90]

—*Gordon B. Hinckley*

THIS DAY IN AMERICAN HISTORY (1866)

Congress authorizes the creation of National Soldier's Homes for military veterans.

Do We Know What the Prophets Have Said About the Constitution?

To all who have discerning eyes, it is apparent that the republican form of government established by our noble forefathers cannot long endure once fundamental principles are abandoned. Momentum is gathering for another conflict—a repetition of the crisis of two hundred years ago. This collision of ideas is worldwide. Another monumental moment is soon to be born. The issue is the same that precipitated the great pre-mortal conflict—will men be free to determine their own course of action or must they be coerced?

We are fast approaching that moment prophesied by Joseph Smith when he said: "Even this nation will be on the verge of crumbling to pieces and tumbling to the ground and the Constitution is upon the brink of ruin, this people will be the staff upon which the nation shall lean, and they shall bear the Constitution away from the very verge of destruction." Are we reading the Constitution and pondering it? Are we teaching its principles to others? Could we defend the Constitution? Do we know what the prophets have said about the Constitution and the threats to it? Have we studied the Federalist papers? It is our sacred responsibility to see that the Constitution is perpetuated so that the Church may more easily flourish in the future. I reverence the Constitution as a sacred document. To me its words are akin to the revelations of God. I testify that God sent some of His choicest spirits to lay the foundations of the government, and he has now sent other choice spirits to help preserve it![91]

—*Ezra Taft Benson*

THIS DAY IN AMERICAN HISTORY (1765)

British Parliament passes the Stamp Act.

God and His Powerful Influence for Good upon This Nation

The Founding Fathers clearly believed in God and His powerful influence for good upon this nation. They knew the need for a moral nation in order for the Constitution to be effective, and that morality was dependent upon religion.

Therefore, they supported religion in general, both in the private and public sectors, as a means to reemphasize and fortify the moral principles upon which this government was built. It was that simple and straightforward, and accordingly, it was clearly understood for the first two hundred plus years of our nation's history.

Nonetheless, in recent times, some have engaged in revisionist history and unwarranted interpretations of the Constitution and have thus supplanted the original intent of our Founding Fathers with secular views that would make this a "nation without God" rather than a "nation under God." This brings to mind the warning of Isaiah: "The nations and kingdoms that will not serve thee [God] shall perish; yea, those nations shall be utterly wasted" (Isaiah 60:12; see also Psalm 127:1). Fortunately, it also brings to mind the converse promise as uttered by the Psalmist: "Blessed is the nation whose God is the Lord" (Psalm 33:12).

Hopefully, we will be a nation "whose God is the Lord," one that encourages religion or, as Justice Douglas said, "respects the religious nature of our people and accommodates the public service to their spiritual needs," not a specific religion but religion in general, and thus a nation that continually reinforces and reenthrones the moral principles adopted by our Founding Fathers. This would not only be consistent with their words and actions but no doubt also be extremely pleasing to the God of heaven, who is the benefactor of all blessings.[92]

—*Tad R. Callister*

THIS DAY IN AMERICAN HISTORY (1775)

Patrick Henry delivers his speech "Give Me Liberty or Give Me Death."

I Will Teach My Firm Conviction

I will develop within me the courage to stand up and defend that which I believe to be right. I will declare my personal witness that the heavens are not closed. The Lord continues to guide and direct all of his children on earth if they will but heed his voice. I will teach my firm conviction that the foundation of any righteous government is the law that has been received from the Lord to guide and direct man's efforts. Righteous government receives direction from the Lord. The scripture President Tanner quoted bears this out, in our country, in the establishment of this government. "And for this purpose have I established the Constitution of this land, by the hands of wise men whom I raised up unto this very purpose, and redeemed the land by the shedding of blood" (D&C 101:80).

I have resolved to do all that is within my power to keep alive the same faith which existed in the hearts and souls of our early Founding Fathers.

It was George Washington who declared, "The people know it is impossible to rightly govern without God and the Bible."

Again from Andrew Jackson the declaration: "The Bible is the rock on which this Republic rests."

I reaffirm before you here today of my faith that the Lord God continues to govern the affairs of his children. His law must be the foundation on which all law is based. We must be willing to support, defend, and live in harmony with His divine law.[93]

—L. Tom Perry

THIS DAY IN AMERICAN HISTORY (1765)

Britain's Parliament passes the Quartering Act, requiring American colonists to house British soldiers.

Traitors to the Spirit and the Genius of the Constitution

I lay these things before you for your information, that you may feel and act understandingly. I have carefully criticized these matters, and examined the views of many of those who are said to be our greatest statesmen on this subject; for I have desired to comprehend the powers of the government and the rights of the people; and I have watched with no little anxiety the encroachments of government and the manifest desire to trample upon your rights. It is for you, however, to maintain them; and if those men that are traitors to the spirit and genius of the Constitution of the United States have a mind to trample underfoot those principles that ought to guarantee protection to every American citizen, we will rally around the standard, and bid them defiance in the name of the Lord God of Israel.

In doing this, we neither forget our duties as citizens of the United States, nor as subjects of the kingdom and cause of God; but, as the Lord has said, if we will keep His commandments, we need not transgress the laws of the land. We have not done it; we have maintained them all the time. When we talk about the Constitution of the United States, we are sometimes apt to quote—"*Vox populi, vox Dei;*" that is, The voice of the people is the voice of God. But in some places they ought to say, VOX POPULI, VOX DIABOLI; that is, the voice of the people is the voice of the Devil.

We are moved by a higher law.[94]

—*John Taylor*

THIS DAY IN AMERICAN HISTORY (1863)

The first six Medals of Honor are awarded by the Secretary of War.

We Cannot Go Back on Principles Such as These

We would like to see [our nation be] the arbiter of peace for all nations. We would like to see the government of the United States true to the Constitution, an instrument inspired by the spirit of wisdom from God. We want to see the benignity, the honor, the glory and the good name and the mighty influence for peace of this nation extended abroad. We want to see the power, the influence for good, for elevating mankind, and for the establishment of righteous principles spread out over these poor helpless peoples of the world, establishing peace, goodwill and intelligence among them, that they may grow to be equal, if possible, to the enlightened nations of the world. . . .

I hope to see the day when the counsels of peace and goodwill from this powerful nation will be so recognized by the people of this continent all the way to the south of us, and by the inhabitants of the islands that border upon our coasts, both east and west, that peace and goodwill and elevation may be brought to pass and established among them through the instrumentality of an enlightened people.

And I hope with all my soul that the members of The Church of Jesus Christ of Latter-day Saints will be loyal in their very hearts and souls, to the principles of the Constitution of our country. From them we have derived the liberty that we enjoy. They have been the means of guaranteeing to the foreigner that has come within our gates, and to the native born, and to all the citizens of this country, the freedom and liberty that we possess. We cannot go back upon such principles as these.[95]

—Joseph F. Smith

THIS DAY IN AMERICAN HISTORY (1830)

The Book of Mormon is published in Palmyra, New York.

The Personal Righteousness of Citizens Will Strengthen a Nation More than the Force of Its Arms

Those who enjoy the blessings of liberty under our national and state constitutions should promote morality, and they should practice what the Founding Fathers called "civic virtue." John Adams, the second president of the United States, declared, "Our Constitution was made only for a moral and religious people. It is wholly inadequate to the government of any other."

Citizens should also be practitioners of civic virtue in their conduct toward our states and our nation. They should obey the laws. They should be ever willing to fulfill the duties of citizenship. This includes compulsory duties like military service and the numerous voluntary actions they must take if they are to preserve the principle of limited government through citizen self-reliance. For example, since U.S. citizens value the right of trial by jury, they must be willing to serve on juries, even those involving unsavory subject matter.

Then there is the matter of voting. I have been alarmed at the steady decline of voter turnout in many parts of the United States, including Utah. Voting is a fundamental right and responsibility that must not be taken for granted. Political participation can be inconvenient. It requires sacrifices of time and resources, but it is essential to our democratic society. Without substantial voter turnout, the people abrogate the great fundamental of popular sovereignty.

It is also part of civic virtue to be moral in our conduct toward all people. We believe with the author of Proverbs that "righteousness exalteth a nation: but sin is a reproach to any people" (Proverbs 14:34). The personal righteousness of citizens will strengthen a nation more than the force of its arms.[96]

—*Dallin H. Oaks*

THIS DAY IN AMERICAN HISTORY (1790)

New York adopts the Bill of Rights.

Walk with Hope and Faith

I lived through the most serious economic depression of modern times. Heaven forbid that we should ever slip again into the financial quagmire of the thirties! Those were days of long soup lines, of suicides that came of discouragement, of a bleakness of life that is incomprehensible to those who didn't experience it. Despite the prevailing cynicism, somehow we survived and stayed alive. We worked at whatever employment we could find, though the pay was meager. But we managed to eat and keep going. In time, opportunities opened here and there. We moved forward with faith in the Almighty, which cultivated a spirit of optimism. In 1982, I attended the fiftieth anniversary party of my university's graduating class and was there reunited with men and women who had become prominent in many undertakings. They had become leaders. They had looked for the positive in life, praying with faith and working with diligence. Despite overwhelming odds, they had moved forward with a spirit of optimism and a willingness to work as hard as they could.

Regardless of our circumstances, we must do the same—go forward with faith and prayer, calling on the Lord for His sustenance and direction. We will discover, as the years pass, that there has been a subtle guiding of our footsteps in paths of progress and great purpose. . . . We must walk with hope and faith. We must speak affirmatively and cultivate an attitude of confidence. We all have the capacity to do so. Our strength will give strength to others, and the cumulative, rippling effect will be tremendous.[97]

—Gordon B. Hinckley

THIS DAY IN AMERICAN HISTORY (1885)

The U.S. Salvation Army is officially recognized.

I Love the Stars and Stripes, and the American Way of Life

Education for citizenship demands more emphasis upon moral and spiritual values. Our government was founded on faith in a Supreme Being as evidenced by the Mayflower Compact, the Declaration of Independence, by George Washington, and Benjamin Franklin in the Constitutional Convention, and by a hundred other incidents prior to, during, and following the birth of this republic. Said the Father of our Country: "We have raised a standard to which the good and wise can repair; the event is in the hands of God."

And Benjamin Franklin, recognizing the apparent inability of the Convention to solve perplexing problems confronting it, stated the faith in an overruling Providence and his assurance that God will answer prayer: "The longer I live, the more convincing proofs I see of this truth: That God governs in the affairs of men. And if a sparrow cannot fall to the ground without His notice, is it probable that an empire can rise without His aid?" God and individual freedom are the fundamental principles in our glorious Republic, and our obligation is to keep in our schools a reverence for Deity and respect for the dignity of the individual man.

I love the Stars and Stripes, and the American Way of Life. I have faith in the Constitution of the United States. I believe that only through a truly educated citizenry can the ideals that inspired the Founding Fathers of our nation be preserved and perpetuated.[98]

—David O. McKay

THIS DAY IN AMERICAN HISTORY (1961)

The 23rd Amendment to the U.S. Constitution is ratified.

Here in This Land Will Be Established the New Jerusalem

I love this nation of which we are a part. To me it is not just another nation, not just a member of a family of nations. It is a great and glorious nation with a divine mission and it has been brought into being under the inspiration of heaven. It is truly a land choice above all others. I thank God for the knowledge which we have regarding the prophetic history and the prophetic future of this great land of America.

When I contemplate the great events that have transpired here, going way back to the days when our first parents were placed in the Garden of Eden, and recall that this garden was here in America, that it was here also where Adam met with a body of great high priests at Adam-ondi-Ahman shortly before his death and gave them his final blessing (D&C 107:53), and that to that same spot he is to return again to meet with the leaders of his people, his children—when I contemplate, my brethren and sisters, that here in this land will be established the New Jerusalem, that here in this land will Zion be built—when I contemplate that prophets of God anciently served here in this land, and that the resurrected Christ appeared unto them—and when I contemplate that the greatest of all visions, the coming of God the Father, and the Son to the boy Prophet in our day took place in this land, my heart fills with gratitude that I am privileged to live here, and that I have the honor and pleasure of not only serving in the Church, but also of serving in the government of this great land. I consider it an honor and privilege.[99]

—*Ezra Taft Benson*

THIS DAY IN AMERICAN HISTORY (1867)

The United States buys Alaska from Russia for $7.2 million, roughly two cents per acre.

To Be on the Lord's Side

Our nation's history is saturated with references to God because His influence has been profound in the discovery, establishment, and preservation of this country. Accordingly, we pay tribute to God through the presence of religious symbols and practices in both private and public places. It is nothing less than historical fiction to think that our government has not supported and encouraged religion for over two hundred years. The initial intent of the Founding Fathers was clear—to promote and encourage religion in both the private and public sectors and, by so doing, reinforce the principles upon which our nation was built, but at the same time never establish a nation religion.

Our Founding Fathers would be shocked to hear some advocate that religion should be spoken only in the confines of one's home or seclusion of a private chapel—that it should be invisible in the public domain. It would be anathema to them and all they stood for.

After a clergyman expressed his hope that the Lord was on the Union's side of the Civil War, Lincoln responded, "I am not at all concerned about that, for I know the Lord is always on the side of the right. But it is my constant anxiety and prayer that I and this nation should be on the Lord's side." How, as a nation, can we be on the Lord's side if our government is neutral in divine matters? The Savior had something to say about those who assumed a neutral position: "He that is not with me is against me" (Matthew 12:30). In essence, once government has excluded God from the public sector, it has chosen a side—the secular side. It has cast its lot with the non-religionists. There is no viable neutral position on the subject. Either God exists or He does not. Either we need God's help to fulfill our nation's destiny or we do not. The Founding Fathers clearly understood God's role in this country's origin and destiny and the need for His continued guidance. For them, it was not a debatable issue.[100]

—Tad R. Callister

THIS DAY IN AMERICAN HISTORY (1948)

The U.S. Congress passes the Marshall Aid Act
(the Marshall Plan) to rebuild Europe.

Civility: That Which Is Most Precious

Civility is the root of the word *civilization*. It carries with it the essence of courtesy, politeness, and consideration of others. How very much of it we have lost in our contemporary society! All of the education and accomplishments in the world will not count for much unless they are accompanied by marks of gentility, of respect for others, of going the extra mile, of serving as a good Samaritan, of being men and women who look beyond our own selfish interests to the good of others. Only as we do so will we find fulfillment. In some respects, it truly is a "jungle out there." The absence of civility creates the jungle. No matter the extent of our education, no matter our achievements in science, business, the professions, or whatever—if that other dimension of which I have spoken is missing, we will lack that which is most precious. We will be deficient in the godly quality of reaching out with respect and kindness, with courtesy and appreciation and maturity, toward our fellow travelers here on planet earth.

I am not suggesting that we be soft and docile. I admire enthusiasm and even assertion in the pursuit of worthy objectives. But I also hope that we will be enthusiastic and aggressive in reaching out to life, to help, to encourage those whose lives we can touch in good ways.[101]

—Gordon B. Hinckley

THIS DAY IN AMERICAN HISTORY (1789)

The U.S. House of Representatives is officially organized.

This Land Is Still a Land Choice Above All Others

War, calamities, pestilence, famine, destruction of our one and other nations—all of these things are startling and staggering the mind. It is little wonder that the coming days strike fear and anxiety into the hearts of men. These times predicted so often by the prophets of the Lord will be grim ones indeed. But it is precisely for this reason that the Lord has given us warning of their coming. When they come upon the world, those Saints who have been looking forth to the signs of the times and making preparations, in terms of their own personal righteousness, will then have strength to endure.

In our own day, the fulfillment of these predictions can be seen coming to pass. War is a common world-wide occurrence; violence, anarchy, and crime abound . . . signs of wickedness that are so prevalent in today's world are indications that mankind is losing the guidance of the Spirit of the Lord. In fact, a little over a year after the Church was organized, the Lord said that he was holding back his Spirit from the world because of the wickedness of its inhabitants. This is so not because the Lord wishes to leave his children without light and guidance, but rather because they will not have his Spirit in their lives. Christ does not withdraw from men; men withdraw from Him, and it is in consequence of this that the inhabitants of this country and the other nations of the world are racing into the maelstrom of destruction.

This land is still a land choice above all others, and it will be a land of liberty and peace for as long as its peoples serve the God of the land, Jesus Christ. However, as they forsake Him and turn to their own gods of material wealth and human learning, the divine decree will once again be invoked, and they, too, "shall be swept off."[102]

—Gerald N. Lund

THIS DAY IN AMERICAN HISTORY (1866)

President Andrew Johnson officially declares the end of the American Civil War.

The Principle of Popular Sovereignty

I mention first what is probably the most important of the great fundamentals of the United States Constitution—the principle of popular sovereignty: The people are the source of government power; it is they who consented to a constitution that delegates certain powers to the government. I stress this fundamental by emphasizing what are not the sources of sovereign power. Sovereignty is not inherent in a state or nation just because it has the power that comes from force of arms. Sovereignty does not come from the divine right of a king, who grants his subjects such power as he pleases or is forced to concede, as in the Magna Carta. And sovereignty does not rest in an aristocracy of self-appointed wise men who think that their high birth or prestigious education gives them the right to prescribe what is best for everyone else. Sovereignty is in the people as a whole, and their sovereignty is supreme, subject only to a few crucial limitations. . . .

The government of the United States had to be ultimately responsible to the will of the sovereign people, but it also had to be stable. Without stability against an aroused majority, government could not give individuals or minorities protection against overreaching by the ruling majority, a reality most evident when an outraged public calls for immediate punishment of one accused but not yet shown guilty of a crime. Government policies should not be tossed about with temporary swings in public opinion. The Constitution had to give government the power to withstand the cries of a majority of the sovereign people in the short run, but it had to be subject to their direction in the long run.[103]

—Dallin H. Oaks

THIS DAY IN AMERICAN HISTORY (1860)

The Pony Express begins delivering between St. Joseph, Missouri, and Sacramento, California.

Patriotism Is Not a Spectator Sport

As a nation, we've been showered with numerous blessings that have been a direct result of our Constitution. Unfortunately, many of us have forgotten that with the receipt of such blessings also comes responsibility. Probably our most important responsibility is to ensure the continuance of freedoms that we have received for our children and for our grandchildren. Patriotism is not a spectator sport. We must become involved in the process of freedom.

Further, we need to understand the great principles of the founding documents. How can we "befriend . . . that law which is the constitutional law of the land" if we are not familiar with it and its genesis? We need to drink deeply at the wellspring of this great document.

We must also recognize that, as President John Adams said, "We have no government armed with power capable of contending with human passions, unbridled by morality and religion." We are facing this situation to a degree in the world today. Therefore, we have the responsibility to remain unspotted from the world, to be upright and honest in all of our dealings, and to *set the example* for that which we have been given. . . .

As Latter-day Saints we should take to heart what the late President David O. McKay counseled: "Next to being one in worshiping God there is nothing in this world upon which this Church should be more united than in upholding . . . the Constitution of the United States" (CR, October 1939, 105). We, as a people, have been the recipients of some of God's most choice blessings, and I believe they came only as a result of the dedication and sacrifice of our forefathers.[104]

—*L. Tom Perry*

THIS DAY IN AMERICAN HISTORY (1789)

The first U.S. Congress begins regular sessions at Federal Hall in New York City.

His Hand Is There in Ways We Scarcely Appreciate

My testimony covers the range of all that I have learned through the Spirit, through the scriptures through life, and through the mentoring of others. Because God's is an inexhaustible gospel, it keeps growing, including Heavenly Father's stretching plan of salvation, which is clearly the best way for His dealings for the human family and to achieve our eternal happiness, justice, and joy.

I exclaim of our Creator's cosmos. It is overwhelming, it is stunning, and it accords completely with Heavenly Father's plans for each of us.

I testify, too, His hand is there in ways we scarcely appreciate—as in the preparation for framing and ratifying and implementing the United States Constitution, in which we see His majesty—as well as those cosmic things of the universe.

I gladly testify of the remarkable way in which the Restoration occurred and marvel at how the Lord, using imperfect people, can proceed with His perfect work. And in particular, I look to the day when mankind will yet proclaim the Book of Mormon from the housetops, providing a more distinct alternative to human indifference, despair, and yearning.[105]

—*Neal A. Maxwell*

THIS DAY IN AMERICAN HISTORY (1778)

North Carolina ratifies the Articles of Confederation.

Lessons from the Berlin Wall

I would like to describe to you, if I may, a place where I took my son—the Berlin Wall. We drove out and walked onto a metal platform and then onto a wooden platform, and then we were up in the air possibly forty or fifty feet. As we looked out across the Berlin Wall, we saw barbed wire. We saw fields that were mined. We saw tank embankments that stopped trucks and tanks from leaving, not from coming into, the walled area. We saw guards with dogs and with searchlights, towers were there were guards looking at us through binoculars as we looked back at them. They had machine guns and guarded the wall.

Let me make this recommendation to any young man or young woman—and I say that to you only after having been in international work for fifteen years. If you ever get disillusioned about your country, please take a trip abroad. Live there, and then after five years, return home, as I did. Then I would like to ask you, as you enter into the sight of the Statue of Liberty, to be emotional. The reason I say that is this: The man who made the Statue of Liberty, Frederic Auguste Bartholdi, had, as a young man, seen a young lady with a torch in her hand jump onto a barricade during a French rebellion. There she was shot, and she died setting the barricade on fire. Thirty years later, as he sailed into the harbor of New York, he conceived the idea of a tribute to America from France, a statue symbolizing *Liberty Enlightening the World*. He thought of the young girl with the torch in her hand, and that is how the statue of liberty was conceived.

All we have talked about to this point is only a preamble as we begin to discuss ourselves and our own free agency, which these documents proclaim and protect. Joseph Smith could not have restored the gospel without freedom of religion. Do you think it an accident that Joseph Smith was born just a few years after our land had become free and after we had gained these documents ensuring our unalienable rights? No, it was not an accident.[106]

—*Robert D. Hales*

THIS DAY IN AMERICAN HISTORY (1789)

The U.S. Senate is officially organized.

Freedom of the Press: A Right Under Threat

In the First Amendment, we have guarantees covering both the freedom of religion and the freedom of the press. Since the founding of this country, it is easy to see the tremendous role freedom of the press has played in the building of this republic. I happen to believe, however, that freedom of the press is probably in greater danger today than at almost any other time in the history of this country. And that brings me great concern for two reasons. First, because I believe, generally speaking, that freedom of the press is inseparably connected with freedom of religion. And when the one suffers, the other almost inevitably will suffer. Secondly, the Lord has said enough to demonstrate to us that the Constitution and its safeguards concerning liberty are inspired and should be upheld.

I should add that I approach this subject as a friend of the court. At least part of my academic and professional experience has been in journalism. I have been a weekly newspaper editor. I am a former member of the Utah State Press Association and of the New England Press Association and a former member of the professional journalism society Sigma Delta Chi. I have been involved intimately with the press in both Boston and New York City.

Under no stretch of the imagination do I want the press to fail. In fact, I believe that it continues to be one of the keys to the future success of our republic. It was Jefferson who said, "Were it left to me to decide whether we should have a government without newspapers or newspapers without government, I should not hesitate to prefer the latter."[107]

—*Loren C. Dunn*

THIS DAY IN AMERICAN HISTORY (1868)

Riots occur in over 100 American cities following the assassination of Martin Luther King Jr.

The Lord in His Wisdom Saw the Necessity of Giving Us a Nation in Which We Could Thrive

We have over three thousand missionaries in the world and many of them will be led to homes which before were closed but will now be open to hear their testimonies. It is our responsibility to carry the message of the gospel not only to the civilized world but also to those who are not considered to be so civilized. All this has been made possible because the Lord in his wisdom saw the necessity of giving us a nation in which we could thrive. In no other nation under heaven could the Church have been organized and gone forward as we have in this nation. The founding of the United States was not an accident. The giving to us of the Constitution of the United States was not an accident. Our Heavenly Father knew what would be needed, and so he paved the way to give us the Constitution. It came under the influence of prayer, and he guided those who framed that wonderful document.

I hope that the membership of this Church will not be deceived into thinking that other plans, other forms of government, other systems of direction whatsoever, are desirable. I want to say to you without any hesitation that no form of government in the world can be compared favorably with the government God gave to us. This is his plan. Then after giving us our civil government, preparing the way for governing ourselves, if you will, he organized the Church and gave it the name of his Beloved Son, and then directed that we share that information with all his children. What a commission, a divine commission![108]

—*George Albert Smith*

THIS DAY IN AMERICAN HISTORY (1913)

The 17th Amendment to the U.S. Constitution is ratified.

The Family Is the Foundation of America's Freedom

It is in our families that the basic morality and righteousness can be taught that will keep America free. Each member of every family plays an important role in America. Throughout this land for several thousand years of history the great fathers and mothers, the noble sons, the patriot sons, the choice daughters, have forged America into what we have today.

It is America's conscience that has preserved her. America is beautiful only when she is good, when her children are laughing in her streets and her love abounds in her families. Without this conscience civilization crumbles, as it has before on this continent. We are all part of America's future. Our job is to remember the lessons of the past, to patch up mistakes and the sins of everything that has gone before. The place to start is within our own families, and as we have counseled, "No success can compensate for failure in the home." That's where we want to leave these people who come and have an opportunity of hearing our message, the most important message that will be taught during our Bicentennial year.

The source of America's greatness is not a new doctrine to us. The Book of Mormon has declared over and over again that the blessings of heaven are contingent upon the righteousness of its people. In fact, this teaching has been attested to in almost every age.

In summary, I have attempted to again remind you of *your* responsibility to preserve the righteousness of the land of America. I have reviewed four thousand years of history, declaring this to be a land of promise, chosen of the Lord for his special purposes. Now we must deal with America's future.[109]

—*L. Tom Perry*

THIS DAY IN AMERICAN HISTORY (1865)

General Robert E. Lee surrenders at Appomattox Courthouse in Virginia.

APRIL 10

Being Disposed to Uphold the Constitution Is a Result of the Gospel of Jesus Christ

There are many in the world who misunderstand the mission of the Church of Christ. To such a desire to say that, as far as I am concerned, if there's anything good in life, any virtue, honesty, integrity, fearlessness to do right; if there is a disposition in me to honor my father and mother and a desire to sustain the priesthood of the living God; if I am disposed to sustain the Constitution of this great country that we live in; if there is a desire in my heart to uphold the great man whom God has honored to preside over the destinies of this nation; if there is within me love for my fellow man and a desire to serve God and keep his commandments, these characteristics have come to me, my friends, as a result of the gospel of Jesus Christ. From childhood I have been taught never to do anything improper or that would harm one of my Heavenly Father's children; but from infancy I have been taught to acquire industry, sobriety, honesty, and integrity, and all virtues possessed by men and woman whom God delights to honor and bless. (CR, October 1906, 46).[110]

—George Albert Smith

THIS DAY IN AMERICAN HISTORY (1869)

Congress increases the number of U.S. Supreme Court judges from seven to nine.

I Am Willing to Be a Sacrifice on the Altar of Virtue, Righteousness, and Truth

I would not have suffered my name to have been used by my friends on anywise, as president of the United States, or candidate for that office, if I and my friends could have had the privilege of enjoying our religious and civil rights as American citizens, even though rights which the Constitution guarantees unto all her citizens alike, but this we as a people have been denied from the beginning. Persecution has rolled up upon our heads from time to time, from portions of the United States, like peels of thunder, because of our religion, and no portion of the government as yet has stepped forward for our relief; and under view of these things, I feel it to be my right and privileged to obtain what influence and power I can lawfully in the United States for the protection of injured innocence, and if I lose my life in a good cause I am willing to be a sacrifice on the altar of virtue, righteousness, and truth, and maintaining the laws and Constitution of the United States if need be for the general good of mankind.[111]

—*Joseph Smith, Jr.*

THIS DAY IN AMERICAN HISTORY (1783)

The Continental Congress proclaims the Cessation of Arms, ending the American Revolutionary War.

Good Form Opens the Way for Good Results

The longer I live, and the more acquainted I am with men and things, the more I realize that these movements, and particularly that instrument called the Constitution of American Liberty, was certainly dictated by the spirit of wisdom, by a spirit of unparalleled liberality, and by a spirit of political utility. And if that Constitution be carried out by a just and wise administration, it is calculated to benefit not only all the people that are born under its particular jurisdiction, but all the people of the earth, of whatever nation, kindred, tongue, religion, or tradition, that may seek to take a shelter under its banner. It seems broad enough, and large enough, to receive and protect all that may be in any way deprived of the common rights of man. It was doubtless dictated by the spirit of eternal wisdom, and has thus far proved itself adequate to the wants of the nation, and to the wants of all mankind that have seen fit to attach themselves to it, to come under its protection, and share in its blessings.

The great question, as has been before observed today more than once, is, not the operations of the instruments, the beauty of the writing, the formation of the language, or the principle of liberty guaranteed therein, but the administration of those principles. For instance, paper itself cannot enforce its own precepts; and unhallowed principles in the people, or in the rulers which they choose, may pervert any form of government, however sacred, true, and liberal. They may overthrow and destroy the practical working of those very principles, which are so true, and so dear to us, and in which we so rejoice. It is the living administration, after all, that is the government, although a good form opens the way for good results, if carried out; but if not carried out, the form becomes a dead letter. Much depends on the feeling and action of the people in their choice of men and measures, and much depends on the administration of those they may choose.[112]

—*Parly P. Pratt*

THIS DAY IN AMERICAN HISTORY (1861)

The Civil War begins at Fort Sumter.

Whenever We Have Good Officers, Strive to Retain Them

I would not speak so plainly, or not that statesman use the same privilege, and that, too, in the halls of legislatures. We can never get a true Republican government upon any other principal. The object those have in view who look and long for the gaudy trash of this world should be removed, that men may occupy the high and responsible seats of the nation who will care for the welfare of the people, and cannot be bought with money, or that which it can be purchased.

Can the Constitution be altered? It can; and when we get a president that answers our wishes to occupy the executive chair, there let him sit to the day of his death, and pray that he may live as long as Methuselah; and, whenever we have good officers, strive to retain them, and to fill up vacancies with good men, until there are none who could let the nation sink for a can of oysters and a lewd woman.

The Signers of the Declaration of Independence and the Framers of the Constitution were inspired from on high to do that work. But was that which was given to them perfect not admitting of any addition whatever? No; for if men know anything, they must know that the Almighty has never yet found a man in mortality that was capable, at the first intimation, at the first impulse, to receive anything in the state of entire perfection. They laid the foundation, and it was for after generations to rear the super structure upon it. It is a progressive – a gradual work. If the framers of the Constitution and the inhabitants of the United States had walked humbly before God, . . . an honest, sober, industrious, enterprising, and righteous people would now have been found from one end of the United States to the other.[113]

—*Brigham Young*

THIS DAY IN AMERICAN HISTORY (1943)

The Jefferson Memorial is dedicated by President Franklin D. Roosevelt in Washington, D.C.

APRIL 14

How Wonderful It Is to Live in This Age

I think how wonderful it is to live in this age; how marvelous it is to be in a country such as we live in, with more liberty and freedom than any other country. If the people of this nation will continue to keep the commandments of God, if they will honor Him by uploading the Constitution of the United States that He had prepared for us by great men whom He raised up, if we will support the law, honor the Constitution, sustain those who are legally elected to reside over us, and if we will pray for them and help them, we will continue to enjoy happiness and God will bless this land, and it will continue to be fruitful of righteousness and of happiness. But if we and the other people who dwell upon the continent, the men and woman of other faiths and other creeds, turn away from the advice of our Heavenly Father, if we discard the Constitution and the blessings that it can bring us, it will only be a little while until America will be in just as dangerous a situation as any other nation of the world has been during the last great world war.[114]

—George Albert Smith

THIS DAY IN AMERICAN HISTORY (1861)

Fort Sumter surrenders to Confederate forces after 34 hours of bombardment.

A Land of Divinity as well as a Land of Destiny

Some otherwise plain and rather ordinary places can become very special to us. Our homes, a hillside, the hospitals where our children were born, the cemeteries where they are laid—these and many more have special meaning not so much for the soil or brick itself but because of what has happened (or will yet happen) there. That meaning has more importance as the events take on eternal as well as temporal significance. . . .

America is such a place, but of course it wasn't always called America nor has it always been identified by a distinctive continental shape. Originally it was simply a portion of that large, single land mass which God in his creative process called "Earth" and which, when completed, was pronounced "good" (Genesis 1:10). Whatever its name and geographical configuration, however, it was from the beginning a land of divinity as well as a land of destiny. . . .

After meticulous preparation and precise timing, the Lord [began] to build on his promised land a congregation that had compacted to pursue "the glory of God and the advancement of the Christian faith." The cultural freedom of the Renaissance and religious freedom of the Reformation underscored the strong sense of personal freedom espoused in the Enlightenment to provide the ideal attitudes and environments for the beginning of this "first new nation." . . .

Indeed it was a beginning, but it was a beginning of the end. The work of pilgrims and Puritans, patriots and politicians had been to prepare the way for prophets of the living God. With what Washington called "the singular interpositions of Providence" a political path had been prepared that would allow the "restitution of all things" (Acts 3:21). Less than a score of years after the Constitutional Convention had concluded its work and freedoms of conscience, speech, press, and worship had been guaranteed in a historic Bill of Rights, the Prophet Joseph Smith was born in clear, graceful Vermont, home of Ethan Allen and his Green Mountain Boys. . . . Thus in one final moment worthy men and righteous principles come together for the restoration of heavenly things. With His center stake in America, God began stretching the cords of his tabernacle to all the world, lengthening the habitation of Israel and establishing Zion wherever the pure in heart dwell.[115]

—*Jeffrey R. Holland*

THIS DAY IN AMERICAN HISTORY (1865)

Abraham Lincoln dies after being shot the previous evening by John Wilkes Booth.

APRIL 16

If We Do Not Practice the Ideals of the Constitution, We Can Become Anonymous and Ineffective

I believe that we should think seriously about the Constitution we dedicate ourselves to understanding and living by the principles it stands for. As the Savior raised up wise men to establish this tremendous idea of government, only wise men and women can maintain it. If we do not practice the ideals of the Constitution, we can become anonymous and ineffective.

Our Forefathers believed that we should always know what is going on in government and should do our best to keep it relatively small and dedicated to protecting each of us in the enjoyment of life, liberty, and property. We must insist that our government refrain from running our individual lives, so long as we are law-abiding. We must not permit government to take responsibilities that we should bear for ourselves.

More than two hundred years ago, one of the Founding Fathers of this great nation, Thomas Jefferson, made this observation: "The natural progress of things is for government to gain ground and for liberty to yield." Our obligation as citizens is to help retain the liberty granted to us in the Constitution.

I encourage each of us to think about government, to participate seriously in every phase of it, and to do our part in blocking its tendency to monopolize our lives. If we will do so, we will please the founders of the Constitution. In short, if we earn again what we have inherited, we will never fail.[116]

—*Joseph B. Wirthlin*

THIS DAY IN AMERICAN HISTORY (1861)

President Abraham Lincoln outlaws business with Confederate States.

If We Do Our Duty, We Can Be Preserved

But many of the prophecies referring to America's preservation are conditional. That is, if we do our duty we can be preserved, and if not, then we shall be destroyed. This means that a good deal of the responsibility lies with the priesthood of this Church as to what happens to America, and as to how much tragedy can be avoided if we do act now. . . . The Prophet Joseph Smith declared it will be the elders of Israel who will step forward to help save the Constitution, not the Church. And have we elders been warned? Yes, we have. And besides, if the Church should ever inaugurate a program, who do you think would be in the forefront to get it moving? . . .

Brethren, if we had done our homework and were faithful, we could step forward at this time and help save this country. That fact that most of us are unprepared to do it is an indictment we will have to bear. The longer we wait, the heavier the chains, the deeper and the blood, the more the persecution, and the less we can carry out our God-given mandate and worldwide mission.[117]

—*Ezra Taft Benson*

THIS DAY IN AMERICAN HISTORY (1861)

Virginia votes to secede.

And So It Is with Us

Now, you remember, doubtless, Pharaoh's treatment of the Israelites, he saw that they were increasing, and he became alarmed. "Why," said he, "If we were going to have a war, these Israelites are becoming so numerous they may join our enemies and take away our kingdom from us. We must stop their increase." And he counseled with his people as to the best method to stop this increase. He issued a decree that all male children that were born of the Israelites should be destroyed and cast into the river Nile, but that the female children should be spared. In this way he hoped to check the increase of the children of Israel in Egypt. There is nothing in history that has come down to us to furnish the grounds or justification for this cruel action on the part of this king. But this action was well adapted to force the children of Israel into the feeling that the government under which they lived was a harsh, a cruel and an unfriendly government, and to create antipathy in their breasts against it. In this way this tyrant—as all tyrants have ever done—in trying to accomplish the object he had in view, took the very means to bring upon himself and his nation the evils that he dreaded; because if he had desired to make the Israelites join the enemies of the nation and be traitors in the midst of the kingdom he could not have taken a more effective method than that which he did take.

And so it is with us. If we had not had a profound attachment to the Constitution of the United States and to the institutions of this government, the course that is taken against us by those who have represented the government has been and is of a character to have driven us into open and avowed enmity to the government years and years ago.[118]

—*George Q. Cannon*

THIS DAY IN AMERICAN HISTORY (1775)

Paul Revere and William Dawes make their famous rides.

There Are Some Fundamental Principles of This Republic Which, Like Eternal Truths, Never Get Out-of-Date

If we would make the world better, let us foster a keener appreciation of the freedom and liberty guaranteed by the government of the United States, as framed by the founders of this nation. . . . But there are some fundamental principles of this Republic which, like eternal truths, never get out-of-date; and which are applicable at all times to liberty-loving peoples. Such are the underlying principles of the Constitution, a document framed by patriotic, freedom-loving men, who we declare were inspired by the Lord.

Members of the Church should have nothing to do with secret combinations and groups antagonistic to the constitutional law of the land, which the Lord " . . . suffered to be established"; and which . . . should be maintained for the rights and protection of all flesh, according to just and holy principles.

That every man may act in doctrine and principle pertaining to futurity, according to the moral agency which I have given unto him, that every man may be accountable for his own sins in the day of judgment.

Therefore, it is not right that any man should be in bondage one to another.

And for this purpose have I established the Constitution of this land, by the hands of wise men whom I raised up unto this very purpose, and redeemed the land by the shedding of blood (D&C 101:77–80).[119]

—David O. McKay

THIS DAY IN AMERICAN HISTORY (1775)

Skirmish at Lexington Green, Massachusetts ("The Shot Heard Round the World").

The Greatest Weapons That Can Be Forged Against Any False Philosophy Are the Positive Teachings of the Gospel of Jesus Christ

The Constitution of the United States has been mentioned several times by speakers in this conference as the basis of wise decisions in fundamental principles as applied to all matters pertaining to law and order, because it was framed by men whom God raised up for this very purpose. But in addition to that inspired document, we must always keep in mind that the greatest weapons that can be forged against any false philosophy are the positive teachings of the gospel of Jesus Christ.

We constantly impress upon all who go out as true ambassadors of the kingdom of God to follow the wise counsel of the apostle Paul, one of the ablest defenders of the faith of all time. In his declaration to the Corinthians he has given us his counsel if we would be as powerful as he in our ministry. This was his secret in combating evil:

"And I, brethren, when I came to you, came not with excellency of speech or of wisdom, declaring unto you the testimony of God.

"For I am determined not to know any thing among you, save Jesus Christ, and him crucified.

"That your faith should not stand in the wisdom of men, but in the power of God." (1 Corinthians 2:1–2, 5.)[120]

—Harold B. Lee

THIS DAY IN AMERICAN HISTORY (2020)

Georgia, Tennessee, and South Carolina are the first states to announce an end to some COVID-19 restrictions.

No True Latter-day Saint Can Be a Communist or a Socialist

I hope that the threat of communism will make you more devoted to the free enterprise system. And more determined to protect and safeguard and strengthen the system under which we have to enjoy the rich blessings which are ours as a great Christian nation. The threat of communism is very real. The threat of socialism is even more real. Communism is more than an economic system.

It is a total philosophy of life, atheistic and utterly opposed to all we hold dear as a great free and Christian nation. No true Latter- day Saint can be a communist or a socialist, because their principles run counter to the revealed word of God and to the constitution of this land which was established by men whom the God of heaven raised up unto that very purpose. And so, my young brethren and sisters, we want you to be happy. We want you to be successful in your chosen field. We want you to be good citizens of this great free land, or other free lands from which you may come. And lastly, and fourthly, we want you to be exalted in the celestial kingdom. That means you live the gospel, every bit of it.

There is a standard of living in America unequaled anywhere in the world. Not because we're smarter, not because we're more not because we have greater capacity than people of other nations, but because we've had a system which is superior. A system which was wisely provided by the Founding Fathers. We must protect and safeguard that system. Sometimes we find people that almost apologize for it.

The free enterprise system, of course it isn't perfect. It's operated by human beings. But it's the best system in operation in this world today. And if we're wise, we'll preserve it, we'll strengthen it, and we'll safeguard it for our children and our children's children. We have an imperfect instrument known as the United Nations. Occasionally that instrument, that agency proposes programs for economic development in various parts of the world. I've been impressed and somewhat amused that generally speaking the United States is asked to provide about 50% of the cost of these projects. When you ask them why, the answer is nearly always the same. Because the United States has about 50% of the wealth of the world.[121]

—Ezra Taft Benson

THIS DAY IN AMERICAN HISTORY (1789)

John Adams sworn in as the first U.S. vice president nine days before George Washington is sworn in as president.

The Constitution Paved the Way for the Restoration

If the Restoration was to happen so that the kingdom of God could spread across the world like a stone cut from the mountain without hands, as Daniel foresaw, then something had to happen first. Absolutely essential to the Restoration was a nation that guaranteed the right of its citizens to free speech, the rights of property, and especially, freedom of religion. Had the Church been restored even in the more enlightened countries of Europe at that time, it would have been quickly crushed by state-sponsored religions, which vigorously opposed the rights of other religions.

When the Founding Fathers created the Constitution in 1787 and added the Bill of Rights in 1879, the separation of church and state was firmly established in the land. Though the Founding Fathers did not realize what would come of their vision, Heavenly Father did. The Constitution, with its first ten amendments, was in place about thirty years before the young Joseph Smith went into a grove of trees and took the first step in opening a new dispensation.[122]

—Gerald N. Lund

THIS DAY IN AMERICAN HISTORY (1864)

First U.S. coin minted with the motto "In God We Trust" (a two-cent coin).

All Such Matters as These Our Constitution Must Not Be Changed

In all that relates to its great fundamentals—in the division of powers and their full independence one from the other, in the equal administration of the laws in the even handed dispensing of justice, in the absence of all class and caste, in the freedom of the press and of speech and of religion—we believe that in all such matters as these our Constitution must not be changed.

Do you not catch a vision of this glory of America, not the glory of a conquest bought with our blood, of a conquest over a torn, maimed, and hating foe, or a conquest that however it may seem, yet nevertheless always leaves the world poorer and more wretched, with more of woe and misery and sin and despair and hate and damnation than before it came; not these conquests. But the conquest of peace and joy, the conquest of bringing more to eat and to wear, of bringing more comfort, more education, more culture the conquest of liberty over tyranny that all men may know and have the free institutions which are ours, the conquest of caste and legalized privileges and of all social inequalities, the conquest of want and misery, of hunger, and nakedness, a conquest of war itself so that peace and 'righteousness shall cover the earth as the waters cover the mighty deep,' a conquest that shall bring a true millennium.[123]

—J. Reuben Clark, Jr.

THIS DAY IN AMERICAN HISTORY (1789)

President-elect George Washington moves into the Franklin House in New York City (the first official residence of a U.S. president).

The Most Ancient and Sacred of Institutions—The Family

I recognize, of course, that there have been illegitimate births, that there have been irresponsible fathers and unprepared mothers, that there has been child abuse and its many and depraved forms throughout history human history. But the degree of its prevalence in this land must become a matter of concern for all of us.

It is so plainly evident that both the great good and the terrible evil found in the world today are the sweet and the bitter fruits of the rearing of yesterday's children. As we train a new generation, so will the world be in a few years. If we are worried about the future, then we must look today at the upbringing of children.

The evils of the world will continue to escalate unless there is an underlying acknowledgment, even a strong and fervent conviction, that the family is an instrument of the Almighty. It is His creation. It is also the most fundamental and basic unit of society. And it deserves—no, it demands—our combined focus and attention. We go to great lengths to preserve historical buildings and sites in our cities. We need to apply the same fervor to preserving the most ancient and sacred of institutions—the family![124]

—*Gordon B. Hinckley*

THIS DAY IN HISTORY (1898)

Spain declares war on the United States, after rejecting an ultimatum to withdraw from Cuba.

We Should Not Be Led Astray by Fallacies

If we failed to sustain the constitutional law of the land, we have transgressed the will of our Heavenly Father.

"I, the Lord God, make you free, therefore you are free indeed; and the law also make a few free.

"Nevertheless, when the wicked rule the people mourn.

"Wherefore, honest men and wise men should be soft for diligently, and good men and wise men you should observe to uphold; otherwise whatsoever is less than these come of evil."

We should not be led astray by fallacies.

In these days of confusion, when the Constitution of our country is assailed, by those who have no understanding of the purpose of God regarding this great country, it behooves those who do understand to consider seriously and faithfully, the benefits that will flow to us by honoring and sustaining the government that was reared under the direction of our Heavenly Father.

We are a peculiar people in many ways, and in this particularly are we peculiar, and that we believe that the Constitution of the United States was inspired by our Heavenly Father, and he has told us that he raised up the very men who should frame the Constitution of the United States. Knowing that, we should not be let stray by the fallacies of individuals whose selfishness inclines them to attack that which are Heavenly Father has prepared for the people of this land.[125]

—*George Albert Smith*

THIS DAY IN AMERICAN HISTORY (1846)

The Mexican War begins.

Living in the Saturday Night of this World's History

We believe we are living in the Saturday night of this world's history, that we are closing the six thousand years of its mortal probation, and that the dawn of the seventh day, or the seventh thousand years, now nearly upon us, will be the Millennium, the reign of peace, when Christ the Ruler and Lord of this world, who labored and suffered and died to redeem its inhabitants from death, will be here in His glory to reign upon the earth King over His people and over the human race.

These simple truths, most of which are plainly spoken of in this holy word of God, the Bible, are distorted by the enemies of the Saints to indicate that they are treasonable to the government under which they live. They say we are traitors because we speak of the kingdom of God; that a kingdom cannot exist within a republic; that it is *imperium in imperio*; that there is no room in this broad land for the Kingdom of our God. They might as well say there is no room in

Christianity for the love of God.

Why, this great government was established for the very purpose of introducing this work. Inspired men like Washington and Jefferson were raised up to frame a Constitution liberal in its provisions, extending the utmost freedom to all men, Christian or heathen, who desired to make this glorious land their home; that they might have the unrestricted right to worship God according to the dictates of their consciences.[126]

—*Orson F. Whitney*

THIS DAY IN AMERICAN HISTORY (2019)

"No religions" (23.1%) tops a survey of American religious identity for the time. Catholics compose 23.0% of the respondents, and evangelicals 22.5% (General Social Survey).

Leaders Who Are Willing to Stand Up for Something

What we desperately need today on all fronts—in our homes and communities, in schoolrooms and boardrooms, and certainly throughout society at large—are leaders, men and women who are willing to stand for something. We need people who are honest; who are willing to stand up for decency, truth, integrity, morality, and law and order; who respond to their consciences even when it is unpopular to do so—perhaps especially when it is unpopular to do so. . . .

Never in the history of the world has there been a more profound need for leaders of principle to step forward. Never before, at least not in our generation, have the forces of evil been so blatant, so brazen, so aggressive as they are at the present time. Things we dared not speak about in an earlier era are now constantly projected into our living rooms. All sensitivity is cast aside as reporters and political pundits speak with a disgusting plainness of things that can only stir curiosity and lead to evil.[127]

—*Gordon B. Hinckley*

THIS DAY IN AMERICAN HISTORY (1777)

Benedict Arnold's troops force the British to retreat in Ridgefield, Connecticut.

APRIL 28

We Must Maintain Our Rights, Not Aggressively, Not in Any Quarrelsome Spirit, but in a Spirit of Quiet Firmness

We are a free people—but other seeks to bring us into bondage as they may—we are a free people with a perfect right to worship our God and to carry to affect the principles that He has revealed. And if the whole world array themselves against us, in the combined power of the nation pits itself against this work, they must go down in the struggle, because they are occupying a false position. If fifty hundred millions of people were to say the contrary, no matter, the principle still remains true, that under the Constitution in this land, a man has a perfect right to do that which God requires his hands as long as he does not intrude upon the rights of his neighbor.

If one man stood alone in this position, and millions of men were to say it is not so, that lone man would still be right. We have that right. God has given it to us under the Constitution of the land in which we dwell, and if men enact laws and pile one law upon another until they reach to the sky, it would not change this. It is an eternal principle, and it will stand—this principle of liberty, the liberty that God has given unto every human being—the right to do that which seems good and his own site, to follow the dictates of his own conscience, as long as, and so doing, he does not trespass upon the rights of his fellow man. We stand by that fearlessly, and stand by for ourselves, and for our children after us. I would not abate one iota, not a hair's breadth, myself, in this feeling. I would feel that I was a traitor to myself and to my posterity if I were to yield in the least upon this. We must maintain our rights, not aggressively, not in any quarrelsome spirit, but in a spirit of quiet firmness, quiet determination to maintain our rights, to contend for them, and to never yield one hair's breadth in maintaining them. This is our duty as individuals and as a people, and in thus determining, we banned ourselves together more closely.[128]

—George Q. Cannon

THIS DAY IN AMERICAN HISTORY (1788)

Maryland receives statehood as the 7th state.

It Is Beyond the Power of Man to Destroy the Principles of the Constitution

It is beyond the power of man to destroy the principles of the Constitution. They may destroy one another, yet the principles contained in that instrument will live, and the God of heaven will maintain them until Jesus Christ comes in the clouds of heaven to set up his throne in Jerusalem, and to rain on the earth a thousand years (JD 22:346, October 23, 1881).

The Constitution must prevail. I would to God that the rulers of our land—the President of the United States, the Congress of the United States, the Supreme Court of the United States—would learn the responsibility the God of heaven will hold them to the administration of those glorious principles laid down in a Constitution of the government of this country. The God of heaven will hold this nation, as well as all other nations, responsible for the manner in which these principles are used. If they misuse them, it will be their loss. If they trampled the Constitution underfoot; if they undertake to deprive any portion of citizens of the rights the Constitution guarantees onto them, they will be held responsible, and will have to pay the bill. When an innocent blood is shed, it cost something; and I would to God that our nation could understand the blessings they enjoy. There is no nation on the face of the earth that has the same liberty that is guaranteed to us by the Constitution of our country (JD 25:11, January 6, 1884).[129]

—Wilford Woodruff

THIS DAY IN AMERICAN HISTORY (1945)

The U.S. Army liberates the Dachau Concentration Camp in Southern Germany.

It Is for Us to Sustain and Maintain the Principles Guaranteed in the Constitution

If the rulers of this nation can afford to tamper with the sacred rights of the people guaranteed by the Constitution of this great nation, and ruthlessly tear down the temple of freedom erected at the cost of so much blood and treasure, instead of anticipated glory, they will bring destruction upon the nation and ruin and infamy upon themselves. The sacred bulwarks of freedom once tampered with, the floodgates of anarchy and confusion will be thrown open and dissolution and ruin will follow in their train and rapid succession. It is for us to sustain and maintain the principles guaranteed in that sacred palladium of human rights—the Constitution of the United States, and to contend inch by inch in every legal and constitutional manner for our own rights and human freedom, leaving misrule, anarchy, violations of law and the trampling under foot of the rights of man and constitutional guarantees to religious fanatics and clamoring demagogues; and if they can afford to tamper with those sacred guarantees, we certainly can afford to have them do it. It is for us to seek more exalted ideas, to abide by constitutional law, to maintain inviolate the principles of human freedom, and to contend with unwavering firmness for those inalienable rights of all men—life, liberty and the pursuit of happiness; and to seek continually to our God for wisdom to accomplish so great, noble and patriotic a purpose.[130]

—*John Taylor*

THIS DAY IN AMERICAN HISTORY (1789)

George Washington gives his first inaugural address.

The Greatest Declaration of Freedom

The men who signed the Declaration of Independence were not just signing a nicely written proclamation with wonderful philosophical and moral ideas. They knew they could be signing their own death sentences. Benjamin Rush, one of the signers, wrote to John Adams, "Do you recollect the pensive and awful silence which pervaded the house when we were called up, one after another, to the table of the President of Congress, to subscribe what was believed by many at that time to be our own death warrants?" They knew that if the little colonies of America did not prevail, they would likely be hanged as traitors to the Crown. Yet they sensed a divine destiny in this country that compelled them to put their pen to perhaps the greatest declaration of freedom and individual rights the world has ever known.[131]

—*Tad R. Callister*

THIS DAY IN AMERICAN HISTORY (1900)

A premature blast collapses a mine tunnel, killing 200 at Schofield, Utah.

There Are Some Fundamental Principles of This Republic

If we would make the world better, let us foster a key appreciation of the freedom and liberty guaranteed by the government of the United States as framed by the founders of this nation. Here again self-proclaimed progressive cry at such old-time adherence is out of date. But there are some fundamental principles of this Republic which, like eternal truth, never get out of date, and which are applicable at all times liberty-loving peoples. Such are the underlying principles of the Constitution, a document framed by patriotic, freedom-loving men, who Latter-Day Saints declare were inspired by the Lord. . . .

It is highly fitting, therefore, as a means of making the world better, not only to urge loyalty to the Constitution and to threatened fundamentals of the United States government, but to warn the people that there's evidence in the United States of disloyalty to try and true fundamentals and government. There are unsound economic theories; there are European "isms," which, termite like, secretly and, recently, quite openly and defiantly, are threatening to undermine our democratic institution.

Today, it's never before, the issue is clearly defined—liberty and freedom of choice, or oppression and subjugation for the individual and nations.[132]

—*David O. McKay*

THIS DAY IN AMERICAN HISTORY (1863)

While attacking Chancellorsville, Virginia, Stonewall Jackson is mortally wounded by his own men.

Defective Personalities Project Themselves into the Affairs of State

The word *civilization* is only used twice in the Book of Mormon (Alma 51:22 and Moroni 9:11), once when its loss is graphically described. It is impressive to note that the loss of civilization was tied to the growing immorality, not to a decline in Nephite art; and the growing anarchy was the outcropping of a decline in their capacity to love, not a decay in their architecture. The author who chronicled this decaying society commented on perversion and violence, not just the failure of the political systems to perform. The inner deficiencies of men impact on the quality of our institutions.

Like it or not, therefore, one of the messages of the scriptures is that defective personalities project themselves into the affairs of state, and their defects are mirrored in the politics of their time; and society, in subtle and direct ways, can pay a terrible price! . . .

Men who are immoral can contribute some good to human affairs, as the Book of Mormon candidly records (Ether 10:11). But to argue that the personal pressures that sin can bring into the life of a ruler do not have a consequence in his management of the affairs of his people is to argue that nothing in a leader's experience (or that is on his mind) has any bearing on what he does. If a leader who is fatigued physically can make bad decisions, a leader who is fatigued spiritually can make them also, and a damaged ego can lead to bad policy.[133]

—*Neal A. Maxwell*

THIS DAY IN AMERICAN HISTORY (1943)

United States food rationing begins during World War II.

This Is a Land Which Is Choice Above All Other Lands

God gave us victory in the Revolutionary War. We are indebted to him for our nation's independence. He has prospered us in every righteous endeavor. He established the Constitution of the United States "by the hands of wise men whom [he] raised up unto this very purpose" (D&C 101:80).

He Himself with His Beloved Son appeared to the Prophet Joseph Smith to open a new dispensation of the gospel of Jesus Christ here in this land. He has established His Church here and has sent and is sending representatives thereof into every nook and corner of the land—and as far as possible to all the earth—to declare and teach the laws of Jesus Christ, the God of this land.

He has revealed anew and repeated over and over again the ancient decree: "This is a land which is choice above all other lands; wherefore he that doth possess it shall serve God or shall be swept off; for it is the everlasting decree of God" concerning this land (Ether 2:10).

This knowledge has been revealed to us that we "may know the decrees of God—that [we] may repent, and not continue in [our] iniquities until the fulness come, that [we] may not bring down the fulness of the wrath of God upon [us] as the inhabitants of the land have hitherto done" (Ether 2:11). . . .

Now my beloved brethren and sisters everywhere, both members of the Church and nonmembers, I bear you my personal witness that I know that the things I have presented to you today are true—both those pertaining to past events and those pertaining to events yet to come. The issue we face is clear and well defined. The choice is ours. The question is: Shall we of this dispensation repent and obey the laws of the God of the land, who is Jesus Christ, or shall we continue to defy them until we ripen in iniquity?

That we will repent and obey and thereby qualify to receive the blessings promised to the righteous in this land, I humbly pray.[134]

—Marion G. Romney

THIS DAY IN AMERICAN HISTORY (1702)

Queen Anne's War begins.

Appraise Any Program, Policy, or Idea Promoted by Any Would-Be Political Leader

It is my conviction that only in this land, under this God-inspired Constitution, under an environment of freedom, could it have been possible to have established the Church and kingdom of God and restored the gospel in its fullness. It is our responsibility, my brethren and sisters, to see that this freedom is maintained, so that the Church can flourish in the future. Today I would like to propose four questions which every Latter-day Saint might well ask as he attempts to appraise any program, policy, or idea promoted by any would-be political leader.

First, is the proposal, the policy, or the idea being promoted right as measured by the gospel of Jesus Christ? I assure you it is much easier for one to measure a proposed policy by the gospel of Jesus Christ if he has accepted the gospel and is living it.

Secondly, is it right as measured by the Constitution of this land and the glorious principles embodied in that Constitution? Now that suggests that we must read and study the Constitution, the Declaration of Independence, and the Bill of Rights, that we might know what principles are embodied therein.

Thirdly, we might well ask the question: Is it right as measured by the counsel of the living oracles of God? It is my conviction, my brethren and sisters, that these living oracles are not only authorized, but are obligated to give counsel to this people on any subject which is vital to the welfare of this people and the upbuilding of the kingdom of God. So, that measure should be applied. Is it right as measured by the counsel of the living oracles of God?

Fourthly, what will be the effect on the morale and the character of the people if this or that policy is adopted? After all, as a Church we are interested in building men and women, building character, because character is the one thing we make in this world and take with us into the next. It must never be sacrificed for expediency.[135]

—*Ezra Taft Benson*

THIS DAY IN AMERICAN HISTORY (1816)

The American Bible Society is organized in New York.

The Constitution Was the Work of His Own Hand

Without the Constitution there would be no government such as the Lord had in mind. The Lord gave us that government by providing the Constitution written by the hands of wise men whom he raised up for this very purpose. It was an act of God. It was another step in establishing the free conditions under which the gospel could be restored and then taken by the believing Gentiles to all other nations.

As the Lord indicated so plainly through Nephi and likewise in his own declaration to the Nephites after his resurrection as quoted above, it was a giant step in the divine plan to fulfill the promise made to Abraham, that God would recover his scattered seed by the preaching of the gospel.

The Constitution provided freedom of religion, speech, press, and assembly. Therefore, under the Constitution the Lord could restore the gospel and reestablish His church. The preparation of the Constitution was the work of His own hand. The restoration of the gospel was likewise His work.

Both were part of a greater whole. Both fit into his pattern for the latter days. There would be no state church in America to interfere.

All men in this land now were given the right to worship God according to the dictates of their own conscience, and that included Joseph Smith and his followers. It is true they were persecuted, as the people of God always have been, but the law—the Constitution—provided the very thing the Lord had in mind: freedom to reestablish His work in these last days, for He had so arranged it.[136]

—*Mark E. Peterson*

THIS DAY IN AMERICAN HISTORY (1861)

Arkansas votes to secede from the Union in the Civil War.

America Is the Cradle of the Church

The United States represents the major source of human and financial resources that go into the expansion of the Lord's work throughout the world. It is very essential that America remain strong in order that the Church can continue to support the Lord's work in all corners of the earth . . . as Saints in these and other lands arrive at the point where they can help in the worldwide expansion of the Lord's work, the Church will have moved into other new lands that will need human and financial support for a long time. To get the Saints in any nation to the point where they can stand on their own feet, so to speak, with their own leaders and supply their own financial resources, represents a long nurturing process.

But until that day comes, it is obvious that the central source of resources for the worldwide Church for the past 146 years has been America—and we think it will continue to be that way for quite some time. So we're anxious to help America be strong and good, because the American Saints are so central to supplying the needs of others throughout the world for the present.

In addition to that central idea we have a basic religious message, a unique message to tell the world—and that is that God's hand was in the founding of America. America is the cradle of the Church. We know that the great reformation of centuries ago was God-inspired. The rediscovery of America by Columbus was God-inspired. The founding of this land with a form of government that would permit the gospel to be restored and be established was God-inspired. This is a great message. A message of fulfilled prophecy. A message that God lives—that He is in our lives, that He is involved in the shaping of history in ways that many people do not know. I tell you, this is great news! The Lord Himself said that He raised up "wise men" for the purpose of founding the United States' constitutional government, a form of government that has been modeled and patterned after all over the world because it provides the kind of freedom, agency, and opportunity our Father's children need in order for them to grow, mature, and develop.[137]

—L. Tom Perry

THIS DAY IN AMERICAN HISTORY (1975)

President Gerald Ford declares an end to the Vietnam Era.

MAY 8

Witnesses of God's Hand

James Madison, the Father of the Constitution, reflected upon the hand of God in the miraculous achievement of such a document: "It is impossible for any man of candour to reflect on this circumstance without partaking of the astonishment. It is impossible for the man of pious reflection not to perceive in it a finger of that Almighty hand which has been so frequently and signally extended to our relief in the critical stages of the revolution." George Washington concurred in this assessment: "[The adoption of the Constitution] will demonstrate as visibly the finger of Providence, as any possible event in the course of human affairs can ever designate it."

The Constitution was not just a patchwork of ideas from other nation's constitutions. James Madison spoke of the uniqueness of this document in the entirety of history: Happy for America, happily, we trust, for the whole human race, [the founders of the nation] pursed a new and more noble course. They accomplished a revolution which has no parallel in the annals of human society. They reared the fabrics of government which have no model on the face of the globe." George Washington added his insight: "[The Constitution] approached nearer to perfection than any government hitherto instituted among men." And John Adams noted that the Constitution was "if not the greatest exertion of human understanding, the greatest single effort of national deliberation that the world has ever seen." In other words, it was inspired. What powerful on-the-scene witnesses of God's hand in the formation of the Constitution! [138]

—*Tad R. Callister*

THIS DAY IN AMERICAN HISTORY (1945)

German General Wilhelm Keital formally surrenders to the Allies—represented by the United States, the UK, France, and the Soviet Union—in Berlin.

The Conquest of Peace and Joy

Do you not catch a vision of this glory of America, not the glory of a conquest bought with our blood, of a conquest over a torn, maimed, and hating foe, of a conquest that however it may seem, yet nevertheless always leaves the world poorer and more wretched, with more of woe and misery and sin and despair and hate and damnation than before it came; not of these conquests.

But the conquest of peace and joy, the conquest of bringing more to eat and more to wear, of bringing more comfort, more education, more culture, the conquest of liberty over tyranny that all men may know and have the free institutions which are ours, the conquest of caste and legalized privilege and of all social inequalities, the conquest of want and misery, of hunger, and nakedness, a conquest of war itself, so that peace and "righteousness shall cover the earth as the waters cover the mighty deep," a conquest that shall bring a true millennium.[139]

—*J. Reuben Clark, Jr.*

THIS DAY IN AMERICAN HISTORY (1914)

President Woodrow Wilson proclaims Mother's Day.

MAY 10

It Was the Voice of the Lord Inspiring All Those Worthy Men

We believe that the Lord has been preparing that when he should bring forth his work, that, when the set time should fully come, there might be a place upon his footstool where sufficient liberty of conscience should exist, that his Saints might dwell in peace under the broad panoply of constitutional law and equal rights. In this view we consider that the men in the Revolution were inspired by the Almighty, to throw off the shackles of the mother government, with her established religion. For this cause were Adams, Jefferson, Franklin, Washington, and a host of others inspired to deeds of resistance to the acts of the King of Great Britain, who might also have been led to those aggressive acts, for ought we know, to bring to pass the purposes of God, in thus establishing a new government upon a principle of greater freedom, a basis of self-government allowing the free exercise of religious worship.

It was the voice of the Lord inspiring all those worthy men who bore influence in those trying times, not only to go forth in battle but to exercise wisdom in council, fortitude, courage, and endurance in the tented field, as well as subsequently to form and adopt those wise and efficient measures which secured to themselves and succeeding generations, the blessings of a free and independent government.[140]

—*Brigham Young*

THIS DAY IN AMERICAN HISTORY (1775)

The Second Continental Congress begins meeting in Philadelphia.

Religious Freedom Is of God; Compulsion of Religion Is of the Devil

Freedom of worship is one of the basic doctrines of the gospel. Indeed, in one manner of speaking it is the most basic of all doctrines, even taking precedence over the nature and kind of being that God is, or the atoning sacrifice of the Son of God, or the vesting of priesthood and keys and saving power in the one true church. By this we mean that if there were no freedom of worship, there would be no God, no redemption and no salvation in the kingdom of God. Let us now reason, as the prophets have done, on this matter. . . .

Lucifer, in the Grand Council when the Great God presented the plan of agency and salvation, proposed instead to save all men. "I will redeem all mankind, that one soul shall not be lost, and surely I will do it," he said (Moses 4:1). That is, none would be damned; damnation would not be a viable alternative to salvation; there would be no agency—no freedom of choice, no election to serve God or to flee from evil and turn to righteousness. But if there is no freedom of choice between damnation and salvation, how can either exist? They are opposites; without one you cannot have the other. Lucifer's proposal to amend the Father's plan could not be; it was philosophically impossible to accomplish. He could not save all mankind, because unless some were damned, there would be no salvation, for nothing can so much as exist unless it has an opposite. Agency and freedom of worship are just that basic and important in the eternal plan of salvation.

Freedom of worship is thus one of the chief identifying characteristics of the true church. Religious Freedom is of God; compulsion in religion is of the devil . . . and so, in expounding upon the eleventh article of faith, we assert with unshakable surety our belief in and allegiance to the doctrine of freedom of worship. We claim it for ourselves; we allow it to others; nay, more, we encourage others to worship as they choose and pledge ourselves to defend them in so doing.[141]

—*Bruce R. McConkie*

THIS DAY IN AMERICAN HISTORY (1858)

Delegates gather in Philadelphia to write the U.S. Constitution.

I Am an American Because . . .

I am an American because I believe in a government of laws and not of men, and in a national allegiance to high principle and lofty ideal instead of to a personal sovereign. . . .

I am an American because I believe that government must derive its "just powers from the consent of the governed" and that branches of government and officers shall have such powers and such only as shall be given by the people; because I believe that the assumption by branches of government or by officers of rights or powers not specifically conferred upon them is usurpation; and because impeachment or other trial lies against any officer who so usurps rights or powers not specifically conferred. . . .

I am an American because I believe in a Bill of Rights which places wholly beyond the reach of lawful government certain matters affecting "life, liberty, and the pursuit of happiness," and specifically the right of freedom of conscience and worship, the right of free speech and a free press, the right peaceably to assemble and petition government, and the right to gain and hold property without molestation except by due process of law. . . .

I am an American because standards of life and of living of the entire American people are far beyond those enjoyed by any other people in any other part of the world, either now or at any other time, which is a living testimony and evidence of the kindly beneficence of our free institutions. . . .

I am an American because my country abolished slavery after it had become deep-rooted and because men still are free to work and are secure in the enjoyment of the products of their labor.

I am an American because I firmly and earnestly believe that the Constitution is an inspired document designed by our Maker to set up a government which would make sure and secure the rights set forth in the Bill of Rights, and particularly the right of freedom of conscience and worship.

I am an American because I believe that the destiny of America is to be the abiding place of liberty and free institutions, and that its own practice and enjoyment of these blessings shall be to the world a beacon light which shall radiate its influence by peaceful means to the uttermost parts of the world, to the uplifting of all humanity.[142]

—*J. Reuben Clark*

THIS DAY IN AMERICAN HISTORY (1958)

The United States and Canada form the North American Air Defense Command (NORAD).

His Peace Is Personal

Prior to His ascension from the Holy Land, the Savior pronounced a unique blessing: "Peace I leave with you, my peace I give unto you: not as the world giveth, give I unto you" (John 14:27).

His peace is not necessarily political; His peace is personal. But that spirit of inner peace is driven away by contention. Contention does not usually begin as strife between countries. More often, it starts with an individual, for we can contend within ourselves over simple matters of right and wrong. From there, contention can infect neighbors and nations like a spreading sore.

As we dread any disease that undermines the health of the body, so should we deplore contention, which is a corroding canker of the spirit. I appreciate the counsel of Abraham Lincoln, who said:

"Quarrel not at all. No man resolved to make the most of himself can spare time for personal contention. . . . Better give your path to a dog than be bitten by him."[143] . . .

My concern is that contention is becoming accepted as a way of life. From what we see and hear in the media, the classroom, and the workplace, all are now infected to some degree with contention. How easy it is, yet how wrong it is, to allow habits of contention to pervade matters of spiritual significance, because contention is forbidden by divine decree:

"The Lord God hath commanded that men should not murder; that they should not lie; that they should not steal; that they should not take the name of the Lord their God in vain; that they should not envy; that they should not have malice; that they should not contend one with another" (2 Nephi 26:32).[144]

—*Russell M. Nelson*

THIS DAY IN AMERICAN HISTORY (1961)

NASA submitted its legislative program for the 87th Congress.

We Can Have Peace in Our Hearts and Peace in Our Homes

Great are the promises concerning this land of America. We are told unequivocally that it "is a choice land, and whatsoever nation shall possess it shall be free from bondage, and from captivity, and from all other nations under heaven, if they will but serve the God of the land, who is Jesus Christ" (Ether 2:12). This is the crux of the entire matter—obedience to the commandments of God.

The Constitution under which we live, and which has not only blessed us but has become a model for other constitutions, is our God-inspired national safeguard ensuring freedom and liberty, justice and equality before the law.

I do not know what the future holds. I do not wish to sound negative, but I wish to remind you of the warnings of scripture and the teachings of the prophets which we have had constantly before us. . . .

I am familiar, as are you, with the declarations of modern revelation that the time will come when the earth will be cleansed and there will be indescribable distress, with weeping and mourning and lamentation (see D&C 112:24).

Now, I do not wish to be an alarmist. I do not wish to be a prophet of doom. I am optimistic. I do not believe the time is here when an all-consuming calamity will overtake us. I earnestly pray that it may not. There is so much of the Lord's work yet to be done. We, and our children after us, must do it. . . .

Let us be prayerful. Let us pray for righteousness. Let us pray for the forces of good. Let us reach out to help men and women of goodwill, whatever their religious persuasion and wherever they live. Let us stand firm against evil, both at home and abroad. Let us live worthy of the blessings of heaven, reforming our lives where necessary and looking to Him, the Father of us all. He has said, "Be still, and know that I am God" (Psalm 46:10).

Are these perilous times? They are. But there is no need to fear. We can have peace in our hearts and peace in our homes. We can be an influence for good in this world, every one of us.[145]

—Gordon B. Hinckley

THIS DAY IN AMERICAN HISTORY (1787)

Delegates gather in Philadelphia to write the U.S. Constitution.

The Constitution Is the Best Instrument in Existence

It may be asked why the framers of the Constitution did not carry out the views enunciated by the declarers of independence, in regard to the inalienable rights of man? . . . It may be asked, if this instrument was imperfect, why do you sustain it? Simply that, with this one fault, it was the best instrument in existence, and it was all and more than the nation has ever lived up to (*JT Papers* 1:282).

We are told, however, that "eternal vigilance is the price of liberty;" and as we possess the best Constitution and the best government in the world, let us preserve it, and transmit it intact, pure and unadulterated to our children (*JT Papers* 1:285).

I have taken the oath of allegiance to the United States government, not being American born, and I have always admired its institutions; and I have been very desirous to see the practice and carrying out of these fundamental principles of our government; I have been anxious to see public affairs conducted in an honorable, intelligent, correct, philosophic, patriotic and statesmanlike form in all things. These have been my sentiments (Hollister 5).[146]

—*John Taylor*

THIS DAY IN AMERICAN HISTORY (1869)

The National Women Suffrage Association forms in New York—co-founded by Susan B. Anthony and Elizabeth Cady Stanton.

MAY 16

Be Examples of Civility

I encourage you to stand clear from the current atmosphere of hate and to refrain from participating in the contentious communications that are so common today. Partly such contentious communications result from modern technology, which fosters conflicts by expanding the audience and the speed of dissemination.

As followers of Christ, we know that all of the inhabitants of this earth are children of God. Use that knowledge to push back against the worldly prejudices that preach hate or hostility toward other nations, ethnic groups, or even political parties.

Remember our Savior's teaching that "he that hath the spirit of contention is not of me, but is of the devil, who is the father of contention, and he stirreth up the hearts of men to contend with anger, one with another" (3 Nephi 11:29).

Followers of Christ should be examples of civility. But beyond this we should remember and follow the Savior's teaching: "By this shall all men know that ye are my disciples, if ye have love one to another" (John 13:35).

Of course this counsel to love, to avoid contention, and to be examples of civility is not meant to discourage us from participating in discussions, debates, and even taking adversarial positions against what we believe to be wrong or inadvisable.

Within the limits of our own resources of time and influence we should take a position, make it known, and in a respectful way attempt to persuade others of its merit, at least for us. Positive action is essential to our responsibility to push back against the world.[147]

—*Dallin H. Oaks*

THIS DAY IN AMERICAN HISTORY (1868)

The U.S. Senate acquits President Andrew Johnson.

Communist vs. Constitution

The Church does not interfere, and has no intention of trying to interfere, with the fullest and freest exercise of the political franchise of its members, under and within our Constitution with the Lord declare: "high established . . . by the hands of wise men who I raised up unto this very purpose," and which, as to the principles thereof, the prophet, dedicating the Kirkland temple, prayed should be "established forever."

But communism is not a political party nor political plan under the Constitution; it is a system of government that is the opposite of our Constitutional government, and it would be necessary to destroy our government before communism could be set up in the United States.

Since communism, established, would destroy our American Constitutional government, to support communism is treasonable to our free institutions, and no patriotic American citizen may become either communist or supporter of communism.[148]

—*Heber J. Grant, J. Reuben Clark, Jr., David O. McKay*

THIS DAY IN AMERICAN HISTORY (1792)

Twenty-four merchants form the New York Stock Exchange at 70 Wall Street.

We Believe that the Constitution Was Brought About by God

No constitution on earth has endured longer than this one. We seek, and usually find, the answers to today's questions in this document of yesterday. It was and is a miracle. Both Washington and Madison referred to it as such. It is an inspired document written under the guidance of the Lord. James Madison, commonly called the father of the Constitution, recognized this inspiration and gave the credit to "the guardianship and guidance of the Almighty Being whose power regulates the destiny of nations, whose blessings have been so conspicuously dispensed to this rising republic."[149]

We believe that the Constitution was brought about by God to ensure a nation where liberty could abound and where his gospel could flourish. Joseph Smith said, "The Constitution of the United States is a glorious standard—it is founded in the wisdom of God—it is a heavenly banner."[150]

Among other things, the Constitution guaranteed the religious freedom that allowed the Reformation to continue and flourish. Many of these great reformers stated that their effort was to reassert the basic Christian teachings of the Bible—but they acknowledged that they possessed no authority to administer the ordinances of the Church, or to reestablish the original church of Jesus Christ.

The Constitution occurred in preparation for a restoration from heaven of the full gospel of Jesus Christ. That restoration began in the United States of America in the 1820s through the instrumentality of the Prophet Joseph Smith, who was chosen by the Lord and who, through personal manifestations from heavenly messengers, received pertinent records which contained the authentic record of early American peoples and God's dealings with them. He received the priesthood and authority to reestablish the church of Jesus Christ in these latter days.[151]

—*N. Eldon Tanner*

THIS DAY IN AMERICAN HISTORY (1652)

Rhode Island enacts the first American law declaring slavery illegal.

We Need to Understand It and the Philosophy that Underlies It

I would further counsel you to pay your honest tithes and contribute generously to the support of the poor and needy through the fast offerings. Then store at least a year's supply of basic food, clothing, and fuel. Then you will find these blessings will accrue:

You will not be confronted with the danger of losing all you have because of inflation or depression.

You will have security that no government can provide, savings and supplies for emergencies.

You can ask God's blessings and his protecting care on you and your family.

You are contributing to the solution of our country's ills, rather than contributing to its problems.

May I humbly urge you to learn about the Constitution, the Declaration of Independence, and other basic documents of our great country so that you can sustain it and the free institutions set up under it. It is a part of my faith that the Constitution of the United States was inspired by God. I reverence it akin to the revelations that have come from God. The Lord declared he established it "by the hands of wise men whom [he] raised up unto this very purpose" (D&C 101:80). Referring to the principles thereof, the Prophet Joseph Smith, dedicating the Kirtland Temple, prayed it should be "established forever" (D&C 109:54).

Before we can intelligently sustain the principles of this divinely inspired document, we need to understand it and the philosophy that underlies it. We will then be in a position to determine encroachments on our liberty when well-intentioned, but unenlightened politicians attempt to circumvent those principles. The greatest watchdog of our freedom is an informed electorate.[152]

—Ezra Taft Benson

THIS DAY IN AMERICAN HISTORY (1883)

"Buffalo Bill" Cody opens his Wild West show.

What Your Opinions Are Today Regarding Life and Its Objectives Will Determine What Our United States Will Be Tomorrow

I think we owe at least the consideration to be loyal to this country and to spurn with all the soul that is within us the scheming disloyal citizens who would undermine our Constitution, or who would deprive the individual of his liberty vouchsafed by that great document, and some of our men who have come up through the public schools are doing just that. Let every loyal member of the Church look down with scorn upon any man or woman who would undermine that Constitution. . . .

More about our country: it has been said that "the destiny of any nation at a given time depends on the opinions of its young men under five and twenty." Never before in the history of our country was the State in greater need of young men who cherish the higher life in preference to the sorted, the selfish, and the obscene. What your opinions are today regarding life and its objectives will determine what our United States will be tomorrow. Tomorrow, then, is something to ponder over.

As precious as life itself is our heritage of individual freedom, for man's free agencies at God-given gift. I'm sensing a responsibility to preserve it for ourselves in our posterity, let students and patriotic people ever keep in mind the warning given by James Russell Lowell: "Our American republic will endure only as long as the ideas of the men who founded it continue to dominate."[153]

—David O. McKay

THIS DAY IN AMERICAN HISTORY (1861)

North Carolina votes to secede from the Union in the Civil War.

The Destruction of the Constitution Must Lead to the Ruin and Destruction of the Union

As it has been in the past, so it will be in the future; the faithful being inspired with the Holy Ghost, will set their hearts upon the redemption of Zion, and relying upon the promises, will turn their faces towards Jerusalem, prayers before, and follow Jesus Christ in life and death. Let the wicked rage and the adversary exert his power, the righteous will gain the victory, and when thrones are cast down the Saints shall prevail.

Let us maintain the Constitution of our country, and all laws enacted in conformity therewith, realizing that the destruction of the Constitution must lead to the ruin and destruction of the Union. Let us honor the rulers of the nation and uphold them, by faith and prayers as long as it is possible to do so. I desire to regard the president as an honorable man. As the chief executive of a great nation, he should have the confidence and respect of the people. Should he select honorable, unbiased gentleman for the Utah commission, as I have reason to hope he will, they can do much towards modifying the unjust law under which they must act, but whether such our appointed or not, we must continue to pray for our enemies and those that despitefully use us, until bye and by we shall learn the lesson so well that when the little stone cut out of the mountains without hands shall roll forth, become a mighty mountain, fill the whole earth, and the Saints of the Most High have the rule and dominion they will never be disposed to oppression.[154]

—*Moses Thatcher*

THIS DAY IN AMERICAN HISTORY (1881)

Clara Barton founds the American Red Cross.

MAY 22

The Church Must Maintain Neutrality

It is part of our faith that the Constitution of the United States was inspired by God. We reverence it akin to the revelations that have come from God. The Church, out of respect for the rights of all its members to heave their political views and loyalties, must maintain the strictest possible neutrality. We have no intention of trying to interfere with the fullest and freest exercise of the political franchise of our members under and within our Constitution, which the Lord declared He established "by the hands of wise men whom [He] raised up unto this very purpose" (D&C 109:54). The Church does not yield any of its devotion to our convictions about safeguarding the American principles, the establishment of government under federal and state constitutions, and the civil rights of men safeguard by these.

We warn our people about false political "isms" that have crept into our midst, revolutionists who use the technique that is as old as the human race—a fervid but false solicitude for the unfortunate over whom they thus gain mastery and control. We have consistently warned our people against the insidious nature of communism, which debases the individual, robs him of his agency, and makes of him an enslaved tool of the state to which he must look for sustenance and religion. Latter-day Saints cannot be true to their faith and lend aid, encouragement, or sympathy to false ideologies such as socialism and communism. The official Church position on communism remains unchanged since it was first promulgated in 1936: "We call upon all Church members completely to eschew communism. The safety of our divinely inspired Constitutional government and the welfare of our Church imperatively demand that communism shall have no place in America."[155]

—Ezra Taft Benson

THIS DAY IN AMERICAN HISTORY (1607)

Colonists make their first landing at Jamestown, Virginia.

Political Allegiance Shall Run Not to Individuals

God provided that in this land of liberty, our political allegiance shall run not to individuals, that is, to government officials, no matter how great or how small they may be. Under His plan our allegiance and the only allegiance we owe as citizens or denizens of the United States, runs to our inspired Constitution which God Himself set up. So runs the oath of office of those who participate in government. A certain loyalty we do owe to the office which a man holds, but even here we owe, just by reason of our citizenship, no loyalty to the man himself. In other countries it is to the individual that allegiance runs. This principle of allegiance to the Constitution is basic to our freedom. It is one of the great principles that distinguishes this "land of liberty" from other countries. Thus God added to His priceless blessings to us.[156]

—*J. Reuben Clark, Jr.*

THIS DAY IN AMERICAN HISTORY (1788)

South Carolina ratifies the U. S. Constitution and receives statehood.

The Constitution Is Perfect so Far as It Pertains to the Right and Privileges of the Children of Men

Many great inglourious principles are contained within the Constitution of our country, not to say that it is perfect, but it is perfect so far as it pertains to the rights and privileges of the children of men. But there is a nucleus of a government, formed since that of the United States, which is perfect in its nature. It is perfect, having emanated from a Being who is perfect. But some may enquire, is it right—is it lawful for another government to be within the United States, of a theoretical nature? Yes, perfectly so! Does not the Constitution of our country guarantee to all religious societies the right of forming any ecclesiastical government they like? Certainly it does, and every intelligent man knows this to be the fact.

The nucleus of such a government is formed, and its laws emanated from the throne of God, and it is perfect, having come from a pure fountain; but does this make us independent of the laws of the United States? No, this new government does not come in contact with the government of the United States. And keeping our covenants, and observing our religious laws and ceremonies, or the laws that God has given to the children of men, we are not required to violate the principles of right that are contained in the Constitution and laws of the United States.[157]

—*Orson Pratt*

THIS DAY IN AMERICAN HISTORY (1775)

John Hancock is unanimously elected as president of the Continental Congress.

May We Keep Always a Deep Sense of Gratitude for a Pioneer Heritage

We charge the Saints to set a proper example in their own personal conduct; to see that their families and home life are in proper order; to be careful not to neglect their family; and to hold family home evenings.

May we keep always a deep sense of gratitude for a pioneer heritage, a love for this country, and a deep-seated reverence for the Constitution of the United States, to the end that we will never forget our civic and political obligations. Our greatest joy comes when, in the years that lie ahead, are you become honored citizens in their communities and active participants in building up the kingdom of God.

If we seek earnestly, we can reach into that spiritual dimension for answers that was secure for us not only great blessings, but also the sublime witness in our hearts that are acts, our life, and our laborers have the seal approval of the Lord and Creator of us all.[158]

—Harold B. Lee

THIS DAY IN AMERICAN HISTORY (1878)

The Constitutional Convention meets its quorum requirement and officially begins in Philadelphia.

We Must Have the Great Guarantees That Are Set Up by Our Constitution

To me the Constitution is a part of my religion. In its place it is just as much a part of my religion as any other part. It is a part of my religion because it is one of those institutions which God has set up for His own purposes, and, as one of the brethren said today, set up so that this Church might be established, because under no other government in the world could the Church have been established as it has been established under this government. . . .

Now, I am not caring today, for myself, anything at all about a political party tag. So far as I am concerned, I want to know what the man stands for. I want to know if he believes in the Constitution; if he believes in its free institutions; if he believes in its liberties, its freedom. I want to know if he believes in the Bill of Rights. I want to know if he believes in the separation of sovereign power into the three great divisions: the Legislative, the Judicial, the Executive. I want to know if he believes in the mutual independence of these, the one from the other. When I find out these things, then I know who it is who should receive my support, and I care not what his party tag is, because, brethren, if we are to live as a Church, and progress, and have the right to worship as we are worshipping here today, we must have the great guarantees that are set up by our Constitution. There is no other way in which we can secure these guarantees. You may look at the systems all over the world where the principles of our Constitution are not controlling and in force, and you will find there dictatorship, tyranny, oppression, and, in the last analysts, slavery. . . .

Today, our duty transcends party allegiance; our duty today is allegiance to the Constitution as it was given to us by the Lord. Every federal officer takes an oath to support that Constitution so given. . . .

God give us wisdom and enable us in these times of trouble and strife clearly to see our way, that we may be instrumental in sustaining the Constitution, in upholding our free institutions, our civil rights, our freedom of speech, of press, of religion, and of conscience. If we shall stand together we shall save the Constitution, just as has been foreseen, and if we do not stand together, we cannot perform this great task.[159]

—*J. Reuben Clark, Jr.*

THIS DAY IN AMERICAN HISTORY (1805)

Lewis and Clark first sight the Rocky Mountains.

I Plead with You Not to Preach Pessimism

Men may fail in this country, earthquakes may come, seas me heave beyond their bounds, there may be great drought, disaster, and hardship, but this nation, founded on principles laid down by men whom God raised up, will never fail. . . . This is a place of the new Jerusalem. This is a place at the Lord said is favored above all other nations and all the world. This is a place where the Savior will come to his temple. This is the land in all the world. Yes, I repeat, men may fail, but this nation won't fail. I have faith in America; you and I must have faith in America, if we understand the teachings of the gospel Jesus Christ. We are living in a day when we must pay to these challenges.

I plead with you not to preach pessimism. Preach that this is the greatest country in all the world. This is the favorite land. This is the land of our forefathers. It is the nation that will stand despite whatever trials or crisis it may yet have to pass through.[160]

—*Harold B. Lee*

THIS DAY IN AMERICAN HISTORY (1935)

The U.S. Supreme Court declares President Franklin D. Roosevelt's National Recovery Act unconstitutional.

America Is the Fulfillment of the Abrahamic Covenant

Few people think of the discovery of America, the Revolutionary War, and the establishment of a constitutional form of government here as being steps toward the fulfillment of the Lord's ancient covenant with Abraham. But it is a fact that they were. The covenant was to be fulfilled through the preaching of the gospel to, and the gathering of, the house of Israel, who were scattered worldwide. Through their acceptance of the gospel, they would receive its blessings and be gathered and would thus have fulfilled upon their heads the promises to Abraham made so long ago. His sheep would recognize the voice of the Good Shepherd and would follow him. But the true gospel had been lost through centuries of apostasy. It could not be given to Israel of today until it was restored, and the restoration could come only under favorable conditions, in a free country, where men could worship God according to the dictates of their own conscience.[161]

—Mark E. Peterson

THIS DAY IN AMERICAN HISTORY (1777)

Washington's Morristown, New Jersey, winter encampment ends.

From Persecution to Providence

Freedom of worship was conceived in Italy during the time of the Renaissance; it gestated in Germany and Western Europe during the Protestant Reformation; but it was born in America after the Constitution of the United States became the supreme law of the land. This establishment of freedom in the New World heaps no credit upon the original colonizers. They neither wanted it nor sought it. Rather, it was forced upon them by political necessity. Political necessity? Nay, by a divine providence, all in preparation for the restoration of the gospel in the dispensation of the fulness of times. Jesus told the Nephites that the Lord would set up in America "a free people by the power of the Father (3 Nephi 21:4)."

Coming to America to escape religious persecution, the original colonists—retaining their various religious persuasions—immediately set up their own separate systems of worship and reached out to condemn and persecute all others. Witches were burned and heretics persecuted as in the Old World. The American colonists had simply transported the traditions of a false and decadent Christendom to new shores. But the Revolutionary War and the need for national survival brought forth the Constitution with this provision: "Congress shall make no law respecting an establishment of religion, or prohibiting the free exercise thereof." Thus, religious freedom was almost thrust upon them by a power beyond their control, and the union of church and state was forever banned in the United States.[162]

—*Bruce R. McConkie*

THIS DAY IN AMERICAN HISTORY (1765)

Patrick Henry delivers his speech "If This Be Treason, Make the Most of It."

Salvation Is Born of Freedom of Choice

My thoughts seem to concentrate on the similarity of two important, heavenly directed events that we, as members of the Church of Jesus Christ, have special reason to be grateful for: the framing of the Constitution of the United States of America and the restoration of the gospel of Jesus Christ—each, in a significant way, sustaining the other. In addition to heavenly direction, both would require a membership of honest, virtuous people if their divine purposes were to be realized.

We attribute the rise of the American nation and its survival to two vital factors. First, God aided the efforts of those who established the republic. . . . Second, America's citizens were known for their righteous conduct and example. . . .

The important human attributes needed for this new nation to really become a cooperating and workable republic of separate states would be manifested by a people who demonstrated by their lives a belief and desire to live in a society of justice for all mankind. Likewise, the Lord, through the Prophet Joseph Smith, recognized that, like the new nation, the restored gospel would have difficulty enduring without men and women of similar integrity and conduct. . . .

People throughout the nation and the free world, are indebted to freedom-loving individuals everywhere who had the faith and integrity necessary to build the foundations of our societies upon fundamental moral values.[163]

—David B. Haight

THIS DAY IN AMERICAN HISTORY (1868)

Memorial Day (then called Decoration Day) is first observed.

People Who Demonstrate by Their Lives a Belief and Desire to Live in a Society of Justice for all Mankind

Freedom of religion, freedom of worship, freedom to choose one's own course is essential to salvation. The very instant that compulsion takes over in the world of worship is the moment when agency ceases to operate and we are no longer free to make the choices that lead to salvation.

Unless we voluntarily choose good rather than evil, light in preference to darkness, Deity's way in preference to the devil's, it is philosophically impossible to be saved. Salvation is born of freedom of choice. Even if we were forced to believe the truth itself, in all its parts, and were compelled to worship in every proper way, it could not save us, for no agency would be involved. Thus, as we have seen, civil control of religion is Lucifer's way of enforcing an enduring state of apostasy and of darkness upon all who are subject to such control. Thus also, as long as government controls our way of worship, Lucifer is in control, and we have no hope except to await the day when the chains will be broken and the bondage will cease.

Civil power does exist the world over. We have no choice but to live in subjection to the laws of that land upon which we dwell, and our great desire and hope, in the midst of a wicked world, is to maintain freedom of worship. Under these circumstances, what must our course be? It must be one of using all our power and influence to keep church and state separated, to sustain civil power in its proper realm, and to stipulate in constitutions, in legislative enactments, in executive decrees, in judicial determinations, in every possible way, that men are free to worship as they will and not be subject to compulsion.[164]

—*Bruce R. McConkie*

THIS DAY IN AMERICAN HISTORY (1900)

U.S. troops arrive in Beijing and help put down the Boxer Rebellion.

JUNE 1

The Basic Law of the Constitution Safeguards Us in Our God-Given Rights

In the wisdom of the Almighty, this ensign of liberty was raised to the nations to fulfill an ancient prophecy that "out of Zion [should] go forth the law, and the word of the Lord from Jerusalem" (Isaiah 2:3). How could this be? The answer is clear: through the Constitution, kings and rulers and the peoples of all nations under heaven may be informed of the blessings enjoyed by the people of this land of Zion by reason of their freedom under Divine guidance, and be constrained to adopt similar government systems and thus fulfill the ancient law to which I have already referred.

My visits to underprivileged countries and among subjugated peoples who have placed their trust in governments of dominating men, rather than in governments of constitutional law, have shown me the importance and the great blessed privilege that is ours to live in this country where the basic law of the Constitution safeguards us in our God-given rights.[165]

—*Harold B. Lee*

THIS DAY IN AMERICAN HISTORY (1792, 1796)

Kentucky (1792) and Tennessee (1796) receive statehood as the 15th and 16th states, respectively.

Rally Around That Sacred Instrument

Need we be surprised that men, as the scriptures say, "should wax worse and worse, deceiving and being deceived?" No. We have preached it—I have preached it upwards of forty years in this nation and in other nations.

Need we be surprised that they should trample under foot the Constitution of the United States? No; Joseph Smith told us that they would do it. Many around me here knew long ago that they would do this thing and further knew that the last people that should be found to rally around that sacred instrument and save it from the grasp of unrighteous men would be the elders of Israel!

When, therefore, we see these things progressing, need we be astonished? I do not think we need to be. Some of our people you know, who are a little shaky and get how? Why a little astride of the fence, and say "good Lord and good devil," not knowing into whose hands they will fall; when they see some of these things transpiring they are filled with amazement; but men who understand themselves, and who are in possession of the gift of the Holy Ghost and the Spirit of the living God, are looking for such things and they are not at all surprised.[166]

—John Taylor

THIS DAY IN AMERICAN HISTORY (1784)

New Hampshire votes in favor of the Constitution and Bill of Rights.

God's Master Plan for America

Historian Henry Steele Commager wrote that the Founding Fathers were "a galaxy of leaders who were quite literally incomparable. What explains this remarkable outpouring of political leadership, this fertility in the production of statesmen—a fertility unmatched since that day? Was it an historical accident?" And yet another historian, Barbara W. Tuchman, noted "it would be invaluable if we could know what produced this burst of talent from a base of only two and a half million inhabitants."

But we do know what produced this burst of talent. It was not a series of random births or "a lucky concatenation of genes." Rather, it was pursuant to God's master plan for America. The Bible tells us that God "hath determined the times before appointed [meaning when we would come to earth] and the bounds of their habitation [meaning where we would be born]" (Acts 17:26). And so, it was with the Founding Fathers. God sent them at a specified time and to a specified place to fulfill their divinely appointed mission. No doubt the words of Mordecai to Queen Esther, who saved her people, are applicable here: "And who knoweth whether thou art come to the kingdom for such a time as this?" (Esther 4:14).

Ben Carson summed it up well when he said, "We must be careful not to allow those who like to rewrite history to silence the voices of those God-fearing visionaries who founded America." In other words, they were men of God.[167]

—*Tad R. Callister*

THIS DAY IN AMERICAN HISTORY (1784)

The ROTC (Reserve Officers Training Corps) Program is established by Congress.

This Is a Nation with a Great Mission

Yes . . . this is a choice land—choice above all others. Blessed by the Almighty, our forebears have made and kept it so. It will continue to be a land of freedom and liberty as long as we are able to advance in the light of sound and enduring principles of right. To sacrifice such principles for momentary expediency—often selfishly motivated—is to endanger our noble heritage and is unworthy of this great American people.

With all my heart I love this nation. I have lived and traveled abroad just enough to make me appreciate rather fully what we have here. To me, this is not just another nation. This is not just one of a family of nations. This is a nation with a great mission for the benefit and blessing of liberty-loving people everywhere. It is my firm conviction that the Constitution of this land was established by men whom the God of heaven raised up unto this very purpose.

The days ahead are sobering and challenging and will demand the faith, prayers, and loyalty of every American. Our challenge is to keep America strong and free—strong socially, strong economically, and above all, strong spiritually, if our way of life is to endure. There is no other way. Only in this course is there safety for our nation.[168]

—*Ezra Taft Benson*

THIS DAY IN AMERICAN HISTORY (1919)

The 19th Amendment to the U.S. Constitution is proposed for ratification.

It's a Commandment to Obey Constitutional Laws

No man need break the laws of the land who will keep the laws of God. But this is further defined by the passage which I read afterwards—the law of the land, which all have no need to break, is that law which is the Constitutional law of the land, and that is as God Himself has defined it. . . . I maintain that The Church of Jesus Christ of Latter-day Saints has ever been faithful to the constitutional laws of our country. . . .

I am bound not only by allegiance to the government of the United States, but by the actual command of God Almighty, to observe and obey every constitutional law of the land. . . .

I wish to enter here my avowal that the people called Latter-day Saints, as has been often repeated from this stand, are the most law-abiding, the most peaceable, long-suffering and patient people that can today be found within the confines of this republic, and perhaps anywhere else upon the face of the earth; and we intend to continue to be law-abiding so far as the constitutional law of the land is concerned; and we expect to meet the consequences of our obedience to the laws and commandments of Godlike men.[169]

—*Joseph F. Smith*

THIS DAY IN AMERICAN HISTORY (1917)

World War I military draft registration begins.

Cleave to the Constitution of the United States and in Doing So, Earn the Blessings of Our Heavenly Father

No nation in the world has a constitution that was given it by our Heavenly Father except the United States of America. I wonder if we appreciate that. The Lord gave us a rule of life for this great nation, and as far as we have lived up to it and taken advantage of it, the nation has grown, and the people have been blessed. But there are many people who prefer, or at least they seem to prefer, something else. . . .

The Constitution of the United States was written, it is true, by men, George Washington, Benjamin Franklin, and others who were their associates, but we have in this book that I have in my hand, the book of Doctrine and Covenants, a revelation in which the Lord tells us that the Constitution of the United States was prepared by men raised up by him for this very purpose.

As Latter-day Saints we ought to know that there is nothing better anywhere else. And so we should cleave to the Constitution of the United States and in doing so, earn the blessings of our Heavenly Father.[170]

—*George Albert Smith*

THIS DAY IN AMERICAN HISTORY (1781)

Colonial forces recapture Augusta, Georgia.

JUNE 7

Ours Truly Is a Land with a Divine Mission

Having come from the Old World to the New World and having been told that this New World was the promised land of the Lord, choice above all others, Nephi was shown its ultimate destiny. Ours truly is a land with a divine mission, highly important to the Lord's latter-day work. It was not only prepared as the place where the gospel would be restored, but it was likewise selected as the site for the New Jerusalem, the Lord's latter-day Zion. The Savior will visit His temple here. It is from this modern Zion in America that the law of the Lord will go forth to all mankind during the millennial reign. As Nephi looked into the future of this hemisphere, he saw that this land, then unknown to the rest of the world, was reserved for the descendants of Lehi until the Lord was ready to take the preliminary steps toward restoring the gospel.[171]

—*Mark E. Peterson*

THIS DAY IN AMERICAN HISTORY (1776)

Richard Henry Lee introduces the Resolution for Independence in the Continental Congress.

Cynicism vs. Concern

I wish to make a distinction here between cynicism and concern. I have concerns about our day—a major one of which I wish to discuss with you in some detail. But I am not cynical, and I ask you not to be. I do not believe that all human conduct is self-serving or that all noble-sounding explanations are contrived and only mask the depravity of human motives. Cynicism is an intellectual cop-out, a crutch for a withered soul, a thin excuse for inaction and retreating commitment. Do not become cynical about government or education or civic affairs or religion or the human race or the time in which you live. Do, on the other hand, be appropriately concerned and actively involved. We will always need responsible, reputable, reasonable social critics who will help in mapping the terrain and marking the pitfalls. But we do not need what Elder Gordon B. Hinckley once described on this campus as "pickle suckers."...

We must have our concerns. Life demands something more than a ubiquitous smile button saying, "Have a nice day." If we need a button at all, I suppose it should say something more like "Make it a nice day." Part of my message this morning is that as we exert virtuous effort in this world, we can rejoice in many good things that are central to our faith in the Lord Jesus Christ, our family and friends and neighbors, our Church activity, and our life together in a choice land and in an age unequaled in the history of this world in its privileges and possibilities. We are not without our solutions. Especially is it true that a faithful Latter-day Saint is not without his or her solutions.[172]

—*Jeffrey R. Holland*

THIS DAY IN AMERICAN HISTORY (1789)

James Madison argues for the Bill of Rights.

Until the Kingdoms of This World Become the Kingdom or Our God

Until He rules whose right it is and subdues all enemies under His feet; until He makes a full end of all nations in the day of His coming; until the kingdoms of this world become the kingdom of our God and of His Christ—there will be conflicts between church and state that defy solutions. Neither the Saints nor Lucifer will yield on the issues involved, and a resolution will be found only after the wicked are destroyed by the brightness of His coming.

In every nation the Saints will use their influence in the cause of righteousness, in the cause of truth, the cause of freedom, the gospel cause. In those same nations, Lucifer will seek to enforce his will. Whenever and wherever he can use either a church or a state as an instrument of damnation, he will do it. We may expect greater opposition and a more definite polarization of the people as the great and dreadful day of the Lord draws nearer. Religious influences will cause political kingdoms to engage in the battle of Armageddon, and there will be martyrdom and destruction on all sides as the gospel is preached in those concluding days of the earth's temporal continuance.[173]

—Bruce R. McConkie

THIS DAY IN AMERICAN HISTORY (1772)

The Revolutionary War's first naval attack takes place near Providence, Rhode Island.

Avoid Extreme or Polarizing Positions

One way our common ground with others can be undermined is if any contending party sows division and separates communities. In condemning and working against racism, we encourage our students, our teachers, and all our members to avoid extreme or polarizing positions and teachings that undermine the U.S. Constitution and other core institutions.

We know that the Constitution was inspired of God despite its birth defect of slavery. Its inspired principles, including the freedoms of speech and religion, and its authorized amendments have allowed subsequent generations to continue to improve and strengthen the rights of all of its citizens. That is part of our history, and it should not be distorted by trying to substitute other motivations for the Constitution of the United States, as some are doing in our time.

A gospel-centered approach to combating racism empowers all parties to support, apply, and teach the power and light of the gospel of Jesus Christ. The Church has made this positive approach in its efforts, both within its membership and with outside organizations.[174]

—Dallin H. Oaks and Clark G. Gilbert

THIS DAY IN AMERICAN HISTORY (1752)

Benjamin Franklin conducts his famous kite-flying experiment.

America Shall Continue to Go Forward with the Blessings of the Almighty

I should like to say a few words about America. I know that there are many here who come from other lands. I think I have been in all of the lands from which you come. I appreciate your people, their innate goodness, their art, their industry, their strength. I have marveled at the beauty of the earth, the wonder and magnificence of God's creations, as I have seen them in every part of the world. No land is without its beauty, no people without their virtues, and I hope that you who come from elsewhere will pardon my saying a few words concerning my own native land, America. I know that she has problems. We have heard so much of them for so long. But surely this is a good land, a choice land, a chosen land. To me it is a miracle, a creation of the Almighty. It was born of travail. The Constitution under which we live is the keystone of our nation. It was inspired of God. Of it, the great Gladstone said, "As the British Constitution is the most subtle organism which has proceeded from progressive history, so the American Constitution is the most wonderful work ever struck off at a given time by the brain and purpose of man" ("Kin Beyond the Sea," *North American Review*, September 1878).

In a few months we shall celebrate the two hundredth anniversary of the founding of the nation. Is it not a miracle that through these two centuries of time our system of government has remained intact, our Constitution has held while storms have beaten about us from within and without? . . .

I doubt not that we shall have days of trial. I am confident that so long as we have more politicians than statesmen, we shall have problems. But I am certain that if we will emphasize the greater good and turn our time and talents from vituperative criticism, from constantly looking for evil, and lift our sights to what may be done to build strength and goodness in our nation, America shall continue to go forward with the blessing of the Almighty and stand as an ensign of strength and peace and generosity to all the world.[175]

—*Gordon B. Hinckley*

THIS DAY IN AMERICAN HISTORY (1776)

A Continental Congress committee is appointed to draft a declaration of independence.

The American Way of Life

Our Constitution and Bill of Rights guarantee to all our people the greatest freedom ever enjoyed by the public of any great nation. This system guarantees freedom of individual enterprise, freedom to own property, freedom to start one's own business and to operate it according to one's own judgement so long as the enterprise is honorable. The individual has power to produce beyond his needs, to provide savings for the future protection of himself and family. He can live where he wishes and pick any job he wants and select any educational opportunity.

The evidence clearly indicates, too, that our most cherished rights and interests—freedom of religion, freedom of speech and of the press, right of assembly, right of petition, right of trial by jury, protection from search and seizure, and freedom of enterprise—are all a part of the American way of life. Can communism, socialism, fascism, the so-called welfare state, or any other coercive system provide these priceless blessings which flow to us as a part of our American way of life? The common denominator of all these systems is the curtailment of individual liberty. Surely, we will all agree that our Constitution and Bill of Rights provide the basis for the only economic system acceptable to true Americans.[176]

—*Ezra Taft Benson*

THIS DAY IN AMERICAN HISTORY (1866)

The 14th Amendment to the U.S. Constitution is proposed.

Reckoning with the Past

I speak of the problem of racism. . . . To do that, we must have clear thinking about how current events should be analyzed and acted upon in view of this nation's shameful history of Black slavery. We need to understand how the founders postponed resolving that moral issue to obtain the ratification of the Constitution for the creation of this nation. As the protests of last summer gained momentum and support across the country, various groups, particularly in the South, began tearing down or replacing statues of prominent figures associated with slavery. Some institutions changed names to refrain from honoring persons who had had any connection with slavery. A small number of persons even took up that cry on this campus, calling for changing the name of some buildings or even the name of Brigham Young University.

Many were distressed at these attempts to erase prominent figures from our history—even history that we would be pleased to change if we could. I wondered, Are the advocates and actors in these efforts aware of what they are attempting to erase? For reasons that every serious student of American history understands, even the Constitution of the United States is stained with concessions to slavery that were made in order to get the whole document ratified. Those textual stains were, of course, removed by the amendments following the Civil War, which cost hundreds of thousands of lives throughout the North and the South. I cannot condone our now erasing all mention and honor of prominent leaders such as George Washington and others who established our nation and gave us our constitution because they lived at a time with legal approvals and traditions that condoned slavery. . . . Let us not "open a quarrel between the past and the present" lest we jeopardize our attempts to improve our future.

This is our current state. We share our history and enjoy the advantages of our constitutional government and the prosperity of this nation. The predecessors of many Americans of different backgrounds made great sacrifices to establish this nation. Whatever those sacrifices—of freedom, property, or even life—let us now honor them for what they have done for us and forgo quarrelling over the past. Ours is the duty to unite and improve the future we will share.[177]

—*Dallin H. Oaks*

THIS DAY IN AMERICAN HISTORY (1866)

The 14th Amendment to the U.S. Constitution is proposed.

Navigating Uncertainty

There is widespread disagreement in our society about the value of long-standing institutions such as religion, marriage, family, constitutional government, and even higher education. The role of these and other institutions in modern society and the values that have long sustained them are being questioned by those who seem willing to ignore not only their spiritual significance but the considerable empirical evidence for their essential role in human flourishing. This raises one of the central challenges of our day—what President Dallin H. Oaks has described as the need to stand for truth with love. There is, as you know, sustained and passionate debate about political questions—and somehow everything seems to have devolved into a polarizing political question. Where will it all lead? Can a healthy pluralism be renewed and sustained?

. . . We must stand for truth in ways that show the love and concern of a true disciple. You who remember the terrorist attacks of 9/11 in 2001 will probably also recall the sense of unity that came to the fore in the United States in the immediate aftermath of those attacks. We witnessed renewed feelings of patriotism, fresh concern for the welfare of one another, and appreciation for first responders and all who make personal sacrifices to help others. A newfound sense that, even more than career success, what truly matters in life are close personal relationships—especially family relationships—seemed to hail a new day. Many resolved to give higher priority to these time-honored mores. But you will also recall how quickly those resolutions and that sense of unity faded. Whatever unity we are left with today seems much less than existed even before 9/11. Can mutual respect amid disagreement be re-enthroned? Can it be sustained?

Going forward, it appears we will be living in a different, more fractious world than any of us have experienced personally heretofore. The leadership . . . of the Church, and all of us individually will need to navigate and make decisions in the presence of uncertainty. . . . It is, in the midst of uncertainty, to focus on what *is* certain—to maintain the eternal verities.[178]

—*D. Todd Christofferson*

THIS DAY IN AMERICAN HISTORY (1775)

The U.S. Army is officially established by Congress—
making it the oldest American military service.

Our Country Was Founded in a Religious Atmosphere

The Latter-day Saints are a chosen people. Their mission is to teach the restored gospel to the world. They feel that responsibility keenly. Their missionary endeavor is evidence of their sincerity and determination to make known truth.

They realize that the souls of men are precious in the sight of God. They know their relationship to God, and they are rightfully called the children of God. He is their Father and is vitally concerned about their welfare. He will hear and answer their prayers. He will come to their rescue in times of need and he will sustain them when they put their trust in him. . . .

Our country was founded in a religious atmosphere. The original colonists who came to America laid their foundations in that background. They came with deep religious convictions. They built churches and schools and worshiped God in their own way. Their quest was religious freedom, and although unknown to them, they prepared the way for the restoration of the gospel of Jesus Christ, which, according to James, is the perfect law of liberty.[179]

—*Alma Sonne*

THIS DAY IN AMERICAN HISTORY (1775)

The Second Continental Congress names George Washington as commander-in-chief.

Our Founding Fathers Were Endowed with Faith

I believe that for the most part our Founding Fathers (whose monumental revolution we again commemorated in the seventies, by the way) were endowed with such faith. Surely they had problems. Taxation *with* representation was not a heck of a lot more fun than taxation *without* it. They had great concerns, but avoided cynicism and rolled up their sleeves. Surely the presidential greatness of Washington and Lincoln must have been in no small measure due to the fact that they were good, thoughtful, dignified, responsible, spiritually sensitive men *before* they were presidents. For all their courage and commitment, neither could be called a lunatic or a zealot; and for all their burdens, they could not be called "pickle suckers" either.

Perhaps we could do not better in this month when we honor their birth than to use their example, as we examine the challenge of the 1970s or the eighties or the nineties, and to remember something of their service and their sacrifice. As I look at your decade—and at those that lie ahead—I am very hopeful and very encouraged because of what I believe. I believe in help from both sides of the veil and in the worth and the possibility of a human soul.[180]

—Jeffrey R. Holland

THIS DAY IN AMERICAN HISTORY (1858)

Abraham Lincoln gives his "A House Divided Against Itself Cannot Stand" speech (while accepting the Illinois Republican Party's nomination for the U.S. Senate).

Freedom Under American Government Ought to Be Universal

This liberty, this freedom, especially under the American government of all nations under heaven, ought to become universal. No man or set of men should attempt to hinder their neighbors from enjoying their religion. . . .

I pray God our Heavenly Father, that His blessing may be over us; that the hearts of the people of our nation and other nations may be open to the light of the gospel, that they may not pursue the course the Jews did, for we know what it has cost them. It will cost this nation or any other nation the same to shed the blood of the servants of God. Whatever course a nation pursues in this respect, it will have to foot the bill. The constitution of our country is one of the best that was ever given to any government. Our forefathers were inspired of God to write that instrument. I have a respect for our government, flag and constitution. I know this nation has been raised up by the power of God for a certain purpose, and that to establish his kingdom upon it, and inasmuch as we do our duty the Lord will sustain us.[181]

—*Wilford Woodruff*

THIS DAY IN AMERICAN HISTORY (1775)

Battle of Bunker Hill.

Believers Can and Must Seek Laws that Will Preserve Religious Freedom

As defenders of the faith, believers can and must seek laws that will preserve religious freedom. Along with the ascendancy of moral relativism, the United States is experiencing a disturbing reduction in overall public esteem for religion. Once an accepted part of American life, religion is now suspect in the minds of many. To them it has become something that must prove its legitimacy as a part of our public life. Some influential voices even question the extent to which our constitution should protect the free exercise of religion, including the right to practice and preach religious principles.

This is a vital matter on which we who believe in a Supreme Being who has established absolute right and wrong in human behavior must unite to insist on our time-honored constitutional rights to exercise our religion, to vote our consciences on public issues, and to participate in elections and debates in the public square and in the halls of justice. In doing so we stand with angels. We must also stand shoulder to shoulder with other believers to preserve and strengthen the freedom to advocate and practice our religious beliefs, whatever they are. For this purpose we must walk together on the same path in order to secure our freedom to pursue our separate ways when that is necessary according to our separate beliefs. Guided by heaven in this righteous cause, our words will be sweet and find place in the hearts of many. . . .

When believers seek to promote their positions in the public square, their methods and their advocacy should always be tolerant of the opinions and positions of others who do not share their beliefs. We should not add to the extremism that divides our society. . . . As believers, we should also frame our arguments and positions in ways that contribute to the reasoned discussion and accommodation that are essential to democratic government in a pluralistic society. By this means we will contribute to the civility that is essential to preserve our civilization.[182]

—*Dallin H. Oaks*

THIS DAY IN AMERICAN HISTORY (1812)

The War of 1812 begins.

JUNE 19

Love of Liberty Inspires My Soul

I would not have suffered my name to have been used by my friends on anywise as President of the United States, or candidate for that office if I and my friends could have had the privilege of enjoying our religious and Civil Rights as American Citizens; even those rights which the Constitution guarantee unto all her citizens alike; but, this we as a people have been denied from the beginning. Persecution has rolled upon our heads from time to time from portions of the United States like peels of thunder, because of our religion, and no portion of the government as yet has stepped forward for our relief. Under view of these things, I feel it to be my right and privilege to obtain what influence and power I can lawfully in the United States for the protection of injured innocence. If I lose my life in a good cause, I am willing to be sacrificed on the altar of virtue righteousness and truth, in maintaining the laws and Constitution of the United States, if need be, for the general good of mankind.[183]

If it has been demonstrated that I have been willing to die for a Mormon, I am bold to declare before heaven, that I am just as ready to die in defending the rights of a Presbyterian, a Baptist, or a good man of any other denomination; for the same principle which would trample upon the rights of the Latter day Saints would trample upon their rights of . . . Roman Catholics or of any other denomination, who may be unpopular and too weak to defend themselves. It is a love of liberty which inspires my Soul, civil and religious liberty to the whole of the human race, love of liberty was diffused into my Soul by my grandfathers, while they dandled me on their knees.[184]

—*Joseph Smith*

THIS DAY IN AMERICAN HISTORY (1778)

Washington's army leaves Valley Forge, Pennsylvania.

Indications of What Is to Come

It is hard to believe that a nation as large and as prosperous and as powerful as the United States is today could lose the power to govern. Even though there are serious problems in this country today, it still has a great governing power and is a world leader in its influence. What conditions could bring such a nation to the brink of destruction? What kinds of crises could strike with such power as to destroy the United States? Although there is much that is not known concerning the specific events that will bring the Lord's prophecies to fulfillment, he has given several indications of what is to come.

In scripture, the Lord said that when the times of the Gentiles were fulfilled, there would be men standing in that generation which would not pass away until they saw an "overflowing scourge coming upon the people, and the devastating results of what would follow. In March of 1829, even before the Church was organized, He said,

"For a desolating scourge shall go forth among the inhabitants of the earth, and shall continue to be poured out from time to time, if they repent not, until the earth is empty, and the inhabitants thereof are consumed away and utterly destroyed by the brightness of my coming" (D&C 5:19).

Webster defines a scourge as "an instrument of punishment or criticism; a cause of widespread or great affliction." This scourge seems to involve many forms of terrible calamities, including great hailstorms, tempests, plagues, pestilence, and war. Such terrible disasters will be such that they will lay to waste those who fight against God and will actually leave mighty cities desolate of their populations. The Lord warned some specific cities, particularly Boston, New York and Albany, of the desolation awaiting them if they did not repent.[185]

—Gerald N. Lund

THIS DAY IN AMERICAN HISTORY (1863)

West Virginia receives statehood as the 35th state.

The Greatest Palladium of Human Rights

Our Heavenly Father raised up the very men that framed the Constitution of the United States. He said He did. He gave to us the greatest palladium of human rights that the world knows anything about, the only system whereby people could worship God according to the dictates of their consciences without, in any way, being molested when the law, itself, was in effect. Now that is what the Lord gave to us. That is the Constitution of this country. Yet, we have people who would like to change that and bring some of those forms of government that have failed absolutely to make peace and happiness and comfort any other place in the world and exchange what God has given to us—the fullness of the earth and the riches of liberty and happiness. . . . I am saying to you that to me the Constitution of the United States of America is just as much from my Heavenly Father as the Ten Commandments. When that is my feeling, I am not going to go very far away from the Constitution, and I am going to try to keep it where the Lord started it. . . .

So let us appreciate it and let us evidence to our Heavenly Father that we do appreciate it, not by talking about it but by letting our light so shine—the light of righteousness, the light of faith, the light of honesty, the light of generosity, the light of truthfulness, all those things that our Heavenly Father indicates that we should manifest to the world—let that light so shine that others seeing our good works will desire to be identified with an organization that seeks to live the commandments of God and honor Him.[186]

—*George Albert Smith*

THIS DAY IN AMERICAN HISTORY (1788)

New Hampshire ratifies the U.S. Constitution, 57–47, and receives statehood as the 9th state.

The Constitution Must Grow and Develop

It is this union of independence and dependence of these branches—legislative, executive, and judicial—and of the governmental functions possessed by each of them, that constitutes the marvelous genius of this unrivalled document. The Framers had no direct guide in this work no historical governmental precedent upon which to rely. As I see it, it was here that the divine inspiration came it was truly a miracle. . . .

Our own prophets have declared in our day the responsibility of the elders of Zion in the preservation of the Constitution. We cannot, guiltless, escape that responsibility, we cannot be laggards nor can we be deserters. . . .

It is not my belief nor is it the doctrine of my church that the constitution is a fully grown document on the contrary we believe it must grow and develop to meet the changing needs of an advancing world. . . .

All such changes must be made to protect and preserve our liberties, not to take them from us. Greater freedom, not slavery, must follow every constitutional change.[187]

—*J. Reuben Clark, Jr.*

THIS DAY IN AMERICAN HISTORY (1868)

Arkansas is readmitted into the Union after the Civil War.

The Sovereign Power Is in the People

Perhaps the most important of the great fundamentals of the inspired Constitution is the principle of popular sovereignty: The people are the source of government power. Along with many religious people, Latter-day Saints affirm that God gave the power to the people, and the people consented to a constitution that delegated certain powers to the government. Sovereignty is not inherent in a state or nation just because it has the power that comes from force of arms. Sovereignty does not come from the divine right of a king, who grants his subjects such power as he pleases or is forced to concede, as in Magna Charta. The sovereign power is in the people. I believe this is one of the great meanings in the revelation which tells us that God established the Constitution of the United States. . . .

In other words, the most desirable condition for the effective exercise of God-given moral agency is a condition of maximum freedom and responsibility. In this condition men are accountable for their own sins and cannot blame their political conditions on their bondage to a king or a tyrant. This condition is achieved when the people are sovereign, as they are under the Constitution God established in the United States. . . .

Popular sovereignty necessarily implies popular responsibility. Instead of blaming their troubles on a king or other sovereign, all citizens must share the burdens and responsibilities of governing.[188]

—Dallin H. Oaks

THIS DAY IN AMERICAN HISTORY (1780)

The Continental Army leaves the Morristown, New Jersey, encampment after one of the harshest winters of the 18th century.

Political Views Should Never Disturb the Harmony of Society

Political views and party distinctions never should disturb the harmony of society. . . .

"A soft answer turns away wrath," says the wise man, and it will be greatly to the credit of the Latter-day Saints to show the love of God by now kindly treating those who may have, in an unconscious moment, done them wrong. For truly said Jesus, "Pray for thine enemies." Humanity towards all; reason and refinement, to enforce virtue, and good for evil, are so eminently designed to cure more disorders of society than an appeal to arms or even argument untempered with friendship and the "one thing needful," that no vision for the future: guide-board for the distant; or expositor for the present, need trouble any one with what he ought to do. His own good, his family's good, his neighbor's good, his country's good, and all good, seem to whisper to every person: the Governor has told you what to do: now do it. The constitution expects every man to do his duty, and when he fails the law urges him: or should he do too much the same master rebukes him. . . . The Latter-day Saints will, at all events, and profit by the instruction: and call upon honest men to help them cherish all the love; all the friendship; all the courtesy; all the kindly feelings and all the generosity that ought to characterize clever people. . . . Our motto then, is, peace with all. If we have joy in the love of God, let us try to give a reason of that joy, which all the world cannot gainsay or resist.[189]

—*Joseph Smith, Jr.*

THIS DAY IN AMERICAN HISTORY (1853)

U.S. makes the Gadsden Purchase—buying 29,670 square miles from Mexico for $10 million.

Religious Freedom Is Woven into the Soul of America

We live in challenging times. Religious freedom is indeed under fire. I am convinced that those who question the value or even the legitimacy of religious freedom do not understand that it is woven into the very soul of America. . . .

The American Revolution cannot be understood without taking into account the religious teachings that motivated patriots to action. . . . The Declaration of Independence reminds us that Americans believed they were "endowed by their Creator with certain unalienable rights." Later, the Constitution would enshrine the first of those unalienable rights—the right to religious freedom.

Even though religious freedoms are the core of what America is and what it stands for, critics now openly ask whether religion belongs in American public life at all. . . . There are concerted efforts to shame and intimidate believers who have traditional moral values and to suppress religious viewpoints and practices regarding marriage, family, gender and sexuality. Worst of all, government sometimes joins in these efforts.

Religious participation in public life is not only part of American history and a constitutionally protected freedom, it's also good for our nation. Religious voices bring a moral—often cautionary—voice to matters of social and public policy that we desperately need. . . .

Things may get worse before they get better. But these are our times. This is our moment to defend our fundamental freedoms. With courage, conviction, and civility—drawing upon our noble heritage as Americans—each one of us can make a profound difference.[190]

—*D. Todd Christofferson*

THIS DAY IN AMERICAN HISTORY (1950)

The Korean War begins.

The Constitution Is Deserving of Our Prolonged Spiritual Applause

The unique founding of this American nation, wherein the Lord revealed that He had established the Constitution of the United States "by the hand of wise men whom [He] raised up unto this purpose." No parallel declaration exists with regard to the constitution of any other nation, ours being the first written constitution. . . . Revealed words, such as 'unto this very purpose,' clearly remind us that God's hand is in the details of such things—sometimes obviously, sometimes subtly. If pondered—bold as to its substance and the miraculous process of its coming forth—the Constitution is deserving of our prolonged spiritual applause.

Think of all the Lord oversaw, including the shaping events which of necessity occurred long before the Constitution was written, ratified, and implemented. First, it was necessary for God to cause a handful of highly talented and 'wise' individuals to be 'raised up'. Second, they needed to live in one geographic area on this planet. Third, this contiguity also had to occur within a short time frame! Fourth, a citizenry had to be prepared who wanted and would then implement self-governance. This incubation was as important as the later ratification. Thus, the words *raised up* involve multiple and concurrent conditions.[191]

—Neal A. Maxwell

THIS DAY IN AMERICAN HISTORY (1917)

The first World War I American soldiers arrive in France.

The United States Is Not the Kingdom of God

We are under the United States, but the United States is not the kingdom of God. It does not profess to be under his rule, nor his government, nor his authority. Yet we are expected as citizens of the United States to keep the laws of the United States, and hence we are, as I said before, an integral part of the government. Very well, what is expected of us? That we observe its laws, that we conform to its usages, that we are governed by good and wholesome principles, that we maintain the laws in their integrity and that we sustain the government, and we ought to do it. But there is a principle here that I wish to speak about. God dictates in a great measure the affairs of the nations of the earth, their kingdoms and governments and rulers and those that hold dominion. He sets up one and pulls down another, according to His will. That is an old doctrine, but it is true today.

Have we governors? Have we a president of the United States? Have we men in authority? Yes. Is it right to traduce their characters? No, it is not. Is it right for us to oppose them? No, it is not. Is it right for them to traduce us? No, it is not. Is it right for them to oppress us in any way? No, it is not. We ought to pray for these people, for those that are in authority, that they may be led in the right way, that they may be preserved from evil, that they may administer the government in righteousness, and that they may pursue a course that will receive the approbation of heaven. . . .

Well, shall we be governed by them? Yes. Shall we obey the law? Yes. Shall I as a citizen of this city obey the laws of this city? Yes. Shall I cause trouble or speak evil of the mayor or city council or any of the administrators of the law? No, I ought to pray for them that they may lead aright and administer justice equitably and act for the welfare and interest of the community wherein they live and for whom they operate. Am I a citizen of the United States? Yes, and I ought to feel the same toward them.[192]

—*John Taylor*

THIS DAY IN AMERICAN HISTORY (1776)

The original rough draft of the Declaration of Independence is read and reviewed by the committee.

Every Line of the Constitution Is not Scriptural

It was a miracle that the Constitution could be drafted and ratified. But what is there in the text of the Constitution that is divinely inspired?

Reverence for the United States Constitution is so great that sometimes individuals speak as if its every word had the same standing as scripture. I have never considered it necessary to defend every line as scriptural. For example, I find nothing scriptural in the compromise on slavery or the minimum age for congressmen, senators, or the president. . . .

I see divine inspiration in what President J. Reuben Clark called the "great fundamentals" of the Constitution. In his many talks on the Constitution, he always praised three fundamentals: (a) the separation of powers into three independent branches of government in a federal system; (b) the essential freedoms of speech, press, and religion embodied in the Bill of Rights; and (c) the equality of all men before the law.[193]

—*Dallin H. Oaks*

THIS DAY IN AMERICAN HISTORY (1919)

World War I officially ends (Treaty of Versailles).

The Constitution Will Be Forsaken by the Country in General

One of the things that has made the United States of America unique in the annals of government is its Constitution. The Church of Jesus Christ of Latter-day Saints teaches that such a document is too unique to have come solely from the minds of men. The Lord has stated clearly in His revelations that He established the Constitution by raising up wise men for that very purpose.

These principles of government by the people for the preservation of freedom are divinely inspired, and the wards and destruction that are coming will not make them any less so. But the prophets have indicated that these principles established in the Constitution will be forsaken by the country in general and that this will be an important factor in bringing about the destruction of the United States.

Many of the prophets have referred to the time when the constitutional principles would be in danger, and it has been clearly prophesied that these principles would be saved or found only in the Church.[194]

—Gerald N. Lund

THIS DAY IN AMERICAN HISTORY (1767)

British Parliament passes the Townshend Revenue Act levying additional taxes on America.

We Want to Be Better Than Any Other Citizens

We profess to be under the government of the United States, and being citizens we want to be good citizens, better than any other citizens, and I believe we are. I firmly believe that we are more loyal and more patriotic to our national government than any other citizens belonging to it. That is my opinion. And I think that we can well afford to observe all of the principles instituted among men by any proper government. . . . For while we are desirous of obeying all of the laws of our country, we cannot violate the law of God.

Should this nation persist in violating their Constitutional guarantees, tear away the bulwarks of liberty, and trample upon the principles of freedom and human rights, that are sacred to all men, and by which all men should be governed, by and by the whole fabric will fall, and who will sustain it? We will, in the name of Israel's God. Of this the Prophet Joseph Smith prophesied long, long ago. This is the position we stand in. And if the government of the United States can afford to oppress us, we can afford to suffer and grow strong.[195]

—*John Taylor*

THIS DAY IN AMERICAN HISTORY (1805)

The Michigan Territory is organized.

Education for Citizenship

In education for citizenship, therefore, why should we not see to it that every child in America is taught the superiority of our Constitution and the sacredness of the freedom of the individual? Such definite instruction is not in violation of either Federal or the State Constitution. Teach that free enterprise is the right to open a gas station or a grocery store, or to buy a farm if you want to be your own boss, or to change your job if you do not like the man for whom you work. . . .

Education for citizenship demands more emphasis upon moral and spiritual values. Our government was founded on the faith in a Supreme Being. . . . God and individual freedom are fundamental principles in our glorious Republic, and our obligation is to keep in our schools a reverence for Deity and respect for the dignity of the individual man. . . .

I love the Stars and Stripes, and the American Way of Life. I have faith in the Constitution of the United States. I believe that only through a truly educated citizenry can the ideals that inspired the Founding Fathers of our nation be preserved and perpetuated. . . .

May our educational system from grade school to university ever seek and merit His divine guidance.[196]

—David O. McKay

THIS DAY IN AMERICAN HISTORY (1971)

The 26th Amendment to the U.S. Constitution is ratified—giving citizens 18 years and older the right to vote.

Upholding the Constitution Preserves Man's Agency

As we look about in the world among the various countries we find philosophies and forms of government the effect of which is to deprive men of their free agency, but by reason of Thy timely warning to us, we know that they are not approved of Thee. Since the God of this choice land is Jesus Christ, we know that His philosophy of free agency should prevail here. Thou didst amply demonstrate this great principle to us by raising up wise men for the very purpose of giving us our constitutional form of government. . . . There are those, our Heavenly Father, both within and without our borders who would destroy the Constitutional form of government which Thou hast so magnanimously given us, and would replace it with a form that would curtail if not altogether deprive man of his free agency. We pray Thee, therefore, that in all these matters Thou wilt help us to conform our lives to Thy desires, and that Thou wilt sustain us in our resolve so to do. We pray Thee that Thou wilt inspire good and just men everywhere to be willing to sacrifice for, support and uphold the Constitution and the government set up under it and thereby preserve for man his agency.

We thank Thee that Thou hast revealed to us that those who gave us our Constitutional form of government were men wise in Thy sight and that Thou didst raise them up for the very purpose of putting forth that sacred document.[197]

—George Albert Smith

THIS DAY IN AMERICAN HISTORY (1788)

Congress accepts the ratification of Constitution.

We Stand in Danger of Losing Our Liberties

The Constitution was framed in order to protect minorities. That is the purpose of written constitutions. In order that minorities might be protected in the matter of amendments under our Constitution, the Lord required that the amendments should be made only through the operation of very large majorities—two-thirds for action in the Senate, and three-fourths as among the states. This is the inspired, prescribed order. But if we are to have an amendment by the will of one man, or of a small group of men, if they can amend the Constitution, then we shall lose the Constitution; because each succeeding person or group who come into a position of place and power where they can "amend" the charter, will want to amend it again, and so on until no vestige of our liberties shall remain. Thus it comes that an amendment of our Constitution by one person or by a group is a violation of the revealed will of the Lord to the Church, as that will is embodied in that inspired Constitution.

Brethren, let us think about that, because I say unto you with all the soberness I can, that we stand in danger of losing our liberties, and that once lost, only blood will bring them back; and once lost, we of this Church will, in order to keep the Church going forward, have more sacrifices to make and more persecutions to endure than we have yet known, heavy as our sacrifices and grievous as our persecutions of the past have been.[198]

—J. Reuben Clark, Jr.

THIS DAY IN AMERICAN HISTORY (1775)

George Washington assumes command of the Continental Army.

Re-Ratifying the Constitution

In a real way, each generation of Americans has its chance to re-ratify the Constitution. We can do this by abiding by its principles and believing our own legacy to posterity—likewise, by both preserving our constitutional rights but also fulfilling our responsibilities. Otherwise, expressions of patriotism are no more than verbal veneration without actual emulation.

Re-ratification will require statesmanship among both the people and the leaders. Statesmanship differs from politics in that it does not treat symptoms but strives to cure the underlying diseases. Our Founding Fathers did statesmanlike work in 1776 and again in 1787, in our time, again regardless of party. We seem preoccupied with treating symptoms, quick fixes, and with getting by a little longer.

Yes, our inspired Constitution has a marvelous system of checks and balances. But if uninspired individuals lack their own checks and balances, the inspired Constitution cannot correct that imbalance. . . . There then happened after his first inaugural something that doesn't happen in our time. The Senate replied to Washington's first inaugural, saying, "We feel, sir, and acknowledge the justness of your observations that the foundations of our national policy should be lain in private morality. If individuals be not influenced by moral principles, it is vain to look for public virtue."

As I close, may I presume to speak for all of us tonight as if to President Washington on this July 4th night of 1993 and say to him, "We feel, sir, the force and acknowledge the justice of your observations about how the foundations of national policy are to be found in private morality." He knew the American people. He knew our beginnings. He knew our constitution. We ignore his prescription at our peril.[199]

—*Neal A. Maxwell*

THIS DAY IN AMERICAN HISTORY (1776)

Congress adopts the Declaration of Independence.

Our Form of Government Superior to Any Other

The governments of the world are varied. We have despotic, monarchical and republican governments, and in order to become a citizen of any one of them we have to obey the laws of that government. A great deal has been said about the form of government, and the constitution under which we live. They have been the praise of all Americans, and perhaps of people living in other portions of the earth. We consider that we have been blessed as a nation in possessing the freedom and privileges guaranteed by the Constitution of the United States. They have been a rich legacy from our fathers. We consider our form of government superior to any other on the earth. It guarantees to us "life, liberty and the pursuit of happiness." . . . Still, I have many times thought that we, as American Citizens, have not prized the gifts and blessings guaranteed to us by the Constitution of our country. For the last few years, especially, the Constitution at times, has been looked upon as a matter of the smallest consequence. In some respects, however, it has been a blessing to us as a people, and it is to the whole nation, as far as it is carried out. But in order to fully receive its blessings we have to honor its precepts.[200]

—*Wilford Woodruff*

THIS DAY IN AMERICAN HISTORY (1775)

The Second Continental Congress drafts the Olive Branch Petition to King George III.

Praising God in the Public Sector

Our public monuments honoring our Founding Fathers and other national heroes, paid for and prompted by our government, are emblazoned with statements referencing God. Among others, we read on the Washington Monument, "Laus Deo," which means "Praise God." Why would we have a permanent public pronouncement to praise God if we are only to do so in private?

On the Jefferson Memorial, we read, "God who gave us life gave us liberty. Can the liberties of a nation be secure when we have removed a conviction that these liberties are the gift of God?" How can a conviction of God's gift of liberty be maintained by our government if the Supreme Court strikes down references to God in public places?

Lincoln's Second Inaugural Address, engraved on the wall of the Lincoln Memorial, mentions God fourteen times and references the Bible four times. Does that sound like the government wanted to remove references to God and the Bible from the public domain, or rather to acknowledge Him and thank Him who was present at every significant step of our nation's founding?

One might well ask: "Why the governmental establishment, maintenance, and publicity of these monuments which support religious principles if government is not in the business of endorsing and encouraging religion in general in the public sector?"[201]

—Tad R. Callister

THIS DAY IN AMERICAN HISTORY (1965)

The 25th Amendment to the U. S. Constitution is proposed for ratification.

Our Civic Duty

The First Presidency wish to bring to the attention of the members of The Church of Jesus Christ of Latter-day Saints their obligations as members of the communities in which they live and as citizens of the nation.

The historic position of the Church has been one which is concerned with the quality of man's contemporary environment as well as preparing him for eternity. (In fact, as social and political conditions affect man's behavior now, they obviously affect eternity.)

The revelations in this dispensation place a sobering responsibility on us as individuals in seeking out and supporting political candidates who are "wise," "good," and "honest." Likewise, the health of our cities and communities is as genuine a concern now as it was in the planning and establishment of Nauvoo or Salt Lake City.

The growing worldwide responsibilities of the Church make it inadvisable for the Church to seek to respond to all the various and complex issues involved in the mounting problems of the many cities and communities in which members live. But this complexity does not absolve members as individuals from filling their responsibilities as citizens in their own communities.

We urge our members to do their civic duty and to assume their responsibilities as individual citizens in seeking solutions to the problems which beset our cities and communities.

With our wide ranging mission, so far as mankind is concerned, Church members cannot ignore the many practical problems that require solution if our families are to live in an environment conducive to spirituality.

Where solutions to these practical problems require cooperative action with those not of our faith, members should not be reticent in doing their part in joining and leading in those efforts where they can make an individual contribution to those causes which are consistent with the standards of the Church.

Individual Church members cannot, of course, represent or commit the Church, but should, nevertheless, be "anxiously engaged" in good causes, using the principles of the gospel of Jesus Christ as their constant guide.[202]

—David O. McKay, Hugh B. Brown, and N. Eldon Tanner (The First Presidency)

THIS DAY IN AMERICAN HISTORY (1981)

President Ronald Reagan nominates Sandra Day O'Conner for the U. S. Supreme Court as the first female court justice.

Latter-day Saints Instrumental in Developing Statesmen

We would hope that we might be instrumental in developing statesmen—men not only with unsurpassed excellence of training in law, but also with an unwavering faith that the Constitution of the United States was divinely inspired and written by men whom God raised up for this very purpose.

Teachers, hold up before your students the prophetic statement of the Prophet Joseph Smith—that if and when our inspired Constitution should hang as by a thread, there would be prepared, well-qualified defenders of the faith of our fathers, the elders of this church, who would step forth and save the Constitution from destruction. . . .

The Constitution was established by the hands of wise men whom God raised up for this very purpose, and they devoutly believe that if it should be in danger of being overthrown, their lives, if need be, are to be offered in defense of its principles.[203]

—Harold B. Lee

THIS DAY IN AMERICAN HISTORY (1776)

The Declaration of Independence is read publicly in Philadelphia.

Be Equally Fair and Impartial

In the Church, there are members who favor the Democratic Party. There are other members who sincerely believe and advocate the principles and ideals of the Republican Party. The First Presidency, the Council of the Twelve, and other officers who constitute the General Authorities of the Church, preside over members of both political parties.

The President is President of the Church, not favoring in this election either political party. The welfare of all members of the Church is equally considered by the President, his Counselors, and the General Authorities. Both political parties will be treated impartially. . . .

It will be equally fair and impartial in the treatment of both political parties. This does not mean however, that error will be condoned. Teachings and ideologies subversive to the fundamental principles of this great Republic, which are contrary to the Constitution of the United States, or which are detrimental to the progress of The Church of Jesus Christ of Latter-day Saints, will be condemned, whether advocated by Republicans or Democrats.[204]

—*David O. McKay*

THIS DAY IN AMERICAN HISTORY (1868)

The 14th Amendment to the U.S. Constitution is ratified.

A Gradual Process

There is a lot of sentiment in this country, outside the Church, in support of our ideals and standards as Latter-day Saints. Let us not fail the Church. Let us not fail ourselves by being so unwise as to feel we have to let down in our standards in order to be accepted by the world. It is not true. The world may not live by our standards, but they have respect and appreciation for those of us who have the wisdom and the courage to maintain those standards.

Someday we may be called upon as a people to exert great influence in helping to preserve the liberties and freedoms and blessings vouchsafed to us as a people in the Constitution of this land. Some of our inspired leaders have had words to say on that subject. I hope and pray that we will be ready when the time comes—in fact, I am inclined to feel sometimes it is going to be a gradual process. Maybe it is underway now. We will not be able to discharge our obligations unless we adhere strictly to the standards and ideals of the church and the kingdom of God. That we may do so with all our hearts and receive the inner satisfaction, the inner peace, and the joy that comes from keeping the commandments of God is my humble prayer. [205]

—*Ezra Taft Benson*

THIS DAY IN AMERICAN HISTORY (1775)

George Washington assumes command of the Continental Army.

Force and Compulsion Will Never Establish the Ideal Society

Today, many nations have lost their independence; men, defeated, have been compelled to labor for their conquerors, property has been seized without recompense, and millions of people have surrendered all guarantees of personal liberty. Force and compulsion will never establish the ideal society. This can come only by a transformation within the individual soul—a life redeemed from sin and brought in harmony with the divine will. Instead of selfishness, men must be willing to dedicate their ability, their possessions, their lives, if necessary, their fortunes, and their sacred honor for the alleviation of the ills of mankind. Hate must be supplanted by sympathy and forbearance. Peace and true prosperity can come only by conforming our lives to the law of love, the law of the principle of the gospel of Jesus Christ.[206]

—*David O. McKay*

THIS DAY IN AMERICAN HISTORY (1780)

French troops arrive to aid the American cause in Revolutionary War in Newport, Rhode Island.

It Was the Design of the Almighty for Our Fathers to Come to America

The Lord Almighty has prepared the way for the coming forth of the kingdom of God in this dispensation by establishing the republican government of the United States; a government affording the widest liberty and the greatest freedom to man that has ever been known to exist among men, outside of those governed by the direct communication of heaven. It was part of the design of the Almighty when He influenced our fathers to leave the old world and come to this continent; He had a hand in the establishment of this government; He inspired the framers of the Constitution and the fathers of this nation to contend for their liberties; and He did this upon natural principles, that the way might be prepared, and that it might be possible for Him to establish His kingdom upon the earth, no more to be thrown down. And when the way was prepared and the time fully come for the restoration of the gospel, God revealed Himself to Joseph Smith, giving to him certain promises concerning the coming forth of the gospel and the establishment of His kingdom in the last days.[207]

—*Joseph F. Smith*

THIS DAY IN AMERICAN HISTORY (1909)

The 16th Amendment to the U.S. Constitution is proposed for ratification.

Don't Walk! Run! Run to Receive the Blessings of Agency

As we walk the path of spiritual liberty in these last days, we must understand that the faithful use of our agency depends upon our having religious freedom. We already know that Satan does not want this freedom to be ours. He attempted to destroy moral agency in heaven, and now on earth he is fiercely undermining, opposing, and spreading confusion about religious freedom—what it is and why it is essential to our spiritual life and our very salvation. . . .

We are responsible to safeguard these sacred freedoms and rights for ourselves and our posterity. What can you and I do?

First, we can become informed. Be aware of issues in your community that could have an impact on religious liberty.

Second, in your individual capacity, join with others who share our commitment to religious freedom. Work side by side to protect religious freedom.

Third, live your life to be a good example of what you believe—in word and deed. How we live our religion is far more important than what we may say about our religion.

My beloved brothers and sisters, don't walk! Run! Run to receive the blessings of agency by following the Holy Ghost and exercising the freedoms God has given us to do His will.[208]

—*Robert D. Hales*

THIS DAY IN AMERICAN HISTORY (1787)

The Northwest Ordinance is adopted.

Reflect on the Foliage of the Precious First Amendment

God raised up both the Founders and the necessary supporting cast. Involved, therefore, were the obvious luminaries—Washington, Adams, Jefferson, Hamilton, Madison, Franklin, and so forth—and also, for example, John Marshall, who was designated by his biographer Jean Edward Smith as the "definer of a nation."

Reflect on the foliage of the precious First Amendment. I read somewhere of the contrast between a banyan tree and a lombardy poplar, a relevant metaphor. The latter, though a thing of beauty and symmetry, does not really offer much shade from the heat of the day or shelter from the storm, whereas a banyan tree is thick with foliage and has sturdy, wide branches. How ironic, therefore, for some to neglect to nourish certain branches of that First Amendment tree under which many would seek shelter later on. A persistent preoccupation with "freedom of speech" to the neglect of other freedoms can diminish the shelter available for religion and other precious freedoms. The intertwining of all our freedoms is greater than we realize. Citizen soil still needs continued preparation to sustain the Constitution.

Clearly, God cares about how power is handled everywhere. It is likewise clear that He also desires to protect all mortals by means of certain rights and principles.[209]

—Neal A. Maxwell

THIS DAY IN AMERICAN HISTORY (1914)

American engineer Robert Goddard is granted the first patent for a liquid-fueled rocket design.

The Constitution Resembles a Theocracy

The Constitution and laws of the United States resemble a theocracy more closely than any government now on the earth, or that ever has been, so far as we know. . . .

The Lord has thus far protected and preserved the human family under their various forms and administrations of government, notwithstanding their wickedness, and is still preserving them. . . .

The Constitution and laws of the United States combine the best form of government in force upon the earth. But does it follow that each officer of the government administers with justice? No; for it is well known throughout our nations that very many of our public officers are as degraded, debased, corrupt, and regardless as men well can be.

I repeat that the Constitution, laws, and institutions of our government are as good as can be, with the intelligence now possessed by the people. But they, as also the laws of other nations, are too often administered in unrighteousness; and we do not and cannot love and respect the acts of the administrators of our laws, unless they act justly in their offices.[210]

—*Brigham Young*

THIS DAY IN AMERICAN HISTORY (1776)

Patriots fend off an attack by Indians and British loyalists dressed as Indians at Lyndley's Fort, South Carolina.

The Greater Purpose of the Constitution

In the providences of the Almighty the constitution of the United States was established to serve an even greater purpose than that of setting up a stable government under which freedom would prevail. It was designed to do far more than guarantee the preservation of natural and inalienable rights to the American people. The Constitution came forth to prepare the way for the restoration of the gospel, the fulfilling of the covenant God made with ancient Israel, and the organization of the church and the kingdom of God on earth in the last days.

America was to be a land of liberty upon which no kings should rule. (2 Nephi 10:11–14.) The nation to possess it was to "be free from bondage, and from captivity, and from all other nations (Ether 2:12)." The Gentiles were to "be established in this land, and be set up as a free people by the power of the Father," so that the Book of Mormon might come forth to the people and the covenants made with ancient Israel be fulfilled (3 Nephi 21:4). "And for this purpose have I established the Constitution of this land, by the hands of wise men whom I raised up unto this very purpose, and redeemed the land by the shedding of blood" (D&C 101:80; 109:54).[211]

—*Bruce R. McConkie*

THIS DAY IN AMERICAN HISTORY (1779)

American "Mad" Anthony Wayne captures Stony Point, New York, during the American Revolution.

The Constitution Is Good Enough for Anybody

I feel to bear my testimony to these things. They are true. God is with this people. And we say to our nation—maintain the Constitution and we are satisfied. Give us the rights of that Constitution and we are satisfied. It is an instrument inspired by the power of God. Our forefathers were inspired when they framed it. . . . The Constitution is good enough for anybody. It is good enough for the Latter-day Saints. We have no principles but what are in accord with the Constitution of the United States and the laws of God. We are perfectly willing to trust ourselves and our interests in the hands of God, and to leave our nation in His hands also; for God will judge our nation; He will judge us; He will judge all the children of men and He will judge righteous judgment. What men sow they will reap. What measure they mete, it shall be measured to them again.

I pray God to bless this nation. I pray God to give our legislators wisdom, that they may maintain the Constitutional principles of the government, the only government on the face of God's earth where the Lord could have established His Church and Kingdom.[212]

—*John Q. Cannon*

THIS DAY IN AMERICAN HISTORY (1945)

President Harry S. Truman, Winston Churchill, and Joseph Stalin meet at the Potsdam Conference in Germany.

Live Under Freedom

I have personally witnessed the heart-rending results of the loss of freedom. I have talked face to face with a Godless, communist leader. It may surprise you to learn that I was host to Mister Khrushchev for a half day when he visited the United States. Not that I'm proud of it. I opposed his coming then, and I still feel it was a mistake to welcome this atheistic murderer as a state visitor. But according to President Eisenhower, Khrushchev had expressed a desire to learn something of American agriculture, and after seeing Russian agriculture, I can understand why. As we talked face to face, he indicated that my grandchildren would live under communism. After assuring him that I expected to do all in my power to assure that his and all other grandchildren would live under freedom, he arrogantly declared in substance: "You Americans are so gullible. No, you won't accept communism outright, but we'll keep feeding you small doses of socialism until you'll finally wake up and find you already have communism. We won't have to fight you. We'll so weaken your economy until you fall like overripe fruit into our hands."[213]

—Ezra Taft Benson

THIS DAY IN AMERICAN HISTORY (1792)

John Paul Jones, Revolutionary War Naval Hero, dies in Paris in 1792.

The Constitution Is Founded in the Wisdom of God

There is a love from God that should be exercised toward those of our faith, who walk uprightly, which is peculiar to itself, but it is without prejudice; it also gives scope to the mind, which enables us to conduct ourselves with greater liberality towards all that are not of our faith, than what they exercise towards one another. These principles approximate nearer to the mind of God, because it is like God, or Godlike.

Here is a principle also, which we are bound to be exercised with, that is, in common with all men, such as governments, and laws, and regulations in the civil concerns of life. This principle guarantees to all parties, sects, and denominations, and classes of religion, equal, coherent, and indefeasible rights; they make our responsibilities one towards another in matters of corruptible things, while the former principles do not destroy the latter, but bind us stronger, and make our responsibilities not only one to another, but unto God also. Hence, we say, that the Constitution of the United States is a glorious standard; it is founded in the wisdom of God. It is a heavenly banner; it is to all those who are privileged with the sweets of its liberty, like the cooling shades and refreshing waters of a great rock in a thirsty and weary land. It is like a great tree under whose branches men from every' clime can be shielded from the burning rays of the sun.[214]

—*Joseph Smith, Jr.*

THIS DAY IN AMERICAN HISTORY (1776)

Congress orders the Declaration of Independence to be inscribed/signed by members.

The Founding of the United States Was Not an Accident

It is our responsibility to carry the message of the gospel not only to the civilized world but also to those who are not considered to be so civilized. All this has been made possible because the Lord in his wisdom saw the necessity of giving us a nation in which we could thrive. In no other nation under heaven could the Church have been organized and gone forward as we have in this nation. The founding of the United States was not an accident. The giving to us of the Constitution of the United States was not an accident. Our Heavenly Father knew what would be needed, and so he paved the way to give us the Constitution. It came under the influence of prayer, and he guided those who framed that wonderful document.

I hope that the membership of this Church will not be deceived into thinking that other plans, other forms of government, other systems of direction whatsoever, are desirable. I want to say to you without any hesitation that no form of government in the world can be compared favorably with the government God gave to us. This is his plan. Then after giving us our civil government, preparing the way for governing ourselves, if you will, he organized the Church and gave it the name of his Beloved Son, and then directed that we share that information with all his children. What a commission, a divine commission!

The Lord says that he is a slothful servant who waits to be commanded in all things (D&C 58:26). When we see all around us the need for living as well as teaching the gospel, it is our duty to set the example. We ought not to be waiting for other people to take the initiative; it should be our responsibility to go forward. Everything that is praiseworthy, everything in civil life, or in religious life that is necessary to make the people happy will come to us as a part of the gospel of Jesus Christ, our Lord. This is his Church; we are His people if we are faithful. I want to say that this Church will continue to grow and expand, and instead of approximately a million souls as we have now, if we shall do our duty, the membership of this Church will continue to increase, and the good men and women, those who are seeking God, will get the inspiration and accept the truth as some of your forebears did.[215]

—*George Albert Smith*

THIS DAY IN AMERICAN HISTORY (1969)

Apollo 11 lands on the moon.

We Have Received a Religion That Admits of Toleration

I have had occasion frequently to talk upon this subject. I have told men that, from my early boyhood, I have been taught to believe that the constitution of the United States was revealed of God, and that the destiny in store for the Latter-day Saints was to uphold constitutional government upon this land; and, that being the case, how could it be reconcilable with the idea that we were disloyal to the government? But there is a class of men who consider everybody disloyal who does not dance to their tunes, and who does not re-echo the sentiments which they express and seem to entertain. We have a class of men among us here who talk about the one-man power and the tyranny that exist in the Utah Territory, but at the same time if an official were to come here and associate with citizens of this territory, "Mormon" citizens I mean, they would put him under a ban and brand him as disloyal and unfit to hold an official position under the government. And why? For years here it has been considered by certain officials as one of the best recommendations to the favor of those in power to hate and abuse the "Mormon" people of Utah Territory; and if a man were to dare to associate with "Mormons," were to speak kindly of or to associate with them, and to treat them as he would other people he would be ostracized and banished, so far as association with them is concerned a non-intercourse act would be passed immediately. And these very individuals talk about the intolerance of the Mormons.

We have these things to contend with, we have these lies to live down, and as far as we are concerned, let them always be lies; let no man have it in his power to say that the Latter-day Saints are an intolerant, proscriptive or an unjust people. Never let this be said of us with truth; but if it be said, let our enemies continue to lie about us until they are tired of it, or until the world become sickened with the falsehoods that are told concerning us. And for us, let us pursue the path that God has marked out, being liberal, truthful, upright, dealing fairly, honestly and tolerantly with every man, so that every class of men who come into our midst may learn that we have received a religion that admits of toleration in the broadest sense of the word.[216]

—*George Q. Cannon*

THIS DAY IN AMERICAN HISTORY (1775)

Benjamin Franklin presents a plan for an American Colonial Confederation.

A Different Kind of Revolution

There seems also to be a great need for a restoration of the national soul of the great land of America and of other lands as well. The Prophet Joseph Smith is quoted as having said that the Constitution of the United States would hang by a thread, but that the elders of the Church would save it. Many have thought that this would be a political saving, and this may be so, but it can come in another way. Could it not also be brought about by members of the Church individually, humbly, wisely, and persuasively adhering to their convictions at all times and under all circumstances? It could be brought about by the young lawyer, standing in the criminal law section of the American Bar Association. During a discussion of so-called "victimless crimes." It can also come about without own physicians, acting individually, but each refusing to perform abortions of convenience. Could it not be with our teachers sharing their examples in individual moral and civil responsibility with our young people as they teach history, chemistry and mathematics? Could it not be with our businessmen refusing to compromise or to be compromised? It could also help if all of our members refuse to patronize stores that sell pornographic materials. Could it not be with those of our numbers who hold positions of honor and trust in government, to function always from a position of personal honor and integrity?

That would be the beginning of a different kind of revolution. It would be a revolution of thought and purpose. It would be a quiet revolution, with each individual acting independently and courageously in his or her own sphere of influence, listening to his or her own peace of conscience.[217]

—*James E. Faust*

THIS DAY IN AMERICAN HISTORY (1893)

Katharine Lee Bates writes "American the Beautiful" in Colorado.

Our Duty Is to Preserve the Christian Principles from Which Spring the Constitution

The Church of Jesus Christ of Latter-day Saints believes with the prophet Lehi that America is a "land of promise, a land choice above all other lands"—a land of liberty unto those who keep the commandments of God. But " . . . if the day shall come that they will reject the Holy One of Israel, the true Messiah, their Redeemer and their God, behold the judgements of him that is just shall rest upon them." (2 Nephi 1:10) The Church believes, also, that before the end of wickedness shall come, and wars shall be no more, this gospel of the kingdom must be preached to all the world. (See Matthew 24:14.)

The Constitution of this government was written by men who accepted Jesus Christ as the Savior of mankind. Let men eyes centered upon him who ever shines as a Light to all the world. Men and women who live in America, "the land of Zion," have a responsibility greater than that yet borne by any other people. Theirs the duty, the obligation to preserve not only the Constitution of the land but also the Christian principles from which sprang that immortal document.

With the Appeals for freedom that you transmit to your fellow countrymen across the sea, send also in messages that connote sincerity never before expressed, an avowed conviction that Christ is the way, the truth, the life, the only safe guide to that haven of peace for which men and women the wide world over are earnestly praying. (See John 14:6.)[218]

To this end let members of the Church, and honest men in every clime accept, not as an abstract, inapplicable saying, but as an eternal and guiding truth, the declaration of the Redeemer: "I am the light of the world; he that followeth me shall not walk in darkness, but shall have the light of life." (John 8:12)[219]

—David O. McKay

THIS DAY IN AMERICAN HISTORY (1777)

King Louis XVI of France agrees to supply the United States during the American Revolution.

The Inspired Constitution: A Latter-day Saint Responsibility

What was God's purpose in establishing the United States Constitution? We see it in the doctrine of moral agency. In the first decade of the restored Church, its members on the western frontier were suffering private and public persecution. Partly this was because of their opposition to the human slavery then existing in the United States. In these unfortunate circumstances, God revealed through the Prophet Joseph Smith eternal truths about His doctrine. . . .

Our belief in divine inspiration gives Latter-day Saints a unique responsibility to uphold and defend the United States Constitution and principles of constitutionalism wherever we live. We should trust in the Lord and be positive about this nation's future. . . .

I see divine inspiration in the vital purpose of the entire Constitution. We are to be governed by law and not by individuals, and our loyalty is to the Constitution and its principles and processes, not to any office holder. In this way, all persons are to be equal before the law. These principles block the autocratic ambitions that have corrupted democracy in some countries. They also mean that none of the three branches of government should be dominant over the others or prevent the others from performing their proper constitutional functions to check one another. . . .

What else are faithful Latter-day Saints to do? We must pray for the Lord to guide and bless all nations and their leaders. This is part of our article of faith. Being subject to presidents or rulers of course poses no obstacle to our opposing individual laws or policies. It does require that we exercise our influence civilly and peacefully within the framework of our constitutions and applicable laws. On contested issues, we should seek to moderate and unify. There are other duties that are part of upholding the inspired Constitution. We should learn and advocate the inspired *principles* of the Constitution. We should seek out and support wise and good persons who will support those principles in their public actions. We should be knowledgeable citizens who are active in making our influence felt in civic affairs.[220]

—*Dallin H. Oaks*

THIS DAY IN AMERICAN HISTORY (1866)

Tennessee readmitted into the Union after the Civil War.

Stand Fast with Love in Proclaiming Truth

As for the Constitution, the constitutional Bill of Rights guarantees [to] protect the good that religious believers and their churches, synagogues, and mosques can do. These protections include the precious freedoms of speech, conscience, and the free exercise of religion. I've spoken often on this subject—in this country and in other countries. It's vital to all of us to understand the importance of these protections and our democratic form of government.

Elder Gilbert: Now, President Oaks, speaking of these three institutions and other truths that we seek to defend, what are ways that you would like to see our young adults in the Church stand fast with love in proclaiming truth?

President Oaks: I have a number of things I would like to urge you to do. The first is avoid overly contentious settings. I encourage you to refrain from participating in the contentious communications that are so common today. Social media can generate conflicts. It can expand the audience and the speed of dissemination. It often fosters careless charges, false representations, and ugly innuendos that intensify the distance between different parties and their communications. I'm not criticizing differences in policies. These need to be debated publicly. What I'm urging our members to do is to stand clear from the current atmosphere of hate and personal meanness in communications. I love Elder Neil L. Andersen's recent statement that, "there are times when being a peacemaker means that we resist the impulse to respond and instead, with dignity, remain quiet." There's great wisdom in that counsel. Second suggestion: Love others; find common ground, even when we disagree. After avoiding contentious settings, we should reach out positively to express our concern and love for those with whom we disagree. We should seek to find common ground on which to stand with those who might otherwise consider us their enemies. Followers of Christ should be examples of civility. We should remember the Savior's teachings: "By this shall all men know that ye are my disciples, if ye have love one to another."[221]

—*Dallin H. Oaks and Clark G. Gilbert*

THIS DAY IN AMERICAN HISTORY (1866)

David Farragut is appointed as the first admiral in the U.S. Navy.

These Are Not Just Human Rights; They Are Divine Rights

The Constitutional Convention gave birth to the document that Gladstone said is "the most wonderful work ever struck off at a given time by the brain and purpose of man." I heartily endorse this assessment. I would like to pay honor—honor to the document itself, honor to the men who framed it, and honor to the God who inspired it and made possible its coming forth. God Himself has borne witness to the fact that He is pleased with the final product of the work of these great patriots.

Our Creator endowed each one of us with certain rights at birth, among which are the rights to life, liberty, speech, and conscience, to name a few. These are not just human rights; they are divine rights. When these rights are not permitted expression by a nation, that nation becomes inhibited in its progress and development, and its leaders are responsible before God for suffocating sacred rights.

This native endowment is what separates man from the animals. It causes men to want to be good and to seek higher aspirations. It creates in man a desire to better his life and his station in life.

It is time we recognize, as a people, that this country rests on divinely inspired and uniquely formulated principles. Until 1791, no nation had all basic rights guaranteed and recognized by written contract. That is what the Constitution is—a contract between a sovereign people and their elected officials. It is high time these principles are not just acknowledged, but carried out. Indeed this is the only real hope for our survival as a free nation.[222]

—*Ezra Taft Benson*

THIS DAY IN AMERICAN HISTORY (1788)

New York ratifies the U.S. Constitution 30–27
and receives statehood as the 11th state.

United States Citizens Should Follow the First Presidency's Counsel to Study the Constitution

U.S. citizens should follow the First Presidency's counsel to study the Constitution. They should be familiar with its great fundamentals. . . . They should oppose any infringement of these inspired fundamentals. They should be law-abiding citizens, supportive of national, state, and local governments.

The Church's official declaration of belief states: "We believe that governments were instituted of God for the benefit of man; and that he holds men accountable for their acts in relation to them. We believe that all men are bound to sustain and uphold the respective governments in which they reside." Those who enjoy the blessings of liberty under a divinely inspired constitution should promote morality, and they should practice what the Founding Fathers called "civic virtue." In his address on the U.S. Constitution, President Ezra Taft Benson quoted this important observation by John Adams, the second president of the United States: "Our Constitution was made only for a moral and religious people. It is wholly inadequate to the government of any other."

As the Lord declared in modern revelation, constitutional laws are justifiable before him, "and the law also maketh you free" (D&C 98:5–8). The self-control by which citizens subject themselves to law strengthens the freedom of all citizens and honors the divinely inspired Constitution.[223]

—*Dallin H. Oaks*

THIS DAY IN AMERICAN HISTORY (1953)

The Koren War ends.

Thus Will the Lord Visit the People

What then will be the condition of that people, when this great and terrible war shall come? It will be very different from the war between the North and the South, do you wish me to describe it? I will do so. It will be a war of neighborhood against neighborhood, city against city, town against town, county against county, state against state, and they will go forth destroying and being destroyed and manufacturing will, in a great measure, cease, for a time, among the American nation. Why? Because in these terrible wars, they will not be privileged to manufacture, there will be too much bloodshed—too much mobocracy—too much going forth in bands and destroying and pillaging the land to suffer people to pursue any local vocation with any degree of safety. What will become of millions of the farmers upon that land? They will leave their farms and they will remain uncultivated, and they will flee before the ravaging armies from place to place; and thus will they go forth burning and pillaging the whole country; and that great and powerful nation, now consisting of some forty millions of people, will be wasted away, unless they repent.[224]

For instance the great, powerful and populous city of New York, that may be considered one of the greatest cities of the world, will in a few years become a mass of ruins. The people will wonder while gazing on the ruins that cost hundreds of millions to build, what has become of its inhabitants. Their houses will be there, but they will be left desolate. So saith the Lord God. That will be only a sample of numerous other towns and cities on the face of this continent. The time will come when there will be no safety in carrying on the peaceable pursuits of farming or agriculture. But these will be neglected, and the people will think themselves well off if they can flee from city to city, from town to town and escape with their lives. Thus will the Lord visit the people, if they will not repent. Thus will He pour out His wrath and indignation upon them.[225]

—*Orson Pratt*

THIS DAY IN AMERICAN HISTORY (1789)

House Select Committee reports on James Madison's proposed amendments to the U.S. Constitution.

A Divine Vision of the Worth of All

The First Amendment to the United States Constitution guarantees the "right of the people peaceably to assemble, and to petition the government for a redress of grievances." That is the authorized way to raise public awareness and to focus on injustices in the content or administration of the laws. And there have been injustices. In public actions and in our personal attitudes, we have had racism and related grievances. As citizens and as members of The Church of Jesus Christ of Latter-day Saints, we must do better to help root out racism.

At the other extreme, a minority of participants and supporters of these protests and the illegal acts that followed them seem to have forgotten that the protests protected by the Constitution are *peaceful* protests. All of us—police, protesters, supporters, and spectators—should understand the limits of our rights and the importance of our duties to stay within the boundaries of existing law. . . .

The United States was founded by immigrants of different nationalities and different ethnicities. Its unifying purpose was not to establish a particular religion or to perpetuate any of the diverse cultures or tribal loyalties of the old countries. Our founding generation sought to be unified by a new constitution and laws. That is not to say that our unifying documents or the then-current understanding of their meanings were perfect. The history of the first two centuries of the United States showed the need for many refinements, such as voting rights for women and, particularly, the abolition of slavery, including laws to ensure that those who had been enslaved would have all the conditions of freedom. . . .

Knowing that we are all children of God gives us a divine vision of the worth of all others and the will and ability to rise above prejudice and racism. As I have lived for many years in different places in this nation, the Lord has taught me that it is possible to obey and seek to improve our nation's laws and also to love our adversaries and our enemies. While not easy, it is possible with the help of our Lord, Jesus Christ. He gave this command to love, and He promises His help as we seek to obey it. [226]

—*Dallin H. Oaks*

THIS DAY IN AMERICAN HISTORY (1958)

The National Aeronautics and Space Administration (NASA) is established.

These Gifts Are Available to All

Members of The Church of Jesus Christ of Latter-day Saints invite all to come unto Christ and enjoy the spiritual feast that His gospel provides. The Saints savor a sweet spiritual nourishment that sustains them through life. This sustenance comes because they have made covenants to take upon themselves the name of the Lord and strive to obey his precepts. Strength comes in recognizing and in being grateful for the Lord's gifts of immortality and the opportunity for eternal life.

These gifts are available to all. Citizens of many countries claim membership in the Church. Regardless of their flag or form of government, they find that allegiance to the Lord does not preclude their being loyal citizens of their nations. Fidelity to God enables one to develop a more profound patriotic allegiance and become a better citizen.

In addition to their national citizenship, members of the Church are also citizens of God's kingdom (see Ephesians 2:19). Their commitment to it, however, may be variable. The great majority seek "first to build up the kingdom of God, and to establish his righteousness" (Joseph Smith Translation, Matthew 6:38). Some allow their allegiance to God and His kingdom to slip below that of other interests in life. They have not yet determined which way they face (see Joel 3:14).

I perceived such confusion in the mind of a newspaper reporter who asked one of our leaders when a representative of such-and-such a country would become a General Authority. While that question was being answered, I thought about our beloved General Authorities born in the countries of Asia; of Europe; of North, Central, and South America; and of the islands of the sea. Though these Brethren come from many nations and speak several tongues, not one of them was called to represent his native country. Presiding quorums of the Church are not representative assemblies. Each leader has been called to face the people as a representative of the Lord, not the other way around. [227]

—Russell M. Nelson

THIS DAY IN AMERICAN HISTORY (1965)

President Lyndon B. Johnson signs the Medicare Bill.

The Constitution of the United States Is a Glorious Standard

I believe that nothing plainer could be written than those statements of our belief (D&C 134). Nothing could be fairer; and no matter what a man's faith, belief, or religion may be, I am sure he can endorse those sentiments given to the Church in 1835. These principles are fundamental to our belief, fundamental to our protection. And in the providences of the Lord, the safeguards which have been incorporated into the basic structure of this nation are the guarantee of all men who dwell here against the abuses and tyrannies and usurpations of times past.

From my childhood days I have understood that we believe absolutely that the Constitution of our country is an inspired instrument, and that God directed those who created it and those who defended the independence of this nation. Concerning this matter it is my frequent pleasure to quote the statement by Joseph Smith, regarding the Constitution:

"The Constitution of the United States is a glorious standard; it is founded in the wisdom of God. It is a heavenly banner; it is, to all those who are privileged with the sweets of liberty, like the cooling shades and refreshing waters of a great rock in a weary and thirsty land. It is like a great tree under whose branches men from every clime can be shielded from the burning rays of the sun."

And such the Constitution of the United States must be to every faithful Latter-day Saint who lives under its protection. We honor the man that God honors. We honor Abraham Lincoln because we believe absolutely that God honored him and raised him up to be the instrument in His hands of saving the Constitution and the Union. That the Lord may help him to think straight, and to pursue a straight course regardless of personal advantage, factional interest, or political persuasion, should be the daily prayer of every Latter-day Saint.[228]

—*Heber J. Grant*

THIS DAY IN AMERICAN HISTORY (1777)

The Marquis de Lafayette, just nineteen years old, is made a major-general in the American Continental Army.

Principles for the Birth and Organization of a New World

It is true that the founders of this nation, as a preliminary step for the introduction of more correct principles and that liberty and the rights of man might be recognized, and that all men might become equal before the law of the land, had that great palladium of liberty, the Constitution of the United States, framed. This was the entering wedge for the introduction of a new era, and in it were introduced principles for the birth and organization of a new world.

The Prophet Joseph Smith said that "the Constitution of the United States was given by the inspiration of God." But good, virtuous and holy principles may be perverted by corrupt and wicked men. . . . This nation abounds with traitors who ignore that sacred palladium of liberty and seek to trample it under foot. Joseph Smith said they would do so, and that when deserted by all, the elders of Israel would rally around its shattered fragments and save and preserve it inviolate. But even this, good as it was, was not a perfect instrument; it was one of those stepping stones to a future development in the progress of a man to the intelligence and light, the power and union that God alone can impart to the human family. And while we acknowledge, as citizens of the United States, the laws and institutions thereof (which by the way are very easily complied with), we have a higher law, more noble principles, ideas that are more elevated and expansive; principles that reach to the whole human family, and which he will continue to reveal to us.

Does that prevent us from obeying the laws of the land? Certainly not. But then, is that a perfect system? I do not think that many of you will say it is, nor do I think that the people of the United States of any political party will tell you it is. I do not wish to cast any reflections or refer to any events that have taken place; I am merely speaking on religious principles, and principles too in which we as Latter-day Saints are interested. We are united, then, as a body politic, as an integral part of this government, and it becomes our duty to submit to the laws and institutions of that government—to all that are constitutional, framed and based upon correct principles, and not in violation of what the fathers of the country instituted.[229]

—*John Taylor*

THIS DAY IN AMERICAN HISTORY (1786)

Shay's Rebellion begins.

Submit Yourselves to Every Ordinance of Man for the Lord's Sake

The twelfth article of faith commits Latter-day Saints to being subject to kings, presidents, rulers, and magistrates, and to obeying, honoring, and sustaining the law. This belief is not unique in Christendom. The Apostle Paul told the early Christians to be subject to principalities and powers and to obey magistrates. The Apostle Peter taught, "submit yourselves to every ordinance of man for the Lord's sake" (see 1 Peter 2:13). . . .

At a clear and extreme level, violations of inalienable rights by a government might excuse citizens from the performance of some obligations of citizenship. But the history of Latter-day Saints' relations to their governments shows that any such exceptions would have to be far more extreme than anything we have experienced in this country. Even when victimized by what they must surely have seen as very severe government oppressions and abridgements of freedom, the Mormon people and their leaders have remained loyal to their established government and its laws. Think of the persecutions in Missouri, the expulsion from Nauvoo, and the repressions suffered in the Utah Territory.

As long as a government provides aggrieved persons an opportunity to work to enlarge their freedoms and relieve their oppressions by legal and peaceful means, a Latter-day Saints' duty is to forgo revolution and disobedience of law. Our doctrine commits us to work from within. Even an oppressive government is preferable to a state of lawlessness and anarchy in which the only ruling principle is force, and every individual has a thousand oppressors. Church members who seek to use LDS doctrine as a basis for concluding that government infringements on inalienable rights have excused them from obeying the law seem to have forgotten the principle of following the prophets. Until the prophets invoke this principle, faithful members will also refrain from doing so. We remain committed to uphold our governments and to obey their laws.[230]

—*Dallin H. Oaks*

THIS DAY IN AMERICAN HISTORY (1788)

North Carolina initially votes 184–84 against ratifying the U.S. Constitution.

God Set Up This People and Their Government

Under our form of government, "We the people of the United States," as the preamble of the Constitution declares, form this government. We alone are sovereign. We are wholly free to exercise our sovereign will in the way we prescribe. The sovereignty is not personal, as under the civil law. The Constitution expressly provides the only way in which we may change our Constitution. The total residue of powers, including all rights and liberties not given up by us to federal or state institutions, is still in us, to remain so till we constitutionally provide otherwise. . . .

Must we go far to see why God set up this people and their government, the only government on the face of the earth—since the Master was here—that God has formally declared was set up at the hands of men whom he raised up for that very purpose and the fundamental principles of which he has expressly approved? Having in mind what the Lord has said about the Constitution and its framers, that the Constitution should be established and should be maintained for the rights and protection of all flesh; that it was for the protection of the moral agency. . . . Speaking for myself, I declare that the divine sanction thus repeatedly given by the Lord Himself to the Constitution of the United States—as it came from the hands of the framers with its coterminous bills of right—makes of the principles of that document an integral part of my religious faith. . . . My faith, my knowledge, my testimony of the restored gospel, based on the divine principle of continuous revelation, compel me so to believe.

Thus has the Lord approved of our political system and approval, so far as I know, such as he has given to no other political system of any other people in the world since the time of Christ. The Constitution as approved by the Lord is still the same great vanguard of liberty and freedom in human government that it was the day it was written. No other human system of government affording equal protection for human life, liberty, and the pursuit of happiness has yet been devised or vouchsafed to man. Its great principles are as applicable, efficient, and sufficient to bring today the greatest good to the greatest number . . . as they were the day the Constitution was signed.[231]

—*J. Reuben Clark, Jr.*

THIS DAY IN AMERICAN HISTORY (1936)

American sprinter Jesse Owens wins the 100-meter race (10.3 seconds) in front of Adolf Hitler at the Berlin Olympics.

They Were Inspired by God

The principles and philosophies upon which our constitutional law is based are not simply the results of the best efforts of a remarkable group of brilliant men. They were inspired by God, and the rights and privileges guaranteed in the Constitution are God-given, not man-derived. The freedom and independence afforded by the Constitution and Bill of Rights are divine rights; sacred, essential, and inalienable. In the 98th section of the Doctrine and Covenants, the Lord indicates that the "law of the land which is constitutional, supporting that principle of freedom in maintaining rights and privileges, belongs to all mankind, and is justifiable before me" (D&C 98:5). . . .

Believe it or not, at one time the very notion of government had less to do with politics than with virtue. According to James Madison, often referred to as the father of the Constitution, "we have staked the whole future of American civilization not upon the power of the government; far from it, we have staked the future of all of our political institutions upon the capacity of each and all of us to govern ourselves according to the Ten Commandments of God."

George Washington agreed with his colleague James Madison. Said Washington, "Reason and experience both forbid us to expect that national morality can prevail in exclusion of religious principle." Nearly 100 years later, Abraham Lincoln responded to a question about which side God was on during the Civil War with this profound thought: "I'm not at all concerned about that, for I know that the Lord is always on the side of right. But it is my constant anxiety and prayer that I and this nation should be on the Lord's side."

Madison, Washington, and Lincoln all understood that democracy cannot possibly flourish in a moral vacuum, and that organized religion plays an important role in preserving and maintaining public morality. Indeed, John Adams, another of America's Founding Fathers, insisted: "We have no government armed with power capable of contending with human passions unbridled by morality and religion."[232]

—M. Russell Ballard

THIS DAY IN AMERICAN HISTORY (1821)

The first issue of the American *Saturday Evening Post* magazine is published.

The Blessings of Our Constitutional Freedoms

The blessings of our constitutional freedoms were secured for us by the bounty of the Almighty through the patriotism and sacrifices of the Founding Fathers. They were preserved for us through the suffering and trials of the Civil War. For them we owe a deep debt of gratitude to God and our forebears.

By the grace of God we occupy this land, the blessings of which are unequaled in any other land. It is difficult for us of this generation to fully appreciate these blessings because they were not won by the shedding of our own blood, sweat, and tears, but by that of others. There are some things, however, that we must no longer fail to appreciate. If we do so, we shall do it at our peril. Chief among these things is man's free agency, which was provided for in the Constitution as it was originally adopted and interpreted. America's destiny requires that the constitutional safeguards of this freedom be appreciated and maintained. It is imperative that they be maintained and observed here in America in order that they may go out from here undiluted to the protection of all flesh. . . .

There are those among us who feel, and perhaps with good cause, that these constitutional freedoms are being, both wittingly and unwittingly, eroded. If this be so, let it be known that with the loss of each constitutional freedom we are surrendering our inheritance in this favored land. Now, my beloved brothers and sisters, young and old, let us—who know and believe so much more than others about the fate and ultimate destiny of America—lead the way by precept and example to the realization of that great destiny.[233]

—*Marion G. Romney*

THIS DAY IN AMERICAN HISTORY (1862)

The U.S. government collects the first income tax.

We Are All a Part of America's Future

Now, what of America's future? How can we best show our appreciation to God for these marvelous blessings of freedom, of a place where his true and everlasting gospel was restored, of the preparation and divine guidance in every event leading to that most significant event? We must remember what the Lord told the Jaredites when they were first brought to this land: "Behold, this is a choice land, and whatsoever nation shall possess it shall be free from bondage, and from captivity, and from all other nations under heaven, *if they will but serve the God of the land, who is Jesus Christ,* who hath been manifested by the things which we have written" (Ether 2:12; italics added). . . .

We are all a part of America's future. Our job is to learn and benefit from the past and to go forward in righteousness, keeping the commandments of God. . . . Also, it is our duty to seek diligently for and support and uphold good, honest, honorable, and wise representatives to govern us. Let me reiterate the message left with the Saints nearly sixty years ago at the general conference in April 1917 when Elder Anthony W. Ivins, after discussing religious liberty and the Constitution, said, "I feel authorized to say . . . that these liberties which have come to men, both religious and civil, have not been established by the Lord to be destroyed, but that they are here to remain until liberty shall prevail from the rivers to the ends of the earth, until God's kingdom shall be established among men, and his will done upon earth as it is done in heaven. Until the universal Fatherhood of God, and brotherhood of man shall be recognized, and the kingdoms of this world become the kingdoms of Christ, who shall reign as Prince of Peace." . . .

Only as we accept and live the teachings of the gospel can the destiny which God planned for America be realized and the world united in peace and brotherhood.[234]

—N. Eldon Tanner

THIS DAY IN AMERICAN HISTORY (1787)

The Constitutional Convention reconvenes.

Champion the Cause of Religious Freedom

Consider with me four ways that society and individuals benefit from religious freedom. First, religious freedom honors the first and second great commandments, placing God at the center of our lives. . . . Whether in a chapel, synagogue, mosque, or tin-roofed hut, Christ's disciples and all like-minded believers can express devotion to God by worship of Him and willingness to serve His children.

Second, religious freedom fosters expressions of belief, hope, and peace. As a church, we join with other religions protecting people of all faiths and persuasions and their right to speak their convictions. This does not mean we accept their beliefs, nor they ours, but we have more in common than we have with those who desire to silence us.

Third, religion inspires people to help others. When religion is given the space and freedom to flourish, believers perform simple and sometimes heroic acts of service. The ancient Jewish phrase "tikkun olam," meaning "to repair or heal the world," is being reflected today in the efforts of so many. . . . The list of what is being done is long, but so are the needs. No question, people of faith, working together, can make significant interventions. At the same time, one-on-one service is often unheralded but quietly changes lives. . . .

And fourth. Freedom of religion acts as a unifying and rallying force for shaping values and morality. In the New Testament we read of many turning away from Jesus Christ, murmuring of His doctrine, "This is an hard saying; who can hear it?" That cry is still being heard today from those who seek to expel religion from discourse and influence. . . . I invite you to champion the cause of religious freedom. It is an expression of the God-given principle of agency. Religious freedom brings balance to competing philosophies. The good of religion, its reach, and the daily acts of love which religion inspires only multiply when we protect the freedom to express and act on core beliefs.[235]

—*Ronald A. Rasband*

THIS DAY IN AMERICAN HISTORY (1964)

The Gulf of Tonkin Resolution is passed by the U.S. Congress.

AUGUST 8

The Political Neutrality of the Church

The work of The Church of Jesus Christ of Latter-day Saints includes sharing the gospel of Jesus Christ, strengthening individuals and families, and caring for those in need. The Church does not seek to elect government officials, support or oppose political parties, or, generally, take sides in global conflicts. The Church is neutral in matters of politics within or between the world's many nations, lands and peoples. However, as an institution, it reserves the right to address issues it believes have significant moral consequences or that directly affect the mission, teachings or operations of the Church.

Government officials and political representatives who are Latter-day Saints make their own decisions. They are not expected or asked to agree with one another or even with a publicly stated Church position. While the Church may communicate its views to them, as it may to any other officials or representatives, it recognizes that these individuals must make their own choices according to their best judgment and considering the constituencies they were elected to represent.

To navigate the application of these principles of political neutrality and participation in an ever-changing and complex world, the First Presidency of The Church of Jesus Christ of Latter-day Saints will continue to seek prophetic wisdom and revelation on these matters.[236]

—*Church Newsroom*

THIS DAY IN AMERICAN HISTORY (1778)

French and American forces besiege Newport, Rhode Island.

It Is Far Too Easy Sometimes to Fall into a Spirit of Mockery

I have a friend who is a member of a political panel that is seen each week on national television. Explaining her role, she said, "We are encouraged to speak before thinking!" We appear to be living in an era in which many are speaking without thinking, encouraging emotional reactions rather than thoughtful responses. Whether it be on the national or international stage, in personal relations or in politics, at home or in the public forum, voices grow ever more strident, and giving and taking offense appear to be chosen rather than inadvertent. . . . We must remain true to the way, the truth, and the life, who is Jesus Christ.

Have we who have taken upon us the name of Christ slipped unknowingly into patterns of slander, evil speaking, and bitter stereotyping? Have personal or partisan or business or religious differences been translated into a kind of demonizing of those of different views? Do we pause to understand the seemingly different positions of others and seek, where possible, common ground? . . .

It is far too easy sometimes to fall into a spirit of mockery and cynicism in dealing with those of contrary views. We demoralize or demean so as to bring others or their ideas in contempt. It is a primary tool of those who occupy the large and spacious building that Father Lehi saw in vision. Jude, the brother of Christ, warned that "there should be mockers in the last time, who should walk after their own ungodly lusts. These be they who separate themselves, sensual, having not the Spirit."

We cannot afford to be caught up in a world prone to give and to take offense. Rather, as the Lord revealed to both Paul and Mormon, we must neither envy nor be puffed up in pride. We are not easily provoked, nor do we behave unseemly. We rejoice not in iniquity but in the truth. Surely this is the pure love of Christ which we represent.[237]

—*Robert S. Wood*

THIS DAY IN AMERICAN HISTORY (1945)

The U.S. drops a second atomic bomb ("Fat Man") on Nagasaki, Japan.

The Constitution Is the Best Human Form of Government Given to the Human Family

We have a constitution that was given by inspiration from God to man. I believe it is the best human form of government that was ever given to the human family

The God of heaven gives all his children this right and privilege, it belongs to the whole human family, every man, woman and child under heaven has the right to worship God according to his desires, according to his own views, and according to the light which he has. The Lord gives all the children of men this right and privilege.

We say to all men, "Enjoy your religion, worship God according to the dictates of your own conscience." We ask the same right as the children of God. We claim this by the Constitution and laws of our country, and upon this principle we have embraced the fulness of the everlasting gospel of Jesus Christ.

God Almighty holds in His hands the destiny of this people, and of all nations, and this generation will yet realize that it is a fearful thing to fall into the hands of the living God. "No weapon that is formed against thee shall prosper; and every tongue that shall rise against thee in judgment thou shalt condemn," saith Isaiah, and I know he was a prophet.[238]

—*Wilford Woodruff*

THIS DAY IN AMERICAN HISTORY (1821)

Missouri Receives statehood as the 24th state.

The Quality of Democracy in America

Our government started out blessed with the rich inheritance of the ages. Its future lay before it, and that justice should rule the hearts of all its people, the Constitution of the United States was written. The influence of our government has been felt time and time again among the nations of Europe, for they have looked to America for the solution of their problems. A few years ago, at Independence Hall in Philadelphia, a great event took place. In that simple and dignified room, where the Declaration of Independence was written and the Constitution of our country.

The peoples of the world have entered our gates, and have found here a new life and happiness. Never had they been so well cared for never had they the chance to live and to look up to their God in hallowed feeling as they were given in this land. No nation of history has given homes to its people as has this our Country. Never has the wealth of land been so equitably distributed; never in all time, have so many people owned their own homes. With individual opportunity, there has gone quite naturally inequality. Inequality is a law of all social life, and to try to do away with inequality among men is to substitute tyranny for liberty.

The quality of democracy in America is that it seeks to protect and preserve that sovereign right of all people to come to a knowledge of their own better selves, and to live their own natural lives. Democracy teaches us that it is not wealth that makes happiness, but the wealth of the spirit, brought about by the opportunity to work on land and in factory, and to enjoy the blessings of church and school. Men may exploit honest labor, but such a thing is foreign to American principles. It is the wealth of America in the hands of men of vision that has built industries, and made it possible for all people to have honest labor, and to live honestly before their God. The schools of America, the churches, the institutions of higher learning have been closed to no one, and the statement of a noted writer on economics that the glory of America is that every head of a family is given an opportunity to own his home, is true. The peasants of Europe, who lived on bread and wine, have found asylum in this land, and the comforts of the humble fire-side.[239]

—*Levi Edgar Young*

THIS DAY IN AMERICAN HISTORY (1885)

One hundred thousand dollars is raised to build a pedestal for the Statue of Liberty.

A Land Choice Above All Other Lands Requires a People Choice Above All Other Peoples

As one reviews the destiny of the nations of the earth and the prophecies concerning the great struggles and universal warfare which is foretold by the prophets, the question naturally comes to mind: "And what of the United States of America? What of this nation, one of the most wealthy and powerful civilizations ever in the unrolling scene of world history? Have the prophets also spoken concerning this land?"

As early as several thousand years before the birth of the Savior, the land which is now called America was designated as a land to be preferred above all others. Both to the Jaredites, who were led out of central Asia at the time of the confusion of tongues, and to the family of Lehi who left Jerusalem about six hundred years before Christ's birth, the Lord testified that the land to which they were going was the promised land, a land so abundant in wealth that all who lived there in righteousness would prosper. Indeed, it was a land which was "choice above all other lands." The millions who have come to this country in this age have found it to be just as the Lord promised.

But such a land was not to be had without some conditions. A land choice above all other lands requires a people choice above all other peoples. The Lord made it very clear that this land was reserved only for a people willing to serve him and keep his commandments. If the people refused to meet those conditions they necessarily would have to lose the privilege of dwelling in the promised land.[240]

—Gerald N. Lund

THIS DAY IN AMERICAN HISTORY (1658)

The first American police force is organized in New Amsterdam (later New York City).

To Be Enjoyed, Freedom Must Be Won Continually

The inspired Founding Fathers formulated a system of government with checks and balances protecting the freedom of the people. But even this was not enough. The first order of the new congress was to draw up a Bill of Rights—ten amendments guaranteeing for all time the fundamental freedoms that the American people insist are theirs by the will of God, not by the will of government.

Yes, the founders of this nation bequeathed to us a heritage of freedom and unity that is our most priceless political possession.

But to be enjoyed, freedom must be won continually. The major responsibility of government is to guard the lives and safeguard the freedom of its citizens. Yet even in the operation of government—especially big government—there are real dangers to our freedom.

Today the scope and variety of governmental operations have become amazingly wide. We are touched by government from before we are born until after we die. Government impinges on our lives every hour of the day and night.

Most of these governmental activities are helpful in greater or lesser degree, of course. But we must face the central problem of just how much of our lives, of our freedom, of our economy, and of our society, we want to entrust to government.

And we must face the further fact of just what division of functions we want to make between Washington and our state capitals. We must be aware of the price we pay when we place more and more of our lives in the hands of centralized government.[241]

—*Ezra Taft Benson*

THIS DAY IN AMERICAN HISTORY (1942)

The Manhattan Project (to develop a nuclear bomb) begins under the direction of General Leslie Groves.

Democracy Is a Condition of the Heart

I thank God that The Church of Jesus Christ of Latter-day Saints is not a political organization; that its members, in affairs ecclesiastical, are not torn by party politics; that they have a common motive of union and unity of purpose which enables them to overcome the bickerings, the jealousies of politics. . . .

A man prominent in the philosophy of the world was invited recently to this State to talk to the people on the troubles of the day, and one thought that I got out of his talk was his definition of democracy. He undertook to tell us that democracy does not consist in a set of rules which provide for the election of representatives of the people, whom we name presidents and senators and representatives, but democracy is a condition of the heart; democracy consists in the recognition, on the part of one person, of the rights of another, and the thought that the common good is the determining principle, or should be, in all government; that men who are placed in prominent positions to direct the destinies of people derive that right from the voice of the people. In other words, that the people is sovereign, and the ruler is the servant of the people.

Our Lord and Master, Jesus Christ, taught that when he said: "He that is greatest among you shall be your servant." Verily this is true.

Democracy is the underlying principle, when it comes to government in The Church of Jesus Christ of Latter-day Saints, and I have stood in this pulpit before and stressed the fact that that democracy is represented in the priesthood of the Church of God.[242]

—*Antoine R. Ivins*

THIS DAY IN AMERICAN HISTORY (1765)

Bostonians protest the Stamp Act under a large elm tree (the Liberty Tree).

Members of Our Church Have Never Offered Any Insult to the Flag of Our Country

Utterances of prominent men in the Church at a time of great excitement have been selected in group, to convey the impression that present members are seditious. Those expressions were made more than thirty years ago, when through the falsehood of recreant officials, afterwards demonstrated to be baseless, troops were sent to this territory and reviewed by the people, and their isolated condition, fifteen hundred miles from railroads, as an armed mob coming to renew the bloody persecution of years before.

At that time excitement prevailed and strong language was used; but no words of disloyalty against the government or its institutions were uttered; public speakers confined their remarks to announcing traitorous officials who are prostituting the powers of their positions to accomplish nefarious ends. Criticism of the act of United States officials was not considered then, neither is it now, as treason against the nation nor as hostility to the government. In this connection we may say that the members of our Church have never offered or intended to offer any insult to the flag of our country; but I've always honored it as an ensign of a laws and liberty.[243]

—Wilford Woodruff, George Q. Cannon, Joseph F. Smith

THIS DAY IN AMERICAN HISTORY (1620)

The *Mayflower* sets sail from Southampton, England, with 102 pilgrims onboard.

AUGUST 16

The Laws of Heaven Command Us

I look upon these things; I reflect upon our government in the manner which has been referred to today; I look at the liberal laws and Constitution that exist in our land, upon which our government is founded; and yet, in the midst of all this, we have not had the privilege of enjoying our rights, or worshipping God, or enjoying our religion, without persecution and oppression. The Lord has frequently given us revelations upon these things, and he has spoken concerning our government and Constitution, and he has said—"Ye are justified in maintaining the Constitution and laws of the land, for they make you free, and the gospel maketh you free; and you shall seek to sustain good and wise men for rulers, and whatsoever is more or less than this cometh of evil." Do you blame the Latter-day Saints? Can the Lord, can angels, or can anybody blame the Latter-day Saints for rejecting such cursed, corrupt scoundrels as we have had here? The laws of Heaven command us not to uphold and sustain men, except they are good men, who will sustain the Constitution of our country; and we are fulfilling the revelations in this respect as in many others, and we are carrying out the requirements of the Constitution of the United States.

We have fulfilled the law of God, and we have always been willing to receive and respect all good and wise men in carrying out the laws and Constitution of our country.[244]

—*Wilford Woodruff*

THIS DAY IN AMERICAN HISTORY (1780)

The British rout Americans soldiers at Camden, South Carolina.

This Is a Christian Nation

This is a Christian nation. Before the Revolution it was so in accord with law; since the Revolution it has remained so in fact. We, the people of the United States, guarantee full religious freedom to all within our jurisdiction, whether they be non-Christian or Pagan. But the nation itself is a Christian nation. Our standards and principles are Christian. Other creeds we protect that all may be free. These facts must never be lost sight of. . . . Thus we of America can stand for no cause which would dethrone Christianity here and put in its place any other creed, whether non-Christian or Pagan; nor can we Christians support a cause or design to set up non-Christian or Pagan states elsewhere in the world. Our duty, divinely imposed is clear on this.

Thus we can stand for no cause and can support no state fostering a cause that would seek to compel the consciences of men, that would set up the state as deity, that would destroy private property, that bulwark of a peaceful, stable ordered society, indeed of civilization itself, that would make men slaves of the state to the destruction of all safety, due protection of life and limb, and all individual liberty, that would blot out the Christian home. All these things are fundamental to this people and to this nation. Again I warn that there are amongst us evil influences plotting and conspiring to destroy all that we hold sacred in our Church and in the nation. If we shall fall asleep to these dangers, we shall some day awaken to find ourselves their slavish victims. We people here in the valleys are a mere handful—a microscopic minority—and yet if we shall, with completely united hearts and hands, put on an armor of righteousness and do battle for righteousness, we shall be the means under God's care and guidance of helping finally to serve and save the world.[245]

—J. Reuben Clark, Jr.

THIS DAY IN AMERICAN HISTORY (1807)

Robert Fulton's steamboat *Clermont* begins first trip up the Hudson River in New York.

Few Nations Enjoy Such Freedom

No nation has such an industrial complex made available to it because of applied science and the harnessing, in part, of electricity. Our transportation system hardly knows any bounds on this sphere. We travel in places, trains, cars, and buses without limitation in our country, and in relative luxury, a luxury scarcely affordable or even accessible to masses of humanity in other countries.

No other country has such an elaborate and universally accessible educational system, where even the humblest among us can climb the ladder of success to the highest rung. The "Horatio Alger" story is yet going on every day in this country.

Few nations enjoy such freedom—freedom to speak, freedom to think, freedom to own property and business or participate in ownership, freedom to worship, freedom to print, freedom to travel at home and abroad, freedom to censure even public officials, and freedom to have the privacy we desire.

No country has been more concerned with "due process" in its judicial system than ours. The protection of human rights, as granted by our Constitution and Bill of Rights, is not just theory. History will record that we bent over backwards to protect the rights of the individual, sometimes even to a fault. No other country has been so generous as America I terms of its money and food. No nation has fought starvation and economic collapse, and come to the rescue of nations struck by natural disaster, as America has.[246]

—*Ezra Taft Benson*

THIS DAY IN AMERICAN HISTORY (1920)

The 19th Amendment to the U.S. Constitution, giving women the right to vote, is ratified.

We Become Smoother by Bumping into Each Other's Rough Edges

We often feel threatened by differences. And we don't have to go far to find them. A family from another country moves next door and doesn't speak your language. A group of Muslims bow and pray in your neighborhood park. A rally on campus challenges your political beliefs. Colleagues at work don't believe in God and question why you do. How should we react to such situations? Evade or engage? The answer may determine whether we flourish or splinter as a society.

The peculiarities of our lives can estrange us from each other. But difference is a matter of perspective, and sometimes the fear of differences threatens us more than the actual differences. A society where many religions, political ideologies, ethnicities and worldviews coexist under one government is called pluralism. The various groups may not agree with each other, but they find ways to live together. Our crowded public square means, for example, that Christians and atheists can't avoid one another and that conservatives and liberals must listen as well as talk. Our differences can enrich our common existence as long as they harm or coerce no one. . . .

In this way, civil society is the engine that keeps the complex parts of society functioning together. Citizens build personal ties that the sectors of government and business cannot. A population of isolated individuals develops into a community when people think outside themselves. Tolerance then grows to understanding. Monologue changes to dialogue. The echo chamber of identical voices transforms into a roundtable of dynamic voices. In a healthy society diverse elements are in constant encounter.

Pluralism is not easy, but pluralism is a reality of modern life. The solutions to its challenges depend on the quality of our deliberation as citizens and neighbors. Professor John Inazu writes, "We can choose to model kindness and charity across deep differences without sacrificing the claims upon which we stake our lives." Pluralism can work if we are confident enough in our own beliefs to let other people confidently express theirs.[247]

—*Church Newsroom*

THIS DAY IN AMERICAN HISTORY (2020)

Apple becomes the first corporation to be valued at $2 trillion.

Every True Latter-day Saint Should Love America

The Lord raised up the Founding Fathers. He it was who established the Constitution of this land—the greatest document of freedom ever written. This God-inspired Constitution is not outmoded. It is not an outdated "agrarian document" as some of our would-be statesmen, socialists, and fellow travelers of the godless conspiracy would have us believe. It was the Lord God who established the foundation of this nation; and woe be unto those—members of the Supreme Court and others—who would weaken this foundation.

I am sorry to say that I am saddened and sick at heart at what I see, at what has happened in the past few years and is happening today in my beloved country. But that is a subject for another time.

It was the Lord who created an atmosphere of freedom here in America so that his Church could be restored in its fullness for the blessing of all mankind. Here in these United States the Lord has established his base of operations in these last days. He selected America. That is why I love the United States of America in a special manner. Every true Latter-day Saint should love America.

No, the Lord's base of operations was not established by the General Authorities of the restored Church. The Lord Himself prepared the way through the centuries. He established his base of operations here in America, and it is the duty of every liberty-loving should, and especially every Latter-day Saint, to help protect, safe-guard, and strengthen the Lord's base of operations, because it is from this base that the glorious saving principles of the eternal gospel are going and will continue to go forth to the world to bless all of our Father's children and to provide a true basis for peace.[248]

—*Ezra Taft Benson*

THIS DAY IN AMERICAN HISTORY (1781)

George Washington begins moving his troops south to fight Cornwallis.

Our Nation Has a Religious Life

I believe that in the heart of the average American there is a deep religious conviction. Our nation has a religious life which must be maintained in determining national questions and controlling national policy. The spirit of mutual respect and good will, of justice and peace, of human brotherhood, is the spirit of the Christian religion, and this spirit teaches us one and all that the object of political activity is not merely to vote or to take sides in elections, but to direct our thoughts and deeds to noble actions and Christian principles. For this reason, we must educate the youth in an understanding of freedom and democracy; we must teach them that the perpetuity of our government depends on a deep conviction of the reality of the kingdom of God and the spiritual quality of life.

We Latter-day Saints believe implicitly in the kingdom of God and that in time it will be established upon the earth with Christ our Lord as King. No more beautiful ideal of government can be known than this. The unity of Christianity is dependent upon the teachings concerning the kingdom and the life of the Savior—the divine birth and the atonement; the resurrection and the assurance that Christ our Lord will come again. In this teaching is envisaged the kingdom of God which becomes our vision. So America has a dream, a vision, the purpose of which is to cause us to understand the spiritual quality of life, for all our civilization must be a spiritual achievement. "Look unto the rock from whence ye are hewn, and remove not the ancient land-mark which thy fathers have set." May the Lord help us to look to the rock and to stand by the land-marks of justice, faith, and the knowledge of the living God. May the Constitution of the United States be preserved and sanctified in the hearts of all Americans. It was George Washington who replied to a question as to whether or not the people would support the Constitution. "Let us raise a standard," said he, "to which the wise and just can repair; the rest is in the hand of God."[249]

—*Levi Edgar Young*

THIS DAY IN AMERICAN HISTORY (1959)

Hawaii receives statehood as the 50th state.

A Land of Freedom

In 1790, at a time when western Europe excluded Jews from the full rights of citizenship, including the ability to hold public office, President George Washington wrote a memorable letter to the Jewish congregation in Newport, Rhode Island. They had written congratulating him on his election. In reply, Washington assured them that "the government of the United States, which gives to bigotry no sanction, to persecution no assistance, requires only that they who live under its protection should [conduct] themselves as good citizens."

He included a prayer for their welfare: "May the children of the stock of Abraham who dwell in this land continue to merit and enjoy the good will of the other inhabitants—while every one shall sit in safety under his own vine and fig tree and there shall be none to make him afraid."[250] No one who knows the difficult history of the Jewish people, or their fate during succeeding generations, can fail to be impressed by Washington's affirmation of religious freedom.[251]

—*D. Todd Christofferson*

THIS DAY IN AMERICAN HISTORY (1902)

Theodore Roosevelt becomes the First American president to ride in a car.

Latter-day Saints Are Loyal to the Constitution

The Mormon people who are citizens of [the United States of] America today are intensely loyal to its Constitution and desire in every way to promote the God-given freedoms it was designed to protect. They have had experience with the tragedy that results when those freedoms are not protected, but this only feeds their determination to do all within their power to protect these freedoms, both for themselves and others, everywhere.[252]

—Spencer W. Kimball

THIS DAY IN AMERICAN HISTORY (1777)

British hear Benedict Arnold's approach and withdraw in Fort Stanwix, New York.

The Law Provides Ways and Means

I hope with all my soul that the members of The Church of Jesus Christ of Latter-day Saints will be loyal in their very hearts and souls, to the principles of the Constitution of our country. From them we have derived the liberty that we enjoy. They have been the means of guaranteeing to the foreigner that has come within our gates, and to the native born, and to all the citizens of this country, the freedom and liberty that we possess. We cannot go back upon such principles as these. We may go back upon those who fail to execute the law as they should. We may be dissatisfied with the decision of judges, and may desire to have them removed out of their places. But the law provides ways and means for all these things to be done under the Constitution of our country, and it is better for us to abide the evils that we have than to fly to greater evils that we know not what the results will be.[253]

—*Joseph F. Smith*

THIS DAY IN AMERICAN HISTORY (1789)

The U.S. House of Representatives passes seventeen amendments to the U.S. Constitution.

The Spirit of America Appeals to the Powers of Heaven

Ours is a land of liberty and freedom, especially a land of religious freedom. Its motto, "In God we trust," might well have come from that remarkable picture—that scene of which we all have read—Jesus the Son of God, in the Garden of Gethsemane upon his knees. That is the spirit which has characterized leading people of the United States in the entire history of our nation.

Have you examined the special stamp issued in 1928 by the United States government? In the left-hand corner is this inscription: "1778"; in the right-hand corner, "1928"—one hundred and fifty years later. Between these two dates are the words "Valley Forge"; and on the stamp, the stamp of the United States government, officially made in the year of our Lord 1928, is Washington, the father of his country, upon his knees. The motto of our country, as it appears upon our dollar, is: "In God We Trust." To this land of liberty—of religious freedom—people came that they might worship God according to the dictates of their own conscience. During the first critical period, they were led by George Washington, who frequently and effectively sought divine aid. . . .

No less a man than Abraham Lincoln, foremost and most typical of Americans, was wont to retire into his office, and there, behind a locked door, to appeal to divine providence for help and guidance. While the fearful Civil War was raging, Lincoln issued a proclamation setting apart the 30th day of April, 1863, as a day of fasting and prayer. In this choice land, "choice above all other lands" (2 Nephi 1:5), he appealed to the people to go into their various places of worship, to assemble around their own hearthstones, and to appeal to the Most High for divine direction. . . .The spirit of America, the spirit of Lincoln, is most distinctively that spirit which appeals to the powers of heaven.[254]

—Richard R. Lyman

THIS DAY IN AMERICAN HISTORY (1814)

British forces burn the Library of Congress in Washington, D.C.

The True Destiny of America Is Religious, Not Political

Since the founding of this country, political leaders have spoken of the greatness of America and of its place in the world as the cradle of freedom and democracy, with a destiny to disseminate these principles throughout the world.

We have witnessed America's attempt at this by various methods, but she is learning by hard and costly experience that freedom cannot be taken or given to any people, nor can it be bought. America of today will need to learn the lesson, as did our Founding Fathers, that freedom must be sought after with courage and sacrifice, and that she cannot maintain it at home or convey it unto others, unless this type of pursuit is involved.

As to the destiny of America, politically speaking, I am not prepared to say, but I do know that long before the ships of Columbus touched the shores of the New World, long before our independence and our Founding Fathers established a new nation, events had long since transpired to give unto this land, which we now call America, its committed purpose and destiny. I have a firm conviction that the true destiny of America is religious, not political; it is spiritual, not physical.

Much has been said by many of the purpose of its founding. The Prophet Joseph Smith himself declared its constitution to be heavenly inspired, and because of this we earnestly pray for its purposeful continuity. But noble and great as are the political phases of its establishment, its real significance lies in its spiritual purpose, for which it was truly founded.[255]

—*Alvin R. Dyer*

THIS DAY IN AMERICAN HISTORY (1873)

The first free kindergarten in the U.S. opens near St. Louis, Missouri.

Our Society Needs Your Voice, Your Experience, and Your Goodness

It is time to get involved and take a stand for religious freedom. There is much you can do to ensure a culture in which religious freedom has an honored place in American life.

Begin by becoming informed. Study the principles of the American founding and teach them in your families. Teach your families to cherish America's heritage of freedom. Teach them the importance of religion to our nation and society. Teach them to respect the faith of all people, even those with very different beliefs. And teach them that respecting religious freedom means tolerating religious beliefs, speech, and practices we disagree with. That is the price of asking others to respect our own freedoms.

Next, speak up. Churches and people of faith must not allow themselves to be intimidated and silenced. Your opinions count. You have a right to speak and to be heard. Make the effort to stay informed about issues of public importance, and then speak out with courage and civility—and I do emphasize civility. Whatever your faith, our society needs your voice, your experience, and your goodness.[256]

—*D. Todd Christofferson*

THIS DAY IN AMERICAN HISTORY (1776)

British forces defeat Americans at the Battle of Long Island.

Apart from God We Cannot Succeed, but as a Partner with God We Cannot Fail

Men receive blessings by obedience to God's law. And without obedience there is no blessing. Before the final triumphal return of the Lord, the question as to whether we may save our Constitutional Republic is simply based on two factors—the number of patriots and the extent of their obedience. That the Lord desires to save this nation which he raised up there is no doubt. But that he leaves it up to us, with his help, is the awful reality.

There is a time and season for all righteous things, and many of life's failures arise when men neither take the time nor find the season to perform their eternal duties. What then in this time and season may best equip us to have our Christian constitutional legacy, while at the same time rescuing our own souls?

In a book, sacred to me as scripture, the Lord states that America is a land choice above all others; and that it shall remain free as long as the inhabitants worship the God of the land—Jesus Christ. Certainly spirituality is the foundation upon which any battle against tyranny must be waged. And because this is basically the struggle of the forces of Christ versus anti-Christ, it is imperative that our people be in tune with the supreme leader of freedom—the Lord our God. And men only stay in tune when their lives are in harmony with God. For apart from God we cannot succeed, but as a partner with God we cannot fail. We must be in the amoral and immoral world—but not of it. We must be able to drop off to sleep at night without having to first sing lullabies to our conscience. [257]

—*Ezra Taft Benson*

THIS DAY IN AMERICAN HISTORY (1957)

U.S. Senator Strom Thurmond begins the longest filibuster in Senate history (24 hours and 18 minutes).

I Believe in Religious Freedom, Religious Belief, Religious Practice

I believe in the great principles laid down in the American Constitution; I believe in religious freedom, religious belief, religious practice. I believe in every principle guaranteed in that document. Well, supposing then that they should send me, as an individual, to prison because of my belief or religious practice; would that alter my belief? No. Would, say, five years in the penitentiary change my belief? No. If they were to inflict the full penalty of the law upon me in every respect, how much would they succeed in converting me that my belief and practice were a crime in the sight of God? Not one iota, forty-five millions of people to the contrary notwithstanding. Why? Because although I am in the minority, I am protected by the Constitution just as much as though I were in the majority; I am an American citizen and I have the rights of an American just as much as though I belonged to the majority.

Well, then, what do you say, shall I renounce my religion, because of this law? No. Shall I advise the Latter-day Saints (an independent people to do as they please so far as their religious views are concerned), to renounce any part of their doctrines because Congress has denounced it? No. I can do no such thing.[258]

—*Orson Pratt*

THIS DAY IN AMERICAN HISTORY (1779)

After Two Settler massacres, American forces burn Indian villages at Newton, New York.

AUGUST 30

God's Gift

An omniscient God who has seen massive and individual human failure—who knows us perfectly—has never displayed contempt for man; neither should we!

God's kingdom has functioned in several political settings, but the revelations for our dispensation have clearly sanctioned 'that law of the Land which is constitutional,' and tell us to do our business by 'the voice of the people.' May we do our part and let our voice shape the voice of the people so that we shall comport ourselves consistently with the divine and tacit compliment God has given us when He gave us agency.[259]

—Neal A. Maxwell

THIS DAY IN AMERICAN HISTORY (1862)

Second Battle of Bull Run at Manassas, Virginia.

The Best Earthly Government in Existence Upon the Face of the Earth

I read that, in the beginning, God created the heavens and the earth (Genesis 1:1). It seemed to be a kind of one-man power that was engaged in the very act of rolling creation into existence. I do not know how much of democracy or of republicanism there was in the beginning. I was not there that I know of, or if I was it is so long since that I have forgotten it. Judging by the accounts we have of matters then, the government was a kind of one-man power; and if we look at things as they really are, Jacob 4:13 we shall find that sin entered the world, and death by sin and that was by one man. Romans 5:12 [says,] "Oh, that was grievous! That drew a veil of gloom over the face of creation." That was one-man power. By and by we read of another one-man power that came along and counteracted this, and that was the Lord from glory—another kind of one-man power.

Now, while I compare these things with the present order of things which exists throughout our world, I do not wish to be understood as depreciating our own government, for it is the best earthly government in existence upon the face of the earth. It was ordained, organized and suffered for a wise purpose in God our heavenly Father (D&C 101:77–80), which, perhaps, I may be able to exhibit to you ere my remarks shall come to a close; but be this as the Lord will, I do not wish to say one word against our government; it is a good government, it answers the times and fills a vacuum that perhaps nothing else could. But I am looking at matters as they were from the beginning.[260]

—*Orson Hyde*

THIS DAY IN AMERICAN HISTORY (2010)

The Iraq War ends.

Founded upon the Principle of Free Agency

Now these wise men that the Lord raised up during the days of Washington, Jefferson, Franklin, Robert Morris, and Hamilton provided a pattern of government for us to follow, a pattern of government which has brought to us numerous blessings, a form of government that has made us the strongest, and, may I say, the richest nation in all the world, because it has been founded upon the principle of free agency. Every individual has had the right to do the thing that he has wanted to do in the fields of industry, agriculture, or whatnot. He has had the right to worship God according to the dictates of his own conscience. He has had the right to own property. He has had the right to speak as he sees fit, and he has enjoyed the privilege of a great and free press.

But, on the other hand, we find that the philosophy of the evil one would teach us that, after all, our government should be centralized in the hands of one or two men. Some advocate changing the form of our government. They advocate regimentation of industry and labor. They advocate that deficit spending is the sure way to prosperity. They would pervert the Constitution. They have endeavored through the various educational systems of this great country to teach us doctrines that are contrary to the doctrines and the principles upon which this great republic is founded. They would restrict us in our religious worship. They would disrupt family relationships. And so as we compare these two great systems, we can readily see that they are but a carryover from that great battle which took place in the spirit world. . . .

When I think of these wise men, George Washington and Jefferson and Franklin, I think of men who were servants of God, raised up for the purpose of establishing the Constitution and establishing this great government. Thomas Jefferson was endowed from on high with prophetic power. . . .

It is of vital importance that in our homes we should teach our children that this great government and its fundamental law were given to us by God, that he inspired men who framed the Constitution of the United States. . . . It is time that in the home we, as parents, take upon ourselves the responsibility of teaching the youth of the land the very truth that God revealed for the establishment of the Constitution of the United States and the organizing of our republic.[261]

—*Joseph B. Wirthlin*

THIS DAY IN AMERICAN HISTORY (1974)

The Currency Act is passed.

The Essence of Religious Freedom

There is another scourge sweeping the globe: attacks on your and my religious freedom. This growing sentiment seeks to remove religion and faith in God from the public square, schools, community standards, and civic discourse. Opponents of religious freedom seek to impose restrictions on expressions of heartfelt convictions. They even criticize and ridicule faith traditions. Such an attitude marginalizes people, devaluing personal principles, fairness, respect, spirituality, and peace of conscience.

What is religious freedom? It is freedom of worship in all its configurations: freedom of assembly, freedom of speech, freedom to act on personal beliefs, and freedom for others to do the same. Religious freedom allows each of us to decide for ourselves what we believe, how we live and act according to our faith, and what God expects of us. Efforts to curtail such religious liberty are not new. Throughout history, people of faith have suffered mightily at the hands of others. Members of The Church of Jesus Christ of Latter-day Saints are no different.

From our beginnings, many seeking God were drawn to this Church because of its teachings of divine doctrine, including faith in Jesus Christ and His Atonement, repentance, the plan of happiness, and the Second Coming of our Lord. Opposition, persecution, and violence plagued our first latter-day prophet, Joseph Smith, and his followers. Amidst the turmoil in 1842, Joseph published 13 fundamental tenets of the growing Church, including this one: "We claim the privilege of worshiping Almighty God according to the dictates of our own conscience, and allow all men the same privilege, let them worship how, where, or what they may." His statement is inclusive, liberating, and respectful. That is the essence of religious freedom.[262]

–Ronald A. Rasband

THIS DAY IN AMERICAN HISTORY (1945)

World War II ends.

SEPTEMBER 3

Our Civic Virtue

It is part of our civic duty to be moral in our conduct toward all people. There is no place in responsible citizenship for dishonesty or deceit or for willful law breaking of any kind. We believe with the author of Proverbs that "righteousness exalteth a nation: but sin is a reproach to any people" (Proverbs 14:34). The personal righteousness of citizens will strengthen a nation more than the force of its arms.

Citizens should also be practitioners of civic virtue in their conduct toward government. They should be ever willing to fulfill the duties of citizenship. This includes compulsory duties like military service and the numerous voluntary actions they must take if they are to preserve the principle of limited government through citizen self-reliance. For example, since U.S. citizens value the right of trial by jury, they must be willing to serve on juries, even those involving unsavory subject matter. Citizens who favor morality cannot leave the enforcement of moral laws to jurors who oppose them.[263]

—*Dallin H. Oaks*

THIS DAY IN AMERICAN HISTORY (1783)

The U.S. and Great Britain sign the Treaty of Paris, ending the Revolutionary War.

Out of the Homes of America Will Come the Future Citizens of America

I was particularly pleased with President Clark's message this morning regarding the fundamentals of our government. In keeping therewith I desire to call attention to the fact that the united, well-ordered American home is one of the greatest contributing factors to the preservation of the Constitution of the United States. It has been aptly said that "out of the homes of America will come the future citizens of America, and only as those homes are what they should be will this nation be what it should be." Of the importance of home and of dangers that threaten the sanctity of marriage, I feel impressed to say a few words this afternoon.[264]

—David O. McKay

THIS DAY IN AMERICAN HISTORY (1918)

The first transcontinental TV broadcast is performed by President Harry S. Truman.

SEPTEMBER 5

A Marvelous Work and a Wonder

Centuries earlier [Lamanite] prophets saw in vision and foretold the coming of Columbus and the colonists, of the Revolutionary War, of the creation of the great Gentile nation of the United States of America; of your scattering, and, above all, and most important to you now, of the gathering of your people and their restoration. Prophecies emanating from our Lord never fail, and the oft-predicted miracle of the 'marvelous work and a wonder' was soon at hand. The war brought independence to the struggling colonies, and a mighty nation was born with a divinely inspired Constitution, granting to its people religious freedom. Early in the nineteenth century preparations were complete for the marvelous miracle. The long-sealed heavens opened. God, the Father, came down with Jesus Christ, whom he introduced to a young modern prophet, Joseph Smith, saying: "This is my Beloved Son."[265]

—*Milton R. Hunter*

THIS DAY IN AMERICAN HISTORY (1775)

The First Continental Congress concludes meeting in Philadelphia.

Planned and Prepared

The Almighty chooses the prophets and apostles who minister in His name and present His message to the world in every age and dispensation. He selects and foreordains His ministers; He sends them to earth at the times before appointed; He guides and directs their continuing mortal preparations; and He then calls them to those positions they were foreordained to receive from before the foundations of the earth. . . .

The work to be done by John the Baptist, by the ancient twelve, by Columbus, by the signers of the Declaration of Independence, and by the framers of the Constitution of the United States were all known and arranged for in advance. And all these are but illustrations and patterns, for all of the Lord's work is planned and prepared in advance, and those who are called and chosen to do the work receive their commission and ordination from him, first in the preexistence and then, if they remain true and faithful, again here in mortality.[266]

—*Bruce R. McConkie*

THIS DAY IN AMERICAN HISTORY (1901)

President William McKinley is shot and assassinated in New York.

The Principle of Right Is Implanted in Our Bosom

In relation to our political position, it is precisely the same. There is an inherent principle of right planted in the human bosom, which God has placed there, and which man never could, cannot now, nor ever will uproot; principles of inherent right which all intelligent men, when they have sought for the truth, with unbiased mind, and desired sincerely to know, have invariably found. Governed by the principles of right, and uninfluenced by party power or wealth there have always been men inspired by an infallible divine afflatus, who have recognized an innate, inalienable principle of justice and equity. . . . The principle of right is implanted in the human bosom and inherent in the human family. . . . The founders of our government, under the inspiration of the Almighty, and goaded by an oppressive power, discovered the same elements, the same principles, the same ideas that we have, and enunciated those eternal principles and made them known to the world—"that all men are born free and equal and have a right to life, liberty and the pursuit of happiness." . . . It is the violation of the natural rights of man that has deluged the earth with blood in all ages. These principles were enunciated also by Joseph Smith, he believed in them, so do we, in the right to think, in the right to speak, in the right to act, in the right to do all things that are right and good and proper, but not in the right to interfere with any other man's rights, any other man's religion, any other man's principles. These are our views. God has planted them in our bosom, they will remain there eternally, for they are principles that dwell in the bosom of God. . . . God has implanted them in our bosoms, and they will grow there and take root and spread and prevail, and the worst wish we have to the human family is that the principles enunciated in our Constitution may reverberate over the wide earth, and spread from shore to shore until all mankind shall be free.[267]

—John Taylor

THIS DAY IN AMERICAN HISTORY (1936)

Hoover Dam (originally Boulder Dam), on the Colorado River, begins operation.

Fostering an Appreciation for the Constitution

I believe that in the hearts of the majority of the inhabitants of this great country that feeling of loyalty persists.

If we would make the world better, let us foster a keener appreciation of the freedom and liberty guaranteed by the government of the United States, as framed by the founders of this nation. There are some self-proclaimed progressives who cry that such old-time adherence is out-of-date. But there are some fundamental principles of this Republic which, like eternal truths, never get out of date; and which are applicable at all times to liberty-loving peoples. Such are the underlying principles of the Constitution, a document framed by patriotic, freedom-loving men, who we declare were inspired by the Lord. . . .

Next to being one in worshiping God, there is nothing in this world upon which the Church should be more united than in upholding and defending the Constitution of the United States.[268]

—David O. McKay

THIS DAY IN AMERICAN HISTORY (1565)

The first permanent European settlement in the U.S. is founded at St. Augustine, Florida.

SEPTEMBER 9

America Was Hidden from the Other Nations Until He Was Ready to Have It Peopled

Brethren and sisters, if there is any doubt in your minds about this being a blessed land in which you live, and that an all-powerful hand controls its destinies, remember that it was the Lord Himself who raised up wise men to give to us our Constitution—the greatest palladium of human rights that any people have ever known.

There are those who would destroy the Constitution of this land; and there are some who would rejoice if they could overthrow this nation, not realizing that our Heavenly Father has given us the best government on earth. No loyal member of this great Church will raise his voice against the government, but he will be found upholding it; he will be found praying for those who have been exalted to the office of presidency and for those who make the laws, under the Constitution. He will petition his Father in Heaven for the governors and legislators of States, and for all those who are chosen from time to time to administer the laws that are calculated to continue unto us our liberty that they may be wise and just and exemplars to the people. If you are doubtful as to the interest of our Heavenly Father in the settlement of this land, read in the first chapter of 2nd Nephi in the Book of Mormon, where the Lord says that it had been his purpose to keep America hidden from the other nations until he was ready to have it peopled.[269]

—*George Albert Smith*

THIS DAY IN AMERICAN HISTORY (1850)

California receives statehood as the 31st state.

Profound Attachment to the Constitution

If we had not had a profound attachment to the Constitution of the United States and to the institutions of this government, the course that is taken against us by those who have represented the government has been and is of a character to have driven us into open and avowed enmity to the government years and years ago. Without that deep-rooted attachment we should have lost all our respect for a government under which we have suffered such cruel wrongs. There could be no better evidence of the kind feeling and the loyalty of the Latter-day Saints to the government of the United States, than the fact that in our breasts and throughout these mountains, there prevails an unquenchable love and respect for the Constitution and the institutions that spring therefrom. . . .

No people in the world have given greater proofs of attachment to their own government, and of devotion to those sacred principles of liberty that we have inherited than the Latter-day Saints have done in these mountains.[270]

—*George Q. Cannon*

THIS DAY IN AMERICAN HISTORY (1945)

First "bug" in a computer program discovered in Massachusetts, when a moth is removed from inside a computer.

The Final Victory Will Be for Freedom

It might hurt your business or your family," says the devil, "and besides, why not let the gentiles save the country? They aren't as busy as you are." Well, there were many businessmen who went along with Hitler because it supposedly helped their business. They lost everything. Many of us are here today because our forefathers loved truth enough that they fought at Valley Forge or crossed the plains in spite of the price it cost them or their families. We had better take our small pain now than our greater loss later. There were souls who wished afterwards that they had stood and fought with Washington and the Founding Fathers, but they waited too long—they passed up eternal glory. There has never been a greater time than now to stand up against entrenched evil. And while the gentiles established the Constitution, we have a divine mandate to preserve it. But unfortunately, today in this freedom struggle, many gentiles are showing greater wisdom in their generation than the children of light. . . .

"Don't worry," says the devil; "the Lord will protect you, and besides, the world is so corrupt and heading toward destruction at such a pace that you can't stop it, so why try?" Well, to begin with, the Lord will not protect us unless we do our part. This devilish tactic of persuading people not to get concerned because the Lord will protect them no matter what they do is exposed by the Book of Mormon. Referring to the devil, it says: "And others will he pacify, and lull them away into carnal security, and they will say: All is well in Zion; yea, Zion prospereth, all is well—and thus the devil cheateth their souls, and leadeth them away carefully down to hell" (2 Nephi 28:21).

I like that word carefully. In other words, don't shake them, you might wake them. But the Book of Mormon warns us that when we see these murderous conspiracies in our midst, we should awaken to our awful situation. Now, why should we awaken if the Lord is going to take care of us anyway? Let us suppose that it is too late to save freedom. It is still accounted unto us for righteousness' sake to stand up and fight. Some Book of Mormon prophets knew of the final desolate end of their nations, but they still fought on, and they saved some souls, including their own, by so doing. For, after all, the purpose of life is to prove ourselves, and the final victory will be for freedom.[271]

—*Ezra Taft Benson*

THIS DAY IN AMERICAN HISTORY (2001)

Terrorists attack New York City and Washington, D.C.

Opposition In Our Day

We are warned not to be "at ease in Zion!" (2 Nephi 28: 24). The Church in its divine mission and we in our personal lives seem to face increasing opposition today. Perhaps as the Church grows in strength and we members grow in faith and obedience, Satan increases the strength of his opposition so we will continue to have "opposition in all things." Some of this opposition even comes from Church members. Some who use personal reasoning or wisdom to resist prophetic direction give themselves a label borrowed from elected bodies—"the loyal opposition." However appropriate for a democracy, there is no warrant for this concept in the government of God's kingdom, where questions are honored but opposition is not (see Matthew 26:24).[272]

—*Dallin H. Oaks*

THIS DAY IN AMERICAN HISTORY (1993)

NASA launches space shuttle *Discovery*.

SEPTEMBER 13

The Constitution Fulfills Its Purpose

There is a great deal of sacredness attached to the Constitution of the United States by this people: that is all right and good. The Constitution is well enough, and so is anything that serves the purpose for which it was created, provided that purpose be a good one. It was designed and created with a good intention. If it serves the purpose and end of its creation, it is good. . . .

Just so with the Constitution of the United States. It was framed by the inspiration of the Almighty, we readily grant. It has served a certain purpose—been a partial shield to the Church in its infancy, or it has been a check upon mobocracy that otherwise would have risen against it. It has not been a protection exactly, but a check; and the Almighty saw fit to bring forth his work under this Constitution. It has served and fulfilled its purpose. . . .

While we walk in the favor of God, we shall have a Constitution.[273]

—*Orson Hyde*

THIS DAY IN AMERICAN HISTORY (1948)

Margaret Chase Smith (from Maine) elected U.S. senator; she was the first woman to serve in both houses of the U.S. Congress.

Divine Destiny

I would like for you to have in mind that there was only one reason why the United States came into being—only one reason. It is a different reason from anything that we know in any other nation. There is a United States only because God planned to restore the gospel in the last days and he had to have a free country in which to do it, with freedom of worship, freedom of the press, freedom of speech, and freedom of assembly.

He declared that he would make this the greatest nation in the world, and this he has done. Ours is, indeed, the greatest nation on earth, and it was made so by the Almighty himself. It was made so to fulfill the divine destiny given to us by the Lord. That is why the Book of Mormon prophets declared that this land is choice above all other lands in the earth.

It is the destiny of America which makes her the greatest nation on earth. No other nation was ever conceived and set up as was ours. No other nation has been given a destiny such as ours.[274]

—*Mark E. Peterson*

THIS DAY IN AMERICAN HISTORY (2001)

Congress authorizes the use of force for war on terrorism.

SEPTEMBER 15

Freedom Is Now Under Fire

Freedom is now under fire. Although religious freedom lies at the core of what America is and what it stands for, critics now openly ask whether religion belongs in American public life at all. Some say that faithful Americans have no business speaking of their beliefs when addressing issues of public concern, even when those issues involve unmistakably moral judgments. Others condemn churches and religious organizations for expressing moral and religious perspectives on matters of public policy—especially when those perspectives conflict with secular viewpoints. Some even claim, with no sense of history, that religious people and institutions violate the constitutional separation of church and state if they bring their beliefs into the public square. A few scholars have gone so far as to argue that religion does not deserve to be tolerated, much less receive special protection.

Recently it has become popular to argue that the freedom of religion is really only the right to worship rather than the right to freely exercise your faith in daily life—as if religion should be kept in the closet or some other private place. Some advocates demean as "discrimination" the long-standing right of religious organizations and schools to have faith-based standards in employment and admissions. Others resort to politically correct name-calling rather than talking about difficult topics in a spirit of mutual respect. Hurtful labels such as "bigot" or "hater" are all too common. There are concerted efforts to shame and intimidate believers who have traditional moral values and to suppress religious viewpoints and practices regarding marriage, family, gender, and sexuality. Worst of all, government sometimes joins in these efforts. . . . Religious freedom is indeed under attack.[275]

—D. Todd Christofferson

THIS DAY IN AMERICAN HISTORY (1776)

The British occupy New York City.

We Love to Be Subject to Laws

There is not another people upon the face of the earth that could have borne what we have, and still remain as loyal to our brethren as we have been and are. They might be displeased with some of the acts of the administrators of the law, but not with the Constitutional laws and institutions of the government.

This people are filled with patience and long-suffering, clinging to the institutions bequeathed to us by our fathers as closely and as tenaciously as ever babe clung to the Maternal breast, and we would that the government had always been so wisely administered as to bind the best feelings of the people together, and to create and still continue to create a union instead of alienation. . . .

We are in the midst of these mountains, and we have good and salutary laws to govern us. We have our Constitutional laws and our Territorial laws; we are subject to these laws, and always expect to be, for we love to be. If there is any man among us who has violated any constitutional law, try the law upon him, and let us see whether there is any virtue in it, before we try the strong arm of despotism and tyranny. I stand for Constitutional law, and if any transgress, let them be tried by it, and, if guilty, suffer its penalty.[276]

—*Brigham Young*

THIS DAY IN AMERICAN HISTORY (1776)

The Continental Army holds their ground during the Battle of Harlem Heights.

SEPTEMBER 17

Remember with Appreciation Before the Lord the Great Blessings of Liberty and Opportunity

The Mormon people who are citizens of [the United States of] America today are intensely loyal to its Constitution and desire in every way to promote the God-given freedoms it was designed to protect. They have had experience with the tragedy that results when those freedoms are not protected, but this only feeds their determination to do all within their power to protect these freedoms, both for themselves and others, everywhere.

We encourage all members, as citizens of the nation, to be actively involved in the political process, and to support those measures which will strengthen the community, state, and nation—morally, economically, and culturally.

President Ronald Reagan has proclaimed the week beginning Sept. 17 (the 195th anniversary of the signing of the Constitution of Sept. 17, 1787) as Constitution Week and has urged all Americans to observe that week by stressing the importance of the Constitution to our individual freedoms and form of government.

In view of this proclamation and because of the high esteem in which the Constitution has been held by members of The Church of Jesus Christ of Latter-day Saints since the days of the Prophet Joseph Smith, we encourage leaders and members of the Church in the United States to heed President Reagan's proclamation and during this week to remember with appreciation before the Lord the great blessings of liberty and opportunity which are guaranteed to the citizens of the United States.[277]

—*Spencer W. Kimball*

THIS DAY IN AMERICAN HISTORY (1787)

The U.S. Constitution is signed.

There Is a Safety in an Informed Public

The sad and shocking story of what has happened in America in recent years must be told. Our people must have the facts. There is safety in an informed public. There is real danger in a complacent, uninformed citizenry. This is our real danger today. Yes, the truth must be told even at the risk of destroying, in large measure, the influence of men who are widely respected and loved by the American people. The stakes are high. Freedom and survival is the issue.

Today we are at war. It is not enough to be against communism. We must shed our complacency and aggressively meet this challenge. . . . There can be no compromise with the communists. They are at war with us—with the entire hard fact, the stronger our position will be. It is a real war. The lines are tightly drawn. The war is more insidious, more devious, more devastating, and more satanical than any war in our history. Moral principles, once universally recognized, are ignored. International law once respected is thrown to the wind.

The socialist-communist philosophy is devastatingly evil—destructive of all that is good, uplifting and beautiful. It strikes at the very foundation of all we hold dear. The communist "has convinced himself that nothing is evil which answers the call of expedient." This is a most damnable doctrine. People who truly accept such a philosophy have neither conscience nor honor. Force, trickery, lies, broken promises—to them such things are wholly justified.[278]

—*Ezra Taft Benson*

THIS DAY IN AMERICAN HISTORY (1783)

President George Washington lays the Capitol building cornerstone.

The Future Rendezvous with History

There is some question . . . as to whether or not the Constitution . . . would be saved by the 'elders' of this Church, or whether 'if the Constitution be saved at all, it will be by the elders of this Church.' Whatever version is correct, we do seem to have rendezvous with history concerning the American Constitution. . . .

We can best prepare ourselves for that time by thinking through our commitment to constitutional government, by involving ourselves in and contributing to the process of that government in appropriate ways, as did Mosiah in Nephite Society and Joseph in Egypt, by understanding the lessons of secular history, and by drawing upon the scriptures in which we have so much longitudinal information about men's past struggles to be free as they faced the issues of their times.

This rendezvous can best be kept by individuals who avoid both naïveté and despair. . . . It can be a rendezvous best kept by men and women who are devoted to the whole document of the United States Constitution; the wise men who authored both the Constitution and the Bill of Rights on which we, as a people, may need to rely were as wise about one part of the First Amendment as another. We cannot seek shelter under the tree of the Constitution if we cut off some of its branches or fail to nourish the whole tree.[279]

—*Neal A. Maxwell*

THIS DAY IN AMERICAN HISTORY (1777)

British General Burgoyne is stopped by Americans during the Battle of Saratoga.

A Prosperous Nation

There has been no nation prospered as our nation has. No government was ever framed by man that is so strong and so good and well adapted to the happiness of human beings as our government is. There never was a better instrument framed for the happiness of man than the Constitution of the United States. The men who framed it were inspired of God. The men who fought the battles of the Revolution were the same. Washington was inspired of God; he was sustained by the almighty arm of God; and the defeats that the mother country received were in accordance with the plan of God. This land was kept for this purpose. For centuries it was hidden from all the nations of the earth. It was not until the 15th century that God inspired Columbus to go forth and seek a passage across the Atlantic, and land upon some of the islands adjacent to this continent. His track was followed by others. All this was in the mind of God. . . . God preserved it; and He has said in the Book of Mormon, that so long as the inhabitants of this land serve the God of the land, who is Jesus Christ—they shall prosper and no nation shall have power over them. . . . Those who contended for liberty in early days were men who desired to serve the Lord. They may have been mistaken in many things, but they were zealous in this and devoted to it, and many of them were willing that every human being should have the rights that they contended for themselves.[280]

—*George Q. Cannon*

THIS DAY IN AMERICAN HISTORY (1787)

The Confederation Congress reads the U.S. Constitution.

SEPTEMBER 21

We Fight for the Soul of America

The doctrine of freedom upon which the government of the United States is founded is interwoven with belief in God and the principles of Christianity. When we fight for freedom of speech, the right to worship, we fight for the preservation of the very soul of America. Lose that soul and we lose our liberty. Contrary to the totalitarian ideal that the individual exists for the State, the doctrine of freedom declares that 'everything must be within humanity, nothing against humanity, nothing outside of humanity.'

Therefore, as against the Tyranny and despotism of totalitarianism and dictatorship, let us willingly and heroically defend the constitution of this land that guarantees to every citizen of the Republic, life, liberty, and the pursuit of happiness, and favors the divine pronouncement that the souls of men are precious in the sight of God.[281]

—*David O. McKay*

THIS DAY IN AMERICAN HISTORY (1922)

President Warren G. Harding signs a joint resolution to establish a Jewish homeland in Palestine.

The Governments of the Earth Are Thrown into Confusion and Division

The nations of the Gentiles are like the waves of the sea, casting up mire and dirt, or all in commotion, and they are hastily preparing to act the part allotted them, when the Lord rebukes the nations, when He shall rule them with a rod of iron, and break them in pieces like a potter's vessel. The Lord declares to His servants, some eighteen months since, that he was then withdrawing his spirit from the earth; and we can see that such is the fact, for not only the churches are dwindling away, but there are no conversions, or but a very few: and this is not all, the governments of the earth are thrown into confusion and division; and destruction, to the eye of the spiritual beholder, seems to be written by the finger of an invisible hand, in large capitals, upon almost everything we behold.[282]

—*Joseph Smith, Jr.*

THIS DAY IN AMERICAN HISTORY (1975)

An assassination attempt on President Gerald Ford fails.

SEPTEMBER 23

Constitutional Safeguards

Freedom of choice, free agency, next to life itself, is the greatest endowment of God to His children. . . .

These lofty concepts [of agency] did not spring from governments, but from the Creator himself, penned into tenets for stabilized government by men whom God raised up for this very purpose. The basic principles underlying these concepts of human government are contained in that great state paper, the Constitution of the United States of America. Written into the Constitution as we have it today are three prime safeguards:

1. There are unique restraints on power that governmental authority may exercise upon citizens, embodied in what is known as the Bill of Rights.

2. There is outlined a division of power between the federal and state governments.

3. There is defined a distinct separation of power among three branches of government—the executive, the legislative, and the judicial—in such a way as to provide checks and balances to control the exercise of governmental power.[283]

—Harold B. Lee

THIS DAY IN AMERICAN HISTORY (1780)

Major John Andre is arrested, which leads to exposure of Benedict Arnold's plans to betray West Point to the British.

The Connection Between Religion and Patriotism

Following the battles of Lexington and Concord, sermons rang out across New England. Clergymen, as one scholar noted, "connected religion and patriotism, and in their sermons and prayers, represented the cause of America as the cause of heaven."[284] Thousands of sermons justified resistance to British tyranny by, as another scholar put it, reaffirming "New England's enduring identity as an embattled people of the Word [of God] who were commissioned to uphold a sacred and exclusive covenant between themselves and God."[285]

The clergymen of New England were not alone in drawing the connection between religion and patriotism. In New Jersey, John Witherspoon—James Madison's tutor at what is now Princeton University—delivered a sermon in 1776 announcing his support for the Revolution. He explained that the union of the colonies against Great Britain resulted from "a deep and general conviction, that our civil and religious liberties . . . depended on [it]."[286]

Capturing the sentiments of that patriotic generation, one historian wrote: "The men of 1776 believed that the good state would rise on the rock of private and public morality, that morality was in the case of most men and all states the product of religion, and that the earthly mission of religion was to set men free. It was no mere pose when they justified resistance to oppression as obedience to God and an appeal to heaven."[287]

—*D. Todd Christofferson*

THIS DAY IN AMERICAN HISTORY (1789)

The Federal Judiciary Act passes, creating a six-member U.S. Supreme Court.

A Nation that Is a Wonder and the Admiration of the Earth

We live in a marvelous age. No people who have dwelt upon the earth have partaken of so many of the comforts and blessings of life. No people have had such opportunities, as are offered to the children of men in the day and age in which we live ; and remarkable as it may seem, you analyze the conditions that exist, every blessing that has come to us has been one that conforms to the ideals of the gospel of Jesus Christ. . . .

Think of the blessings that came to America. How Columbus was inspired to go out upon the great waters and find his way to this western land. Then the settlers of Jamestown, the pilgrim fathers, and all those early pioneers who came to America because they desired to serve God according to the dictates of their conscience. The Lord blessed them and finally raised up a nation that is the wonder and the admiration of the earth. Those men who framed the Constitution of the United States were not only wise in the things of this world, but they were inspired by our Heavenly Father who raised them up for that very purpose. This marvelous government that we enjoy in this favored land of liberty, was given to man that it might be a blessing to him. Here men and women are permitted to worship God according to the dictates of their conscience. Our Heavenly Father will not coerce or compel mankind, but in loving kindness has given to them from the age when the world was first peopled until now, opportunity to know the truth.[288]

—George Albert Smith

THIS DAY IN AMERICAN HISTORY (1789)

The Bill of Rights is approved by Congress.

Shall We Forsake?

Shall we forsake the institutions of this country because of the acts of those men? No, we will cleave to them and sustain them. Shall we deprive other men of their political rights? No, we will not. Shall we deprive any man of his social rights? No, we will not. Shall we deprive any men of their religious rights? No, we will not. They may do as they please in Washington and other places; but we will do right towards all men. Our motto is, Freedom, Liberty and Rights of Conscience to all people; as Brother Parley P. Pratt has it in one of his poems:

'Indian, Muslim, Greek or Jew, Freedom's banner waves for you.'

This is the kind of feeling we entertain in regard to this subject. We all have faults, and perhaps this government is one of the best governments we could have in the world; and we will sustain it. And then, we will contend for our rights legally, properly, orderly and constitutionally. Honorable and decent men, men that will do right we will maintain all the time. But this nation is laying the axe at the root of the tree and they then will crumble to pieces by and by. . . . And they will tear away one plank of liberty after another, until the whole, fabric will totter and fall; and many other nations will be cast down and empires destroyed; and this nation will have to suffer as others will. And it will be as Joseph Smith once said, 'When all others forsake the Constitution, the Elders of this Church will rally around the standard and save its tattered shreds.' We will come to its rescue and proclaim liberty to all men.[289]

—*John Taylor*

THIS DAY IN AMERICAN HISTORY (1777)

British Forces occupy Philadelphia.

Free Agency and Free Enterprise: The Foundations of a Great Nation

But these two essentials of a free people are being more and more restricted in this country. They have been practically destroyed in Russia and some other communistic controlled countries where it is claimed a people's democracy rules—a highly absurd claim in the light of the facts.

What do I mean by the words "free enterprise"? I mean individual freedom of action and of opportunity. Everyone born in mortality, according to our teachings, comes from God, our Father, with the priceless gift of "free agency" and will be held accountable for its use. Naturally, in the exercise of this gift one may not, without sinning against God and man, do anything knowingly to hurt, or injure a fellow human being. Further, our Church teaches that the Constitution of the United States as given to us by the Founding Fathers of our republic is a divinely inspired document, designed to protect the citizens in the enjoyment of their inalienable rights among which are "life, liberty, and the pursuit of happiness." Hence, are not restrictions to our freedom of action, insofar as we do not harmfully interfere with others, violative of the spirit of the Constitution and our Bill of Rights?

America has become great in many lines of human endeavor, in fact the greatest nation on earth, due unquestionably to its free enterprise or capitalistic system. This system is our pride and the envy of some other peoples.[290]

—*Joseph F. Merrill*

THIS DAY IN AMERICAN HISTORY (1779)

John Adams is appointed to negotiate Revolutionary War peace terms with Great Britain.

The Everlasting Decree of God for America

And he had sworn in his wrath unto the brother of Jared, that whoso should possess this land of promise, from that time henceforth and forever, should deserve him, the true and only God, or they should be swept off when the fulness of his wrath shall come upon them. And now, we can behold the decrees of God concerning this land, that it is a land of promise; and whatsoever nation shall possess it shall serve God, or they shall be swept off. . . . For it is the everlasting decree of God. And it is not until the fulness of iniquity among the children of the land, that they are swept off (Ether 2:8-10)."

That is the everlasting decree of God for all who possess this land. And the Book of Mormon records the literal fulfillment of this promise to two great and mighty nations. One has only to read the final destruction of both the Jaredite and Nephite nations to know that God's decree is not one to be set aside.

In his preface to the Doctrine of Covenants, the Lord warned the people living in our time that the level of wickedness was rising, and would soon bring the divine promise into play once again if they did not repent.

If the generation which now inhabits the promised land does not serve the only true and living God they too shall be swept off when their iniquity is full. The outlook is not very optimistic, for the prophets have been testifying that the wickedness in this age is rampant.[291]

—Gerald N. Lund

THIS DAY IN AMERICAN HISTORY (1781)

American and French soldiers begin the siege of Yorktown, Virginia.

Scriptural Stature

I have always felt that the United States Constitution's closest approach to scriptural stature is in the phrasing of our Bill of Rights. Without the free exercise of religion, America could not have served as the host nation for the restoration of the gospel, which began just three decades after the Bill of Rights was ratified. I also see scriptural stature in the concept and wording of the freedoms of speech and press, the right to be secure against unreasonable searches and seizures, the requirements that there must be probable cause for an arrest and that accused persons must have a speedy and public trial by an impartial jury, and the guarantee that a person will not be deprived of life, liberty, or property without due process of law. President Ezra Taft Benson has said, "Reason, necessity, tradition, and religious conviction all lead me to accept the divine origin of these rights."

The Declaration of Independence had posited these truths to be "self-evident," that all men "are endowed by their Creator with certain inalienable Rights," and that governments are instituted 'to secure these Rights." This inspired Constitution was established to provide a practical guarantee of these God-given rights (see D&C 101:77), and the language implementing that godly objective is scriptural to me.[292]

—*Dallin H. Oaks*

THIS DAY IN AMERICAN HISTORY (1789)

The U.S. Congress officially recognizes the U.S. Army.

The Inseparable Bond Between Christianity and Democracy

For it is out of that religion [Christianity] common that the whole concept of the common brotherhood of men as the children of the same God derives, each equal before the law. So intimately are the two intertwined that democracy and the Christian religion must survive or perish together. Neither has worked perfectly in human hands. But the failure of the perfect working of the principles of free government probably is fairly in proportion to the failure of men to live the Christian religion. The perfect working of the latter would insure the perfect working of the former. We may not, except at our peril, discard either of them. Together they have provided an atmosphere in which, in spite of imperfections, we have lived and flourished as has no other nation in recorded history. It is important to note that in those countries where freedom has perished, there has gone side by side with its decline, a breaking down and denial of the Christian religion, and in that country where the breakdown has been most complete, there has been accomplished the most thorough regimentation of the bodies and spirits of men. But a superficial, unbelieving profession of the Christian faith will not withstand the disintegrating forces at play in the world today. Only a genuine, deep-seated religious conviction carried over into practice can do that.

The disciples who established the Ancient Church were not men who rationalized Jesus and his doctrines away, nor were satisfied with proclaiming him merely a great ethical teacher. When Jesus asked his disciples, "Whom do men say that I am?" (Mark 8:27.) Peter gave him the various conjectures that men had ventured concerning him. Jesus then put it to him directly, "But whom say ye that I am?" Peter answered without equivocation or hesitancy, "Thou art the Christ, the son of the living God." (Matthew 16:13–16.) That is the kind of living faith which carried the Christian religion into ascendancy in the western world and ultimately gave to the world our democracy. It is the only kind of faith that can save the world from the unchristian doctrine of regimentation and authoritarian dominance over the lives of men.[293]

—*Albert E. Bowen*

THIS DAY IN AMERICAN HISTORY (1889)

The Wyoming State Convention approves the Constitution granting women the right to vote.

OCTOBER 1

Calculated to Ensure Liberty Not License

Our feet have been planted upon this sacred soil for a wise purpose. This land has been dedicated for the blessing of mankind. The Constitution and the laws that have been enacted under its provisions are calculated to ensure liberty, not license, to all who dwell here. This Church with which we are identified stands, if it stands for anything, for the perpetuation of the liberties of all mankind. We should not listen to those who find pleasure in teaching sedition. Neither should we follow those who claim to be citizens of this land, who go about violating the laws that govern it. There are many who are failing to do their duty as citizens who have the right of franchise, but who are unworthy of that blessing that has come to those who live in this wonderful country. . . .

Upon you men of Israel—to whom the priesthood of the Holy One has been given—there rests an obligation. You must serve the Lord and keep his commandments. It matters not what others may do, but for you there is only one course, and that is to be obedient to law, and to sustain the Constitution of this great land, and to sustain those influences and powers wherever they may be, that are calculated to uplift the human family.[294]

—*George Albert Smith*

THIS DAY IN AMERICAN HISTORY (1979)

After 70 years of American control, the Panama Canal Zone is formally handed over to Panama.

In Their Excellence to Regulate Rulers as Well as the Ruled

Go back in the history of the world and you will see that the greatest nations that ever existed, as soon as they commenced to pervert justice, crush truth and right, persecute God's people and exalt iniquity, then commenced their downfall, and their way was down, down, down, to demolition and destruction, until more substantial and better elements were found in their ruins with which to raise up and create something new. It was that excellence and purity which God saw in the Puritan fathers that came over to this country for the love of the truth, and to worship God according to the dictates of their own consciences—it was that excellence that preserved them and established them here, and as long as they maintained the principles of liberty, allowed others to enjoy the same rights that they themselves enjoyed, just so long did they prosper. They were powerful in that they had influence and faith to receive inspiration from God, to draw up and establish the greatest Constitution that has ever been known on the earth—the grandest combination of loyal principles and fundamental truths that has been established by man, since the days of Noah. . . . That glorious Constitution was made to regulate rulers as well as the ruled. It was so constructed that those who should be appointed to rule over the people should not be their masters, but their servants.[295]

—*Franklin D. Richards*

THIS DAY IN AMERICAN HISTORY (1895)

The Cuban Missile Crisis begins.

This Nation Did Not Come into Being by Chance

From ancient American prophets, we learn that this United States of America was established by God for a divine purpose, and that great blessings, which all must admit, as we review the history of this nation, have so far been literally fulfilled; yet the fulfillment of future promise of blessings is conditional upon the continued righteousness of its people. . . .

This nation did not come into being by chance. God declared that the gentiles who came here were to be brought out of captivity by his hand. The prophecies previously quoted concerning the establishment of this nation have been fulfilled to the letter. The people coming here in the beginning did so to find religious freedom. . . .

The Declaration of Independence came from a determined people. The successful Revolutionary War which followed united the colonies; and the gentile nation of destiny and of divine purpose, as foretold by the prophets, was born. A Constitution was needed to set forth the purposes, obligations, and the guide lines for the new nation. God was prepared and ready and did not neglect this newborn nation which he had ordained to be established thousands of years previously.[296]

—*Delbert L. Stapley*

THIS DAY IN AMERICAN HISTORY (1863)

The first cartoon comic strip is printed in an American newspaper.

When the Lord Speaks, What He Promises Has Always Been Fulfilled

The world would not be taken by surprise if they paid attention to the leadership that the Lord provided. So we look down over the vista of time. . . .

In the year 1830 [God] established His church here upon the earth. That did not come by accident—it did not come by surprise. It had all been predicted—all these things that are contained in the Old and New Testaments. . . . I am trying to call your attention to the fact that when the Lord speaks, what He promises has always been fulfilled. . . .

You may follow the record, and you will discover that such things have never happened to a people who were keeping the commandments of God. The destruction has come to those who were failing to pay attention to what the Lord desired. This nation was raised up in order that men might worship God according to the dictates of their conscience–this nation of which we are a part. God raised up the very men who prepared the Constitution to declare to us our privileges and our liberties. It was not an accident.[297]

—George Albert Smith

THIS DAY IN AMERICAN HISTORY (1777)

Americans are driven off at the Battle of Germantown.

OCTOBER 5

A Government as Weak as Water

These corruptions flow very naturally from the indebtedness contracted to obtain power. In elections, the successful become indebted to their friends, and they promise them the patronage of the President, that they shall be sent as a minister to such or such a country, or be appointed a judge here or there, or a governor yonder. They cannot obtain their election without paying largely for it, both in promises and money; and to recover the means, they must either become thieves or repudiate their debts. "Such a one owes me so much for contributing to his election and he will not pay me." It often happens that he cannot, unless he steals it.

The whole government is gone; it is as weak as water. I heard Joseph Smith say nearly thirty years ago, "they shall have mobbings to their hearts' content, if they do not redress the wrongs of the Latter-day Saints." Mobs will not decrease but will increase until the whole government becomes a mob, and eventually it will be State against State, city against city, neighborhood against neighborhood, Methodists against Methodists, and so on.[298]

—*Brigham Young*

THIS DAY IN AMERICAN HISTORY (1857)

Captain Lot Smith and Utah militia soldiers destroy a U.S. Army supply wagon train during the Utah War.

If Christianity Is Safe, Then Is Democracy Safe Also

I do not think it necessary to enter into any argument to convince this congregation of thoughtful, observing people, that the spirit of Anti-Christ is in the world today, and is making the greatest effort to obtain world dominion, and the overthrow of Christianity that has ever been made since the beginning of time. . . .

My brethren and sisters, we have heard a great deal since, the beginning of this devastating war, in regard to making the world safe for democracy. My appeal to you this morning is to make the world safe for Christianity, for if Christianity is safe, then is democracy safe also. Then is representative government by the people, and for the people, safe. Then are the principles of charity, and mercy, and justice safe, for these, and every other thing which the heart of man may desire in righteousness are made safe when the doctrines taught by the Redeemer are acknowledged to be the supreme law, and he the Lawgiver.

So I appeal to you to reflect, and to resolve, in the words of Moroni; which I have read, that so long as there is a band of Christians left in the world, they will gird on their armor, the armor of righteousness, that the word of the Lord may be advocated in every nation, and if necessary the arm of every Christian be steeled to fight for the perpetuity of these eternal truths upon which the salvation of the world depends today. God give victory to the armies which are fighting in defense of these principles. May he give strength to the Latter-day Saints to .properly perform their part in this great struggle, and above all may he give power to spread these truths among all nations, until the world shall be converted, God's kingdom come, and his will be done upon earth, as it is in heaven, I pray.[299]

—*Antoine R. Ivins*

THIS DAY IN AMERICAN HISTORY (1961)

President John F. Kennedy advises Americans to build nuclear fallout shelters.

OCTOBER 7

The Importance of Religion in National Understanding

It is no surprise that just weeks before the Declaration of Independence was signed, Virginia adopted a bill of rights, largely penned by George Mason. Its ringing affirmation of religious liberty remains an inspiration:

"Religion, or the duty which we owe to our Creator, and the manner of discharging it, can be directed only by reason and conviction, not by force or violence; and therefore all men are equally entitled to the free exercise of religion, according to the dictates of conscience."[300]

And of course the Declaration itself reminds us that Americans believed they were "endowed by their Creator with certain unalienable rights." Later the Constitution would enshrine the first of those unalienable rights—the right to religious freedom.

These formative experiences of colonization and revolution solidified the importance of religion in our national understanding. The French political thinker Alexis de Tocqueville, visiting America during the 1830s, reported that Americans considered religion indispensable to freedom. Tocqueville wrote: "I stop the first American whom I meet, . . . and I ask him if he thinks religion is useful for the stability of law and the good order of society; he immediately responds that a civilized society, but above all a free society, cannot subsist without religion."[301, 302]

—*D. Todd Christofferson*

THIS DAY IN AMERICAN HISTORY (1765)

The Stamp Act Congress begins meeting.

A Patriotism Born of an Understanding of the Ultimate Destiny of This Land

A pronouncement of the faith and understanding of the Latter-day Saints concerning the destiny of this land of America comes at a time when it may not be easy for those without this understanding to have full faith and confidence in the future of our democracy. We in America have viewed great depressions; we remember the armies of the unemployed and restless who have frequently raised strange flags of sedition above fearful masses of people.

[These] and other similar conditions indicate to the thinking person a day of reckoning that may result in near-chaotic conditions that God in His mercy may not turn aside from us. Indeed, it has been said by a prophet in our generation that the time would come when the destiny of this nation would hang as by a single thread, but that it would be saved by the people who possessed faith in America and in her destiny.

And what is to be that destiny? It is the patriotism possessed by this people and an expression of their faith in the promises of the Lord concerning the place that this great country and its people may occupy in the moving drama of God's dealings with men and nations. We Latter-day Saints believe that we have come to a time when we need to do more to demonstrate our patriotism than merely wave the flag and doff our hats at its passing and join lustily in singing the strains of patriotic songs. We believe that the American people must subscribe to a patriotism born of an understanding of the ultimate destiny of this land. . . .

To the pioneers of 1847, this land of America was to be a choice land above all other lands as an inheritance to the faithful of the Lord. It was to be a land of liberty upon which no king should ever rule. It would be so fortified against all other nations that whosoever would raise up a king or would fight against this nation should perish, because the Lord, the king of heaven, was to be their king. (See 2 Nephi 10:10–14.) To them, this was the land of Zion, a land of peace, a city of refuge, a place of safety.[303]

—Harold B. Lee

THIS DAY IN AMERICAN HISTORY (1871)

The Great Chicago Fire begins.

OCTOBER 9

The Best Spirits the God of Heaven Could Find on the Face of the Earth

I am going to bear my testimony to this assembly, if I never do it again in my life, that those men who laid the foundation of this American government and signed the Declaration of Independence were the best spirits the God of heaven could find on the face of the earth. They were choice spirits, not wicked men. General Washington and all the men that labored for the purpose were inspired of the Lord.

Another thing I am going to say here, because I have a right to say it. Every one of those men that signed the Declaration of Independence, with General Washington, called upon me, as an Apostle of the Lord Jesus Christ, in the temple at St George, two consecutive nights, and demanded at my hands that I should go forth and attend to the ordinances of the House of God for them. . . . Brother McAllister baptized me for all those men, and then I told those brethren that it was their duty to go into the temple and labor until they had got endowments for all of them. They did it. Would those spirits have called upon me, as an Elder in Israel, to perform that work if they had not been noble spirits before God? They would not. I bear this testimony, because it is true. The Spirit of God bore record to myself and the brethren while we were laboring in that way.

What has been said with regard to this nation and to our position is coming to pass. All the powers of earth and hell will not stay the hand of Almighty God in the fulfillment of those great prophecies that have to come to pass to prepare the way for the coming of the Son of Man.[304]

—*Wilford Woodruff*

THIS DAY IN AMERICAN HISTORY (1779)

Failed American Attempt to recapture Savannah, Georgia.

We Have a Divine Duty to Preserve That Constitution

Not only should we have strong spiritual homes, but we should have strong temporal homes. We should avoid bondage by getting out of debt as soon as we can, pay as we go, and live within our incomes. There is wisdom in having on hand a year's supply of food, clothing, and fuel, if possible, and in being prepared to defend our families and our possessions and to take care of ourselves. I believe a man should prepare for the worst while working for the best. Some people prepare and don't work, while others work but don't prepare. Both are needed if we would be of maximum service to our God, our family, and our country.

It is a part of my religious belief that America is a land choice above all others, that we are not just another of the family nations, but that we have been singled out to perform a divine mission for liberty-loving people everywhere. Those who founded this republic were wise men raised up by our Father in heaven to perform that very task, and the Constitution of this land was inspired by God. We have a divine duty-even a destiny-to preserve that Constitution from destruction and hold it aloft to the world.

A book that I accept as scripture tells of two ancient American civilizations that were destroyed as a result of murderous conspiracies lusting for power and seeking to overthrow freedom. That book warned that when we should see a similar situation developing in our land in our day, we would be under commandment of the Lord to awake to our awful situation. That day is upon us, and those of us who are awake to our situation have a moral obligation to do all we can to awaken our fellow citizens.[305]

—*Ezra Taft Benson*

THIS DAY IN AMERICAN HISTORY (1789)

The last official business is conducted under the Articles of Confederation

OCTOBER 11

A Haven from the Scorching Sun of Turmoil and Oppression

To the membership of The Church of Jesus Christ of Latter-day Saints, the Constitution of the United States is as a tree of liberty under whose cooling branches one might find a haven from the scorching sun of turmoil and oppression and have his rights protected according to just and holy principles. To them, the Constitution was established by the hands of wise men whom God raised up for this very purpose, and they devoutly believe that if it should be in danger of being overthrown, their lives, if need be, are to be offered in defense of its principles. (See D&C 101:77–80.)

What wonder, then, that with this sublime faith in America and this understanding of her future destiny, the intrepid, reverent band that entered the Salt Lake Valley in 1847 should have first hoisted on a topmost peak of the valley the flag of the United States, and that written into their basic doctrines was the declaration that "we believe in being subject to kings, presidents, rulers, and magistrates, in obeying, honoring, and sustaining the law" (Article of Faith 12), to attest to their faith in the divine decrees of God concerning this nation. Indeed, they believed and taught that "no man [should] break the laws of the land, for he that keepeth the laws of God hath no need to break the laws of the land" (D&C 58:21); that "governments were instituted of God for the benefit of man; and that he holds men accountable for their acts in relation to them, both in making laws and administering them, for the good and safety of society" (D&C 134:1), and that thus should men rule "until [the Master] reigns whose right it is to reign, and subdues all enemies under his feet (D&C 58:22).

It is not surprising that as a result of such teachings there should have been developed in the communities fostered by the pioneers a sincerity of purpose and a patriotic loyalty to government that was to stand for generations yet unborn to follow.[306]

—*Harold B. Lee*

THIS DAY IN AMERICAN HISTORY (1776)

Benedict Arnold's forces are defeated near Lake Champlain, delaying the British advance.

No Item of Inspiration Is Held More Sacred with Us

To accuse us of being unfriendly to the government, is to accuse us of hostility to our religion, for no item of inspiration is held more sacred with us than the Constitution under which she acts. As a religious society, we, in common with all other denominations, claim its protection; whether our people are located in the other states, or territories, as thousands of them are, or in this territory, it is held as a shield to protect the dearest boon of which men is susceptible, his religious views and sentiments.

The government of the United States has never engaged in a crusade against us as a people, although she has remained silent, or refused us, when appealed to for redress of grievances. . . . Under these circumstances, what course is left for us to pursue? I answer that, instead of seeking to destroy the very best government in the world, as seems to be the fears of some, we, like all other good citizens, should seek to place those men in power who will feel the obligations and responsibilities they are under to a mighty people; who would feel, and realize the important trusts reposed in them by the voice of the people who call them to administer law under the solemn sanction of an oath of fidelity to that heaven inspired instrument, to the inviolate preservation of which we look for the perpetuity of our free institutions. . . .

I believe it is legal to exercise all the power and influence which God has given me for the preservation of virtue, truth, and holiness; and because we feel sensitive, upon points such as these, should it be construed that we are enemies to the federal government? Our history proves that for such things we have been persecuted even unto death, but this deters me not. I would rather have God my friend, and all the world enemies, than be a friend with the world, and have God my enemy; and in this view of the case the government should also be our friends, for assuredly in the preservation of virtue, morality, and intelligence she may look for the perpetuity of her free institutions, and preservation of her liberty.[307]

—*Brigham Young*

THIS DAY IN AMERICAN HISTORY (1892)

The Pledge of Allegiance is first recited in public schools.

OCTOBER 13

The Elders of Israel Are Commanded to Warn the World

A terrible day of reckoning is approaching the nations of the earth; the Lord is coming out of his hiding place to vex the inhabitants thereof; and the destroyer of the gentiles, as prophesied of, is already on his way. . . . Already combinations are being entered into which are very ominous for the future prosperity, welfare, and happiness of this great republic. The volcanic fires of disordered and anarchical elements are beginning to manifest themselves and exhibit the internal forces that are at work among the turbulent and unthinking masses of the people.

The angels of God are waiting to fulfill the great commandment given forty-five years ago, to go forth and reap down the earth because of the wickedness of men. How do you think eternity feels today? Why, "there is more wickedness a thousand times over, in the United States now, than when that revelation was given. The whole earth is ripe in iniquity; and these inspired men, these Elders of Israel, have been commanded of the Almighty to go forth and warn the world, that their garments may be clean of the blood of all men."[308]

—*John Taylor*

THIS DAY IN AMERICAN HISTORY (1792)

The cornerstone is laid for the White House (originally called the Executive Mansion).

They Shall Be Broken Up

I arrived safely at Nauvoo, after a wearisome journey, through alternate snow and mud, having witnessed many vexatious movement sin government officers, whose sole object should be the peace and prosperity and happiness of the whole people; but instead of this, I discovered that popular clamor and personal aggrandizement were the ruling principles of those in authority; and my heart faints within me when I see, by the visions of the Almighty, the end of this action, if she continues to disregard the cries and petitions of her virtuous citizens, as she has done, and is now doing.[309]

I prophesy in the name of the Lord God of Israel, unless the United States redress the wrongs committed upon the Saints in the state of Missouri and punish the crimes committed by her officers that in a few years the government will be utterly overthrown and wasted, and there will not be so much as a potsherd left.[310]

While discussing the petition to Congress, I prophesied by virtue of the holy priesthood vested in me, and in the name of the Lord Jesus Christ, that if Congress will not hear our petition and grant us protection, they shall be broken up as a government.[311]

—*Joseph Smith, Jr.*

THIS DAY IN AMERICAN HISTORY (1774)

The Declaration of Rights and Grievances is passed.

The World Is Full of Confusion

Were we surprised when the last terrible war took place here in the United States? No; good Latter-day Saints were not, for they had been told about it. Joseph Smith had told them where it would start, that it should be a terrible time of bloodshed and that it should start in South Carolina. But I tell you today the end is not yet. You will see worse things than that, for God will lay his hand upon this nation, and they will feel it more terribly than ever they have done before; there will be more bloodshed, more ruin, more devastation than ever they have seen before. Write it down! You will see it come to pass; it is only just starting in.

And would you feel to rejoice? No; I would feel sorry. I knew very well myself when this last war was commencing, and could have wept and did weep, over this nation; but there is yet to come a sound of war, trouble and distress, in which brother will be arrayed against brother, father against son, son against father, a scene of desolation and destruction that will permeate our land until it will be a vexation to hear the report thereof.[312]

The world, as I have said, is full of confusion, and there will be worse confusion by and by. We had a great war upon this continent some years ago; but there will yet be wars pass through these United States, and through other nations, until it will be mournful to hear the report of the bloodshed, the sorrow and the trouble that will be caused thereby.[313]

—*John Taylor*

THIS DAY IN AMERICAN HISTORY (1951)

The TV show "I Love Lucy" debuts.

The Lord Will Fulfill Prophecy Concerning This Nation

He will speedily fulfill the prophecy in relation to the overthrow of this nation, and their destruction. We shall be obliged to have a government to preserve ourselves in unity and peace; for they, through being wasted away, will not have power to govern; for state will be divided against state, city against city, town against town, and the whole country will be in terror and confusion; mobocracy will prevail and there will be no security, through this great Republic, for the lives or property of the people.

When that time shall arrive, we shall necessarily want to carry out the principles of our great Constitution and, as the people of God, we shall want to see those principles magnified, according to the order of union and oneness which prevails among the people of God.[314]

—*Orson Pratt*

THIS DAY IN AMERICAN HISTORY (1859)

Abolitionist John Brown leads a raid on the federal arsenal at Harpers Ferry, Virginia.

OCTOBER 17

Religion and Religious Freedom Are Deeply Connected to Both the Formation of America and Our Ongoing Effort

Religious convictions and language set the terms of the national debates over slavery, emancipation, and the Civil War.

Within my lifetime, the civil rights movement depended on the persuasive power of ministers and the language of religious belief. Martin Luther King Jr. wrote from the Birmingham jail, for instance, that "human progress . . . comes through the tireless efforts and persistent work of men willing to be co-workers with God."[315]

So religion and religious freedom are deeply connected to both the formation of America and our ongoing effort, in the words of the Constitution, "to form a more perfect Union [and] establish Justice."[316] As one historian summarized:

"American churchmen and American churches have, throughout our history, played an important role in public affairs. . . . The churches have usually assumed that their mission includes active participation in the formulation and fulfilment of moral principle. Whether the cause has been abolition, prohibition, or integration, the churches and their leaders have played a central, sometimes a crucial, role in translating what the churches conceived to be moral principle into rules of law."[317]

Religious participation in public life is one of the golden threads in our national tapestry. It is also, of course, a cherished constitutional right.[318]

—*D. Todd Christofferson*

THIS DAY IN AMERICAN HISTORY (1777)

British General Burgoyne surrenders to General Gates at Saratoga, New York.

Inspired Constitution, and Therefore, What?

U.S. citizens have an inspired Constitution, and therefore, what? Does the belief that the U.S. Constitution is divinely inspired affect citizens' behavior toward law and government? It should and it does.

U.S. citizens should follow the First Presidency's counsel to study the Constitution. They should be familiar with its great fundamentals: the separation of powers, the individual guarantees in the Bill of Rights, the structure of federalism, the sovereignty of the people, and the principles of the rule of the law. They should oppose any infringement of these inspired fundamentals.

They should be law-abiding citizens, supportive of national, state, and local governments. . . .

As the Lord declared in modern revelation, constitutional laws are justifiable before him, "and the law also maketh you free." (D&C 98:5–8.) The self-control by which citizens subject themselves to law strengthens the freedom of all citizens and honors the divinely inspired Constitution.[319]

—*Dallin H. Oaks*

THIS DAY IN AMERICAN HISTORY (1876)

U.S. formally takes possession of Alaska from Russia.

Can the American Nation Escape?

I warn future historians to give credence to my history; for my testimony is true, and the truth of its record will be manifest in the world to come. All the words of the Lord will be fulfilled upon the nations, which are written in this book. The American nation will be broken in pieces like a potter's vessel and will be cast down to hell if it does not repent–and this, because of murders, whoredoms, wickedness and all manner of abominations for the Lord has spoken it.[320]

I ask myself the question, "Can the American nation escape?" The answer comes, "no." Its destruction, as well as the destruction of the world is sure; just as sure as the Lord cut off and destroyed the two great and prosperous nations that once inhabited this continent of North and South America, because of their wickedness, so will He them destroy, and sooner or later they will reap the fruits of their own wicked acts, and be numbered among the past. . . .

There are changes awaiting us, they are even nigh at our very doors, and I know it by the visions of heaven; I know it by the administrations of angels, and I know it by the inspiration of heaven, that is given to all men who seek the Lord; and the hand of God will not stay these things. We have no time to lose.[321]

–*Wilford Woodruff*

THIS DAY IN AMERICAN HISTORY (1781)

Cornwallis surrenders at Yorktown, Virginia.

We Must Always Remember God Rules in the Affairs of Men

Under the blessings of liberty secured by the Constitution, we must continue to pursue excellence and progress, but we must recognize that to move forward we must ever hold fast to those moral laws of the Lord which do not change.

There must be a dedication to observing and honoring the law of the land. We must always remember God rules in the affairs of men, and that he is truly the Heavenly Father of all mankind.

It (the Constitution), gave us, for perhaps the first time in history, a republic with the three basic divisions of the government—the legislative, executive, and judicial—mutually, and completely independent the one from the other, under which it is not possible for any branch of government legally to set up a system by which that branch can first conceive what it wants to do, then make the law ordering its doing, and then, itself, judge its own enforcement of its own law, a system that has always brought extortion, oppression, intimidation, tyranny, despotism—a system that every dictator has employed and must employ.

We urge members of the Church and all Americans to begin now to reflect more intently on the meaning and importance of the Constitution, and of adherence to its principals, in giving strength not only to this country but to the entire family of nations.[322]

—Harold B. Lee, N. Eldon Tanner, Marion G. Romney

THIS DAY IN AMERICAN HISTORY (1774)

Articles of Association (prohibiting trade with Great Britain) is signed.

OCTOBER 21

For You There Is Only One Course, and That Is to Be Obedient to Law

Upon you, there rests an obligation. You must serve the Lord and keep his commandments . . . for you there is only one course, and that is to be obedient to law, and to sustain the Constitution of this great land

Men have assumed, of their own wisdom, to point the way, and they have forgotten the teachings of the Creator and in their pursuit of the gifts of our Father in heaven, they have forgotten the giver.

The Constitution and the laws that have been enacted under its provisions are calculated to ensure liberty, not license, to all who dwell here. This Church with which we are identified, stands, if it stands for anything, for the perpetuation of the liberties of all mankind. We should not listen to those who find pleasure in teaching sedition. Neither should we follow those who claim to be citizens of this land, who go about violating the laws that govern it. There are many who are failing to do their duty as citizens who have the right of franchise, but who are unworthy of that blessing that has come to those who live in this wonderful country.

There should go forth from this great Church an influence intended to leaven the whole lump. We have received knowledge and information that our Father's children elsewhere know not of. We are in the position of Noah, who, in his day, went to and fro in the world, proclaiming the truth, calling all men to turn from the error of their way, warning them of the impending judgments that would fall upon them if they failed to repent ; but, in due time those who refused to reform, their lives and failed to listen to that servant of the Lord, became absolutely unfit to inhabit this earth and they were overwhelmed by the flood, while the eight who were righteous were preserved from that awful calamity.[323]

—George Albert Smith

THIS DAY IN AMERICAN HISTORY (1771)

The first World War I American soldiers enter the front lines at Sommerville, France.

Morality Flourishes When the Rank and File Are Free

Virtues, like love and liberty and patriotism, do not exist in general, they exist in particular. If morality exists at all, it exists in the individual heart and mind of the ordinary citizen. Morality flourishes when the rank and file are free. It flourishes where a conscience is clear, where men have faith in God and are obedient to the restraints he has set upon human conduct.

As President Thomas S. Monson taught us in one of his last conference messages, we should "[show] our love in day-to-day interactions. . . . Love is the very essence of the gospel, the noblest attribute of the human soul."

We should also hold to truth, even in our outreach to others. Loving those with different views and avoiding contention are both examples of civility. And they do not mean we should refrain from participating in discussions, debates, and even taking positions against what we believe to be wrong or inadvisable.[324]

—Dallin H. Oaks and Clark G. Gilbert

THIS DAY IN AMERICAN HISTORY (1836)

Sam Houston is inaugurated as the first elected president of the Republic of Texas.

OCTOBER 23

We Again Warn Our People in America of the Threat Against Our Constitution

We again warn our people in America of the constantly increasing threat against our inspired Constitution and our free institutions set up under it. The same political tenets and philosophies that have brought war and terror in other parts of the world are at work amongst us in America. The proponents thereof are seeking to undermine our own form of government and to set up instead one of the forms of dictatorships now flourishing in other lands. These revolutionists are using a technique that is as old as the human race—a fervid but false solicitude for the unfortunate over whom they thus gain mastery, and then enslave them.

They suit their approaches to the particular group they seek to deceive. Among the Latter-day Saints they speak of their philosophy and their plans under it, as an ushering in of the United Order. Communism and all other similar isms bear no relationship whatever to the United Order. They are merely the clumsy counterfeits which Satan always devises of the gospel plan. Communism debases the individual and makes him the enslaved tool of the state to whom he must look for sustenance and religion; the United Order exalts the individual, leaves him his property, "according to his family, according to his circumstances and his wants and needs" (D&C 51:3), and provides a system by which he helps care for his less fortunate brethren; the United Order leaves every man free to choose his own religion as his conscience directs. Communism destroys man's God-given free agency; the United Order glorifies it. Latter-day Saints cannot be true to their faith and lend aid, encouragement, or sympathy to any of these false philosophies. They will prove snares to their feet.[325]

—*J. Reuben Clark, Jr.*

THIS DAY IN AMERICAN HISTORY (1954)

The U.S., Britain, and France agree to end the occupation of Western Germany.

The Constitution Is an Instrument Inspired by the Power of God

We say to our nation—maintain the Constitution and we are satisfied. Give us the rights of that Constitution and we are satisfied. It is an instrument inspired by the power of God. Our forefathers were inspired when they framed it. Yet it is marvelous to reflect upon some principles that have been laid down . . . even by the Supreme Court of the United States. In effect it has said that we may think as we please, but must not act.

I would ask . . . was that all Thomas Jefferson, and others had in their minds when they framed the clause in reference to religious liberty? What about men acting? If it was only intended that men should think and not act, why not say so in the instrument? Why should it be stated that "Congress shall make no law respecting an establishment of religion, or prohibiting the free exercise thereof," if men were not to be allowed to act? Why, in the exercise of their religion, men must act: and it is straining points, it is overstepping the bounds of the Constitution to pass laws taking away the rights and privileges of any people because of their religion—because they happen to differ from their neighbors.

Where will such a course land our government? I will tell you what it will do. It will rend the government in twain like unto a potter's vessel. It will lay the nation in the dust. It will overthrow the government. . . .The Constitution is good enough for anybody. It is good enough for the Latter-day Saints. We have no principles but what are in accord with the Constitution of the United States and the laws of God. We are perfectly willing to trust ourselves and our interests in the hands of God, and to leave our nation in His hands also; for God will judge our nation. . . .

I pray God to bless this nation. I pray God to give our legislators wisdom, that they may maintain the Constitutional principles of the government, the only government on the face of God's earth where the Lord could have established His Church and Kingdom.[326]

—John Q. Cannon

THIS DAY IN AMERICAN HISTORY (1861)

The first transcontinental telegram is sent from San Francisco to Washington, D.C.

OCTOBER 25

Righteousness Must Begin with Each Person

Every nation is made up of its individual citizens. When its citizens are evil, the nation is evil. When they are righteous we have an upright nation.

Then righteousness must begin with each person. Each must regard himself as a part of the salt of the earth which is intended to give a sweet savor to his fellowmen. Especially should every follower of Christ be as salt that provides a sweet savor.

But we must remember the Lord's warning: "If the salt have lost his savor wherewith shall it be salted? it is thenceforth good for nothing, but to be cast out, and to be trodden under foot of men" (Matthew 5:13).

And again, what was it Lincoln said? "If we do not do right, God will let us go on our own way to ruin." And that is true, for God will force no man to heaven.[327]

—Mark E. Peterson

THIS DAY IN AMERICAN HISTORY (1765)

The Stamp Act Congress concludes its meeting.

Religious Freedom and the Practice of Religion Strengthen Society

Religious freedom is the cornerstone of peace in a world with many competing philosophies. It gives us all space to determine for ourselves what we think and believe—to follow the truth that God speaks to our hearts. It allows diverse beliefs to coexist, protects the vulnerable, and helps us negotiate our conflicts. . . .

A robust freedom is not merely what political philosophers have referred to as the "negative" freedom to be left alone, however important that may be. Rather, it is a much richer "positive" freedom—the freedom to live one's religion or belief in a legal, political, and social environment that is tolerant, respectful, and accommodating of diverse beliefs.

We use our freedom of religion and belief to establish our core convictions, without which all other human rights would be meaningless. How can we claim the freedom of speech without being able to say what we truly believe? How can we claim the freedom of assembly unless we can gather with others who share our ideals? How can we enjoy freedom of the press unless we can publicly print or post who we really are?

The good news is that there has been remarkable progress in the spread of religious freedom. I have seen this progress in my own lifetime. . . . Strong reasons undergird the progress made and should motivate us to do even more. Religious freedom strongly correlates with a host of positive economic, public health, and civic benefits. In general, religious individuals have better family lives, stronger marriages, less substance abuse and crime, higher educational levels, a greater willingness to volunteer and donate to charities, better work habits, longer lives, better health, greater income, and higher levels of well-being and happiness. Clearly, religious freedom and the practice of religion strengthen society.[328]

—*D. Todd Christofferson*

THIS DAY IN AMERICAN HISTORY (1774)

The First Continental Congress concludes meeting in Philadelphia.

OCTOBER 27

We Believe and Worship as We Choose

The fathers of the revolution fought and bled to secure this holy right to their children so long as the world should last or the government continue. We are therefore bold in declaring our principles, and in defending our rights. There are countries in the world where imprisonment would be the penalty of the free expression of principles and rights; but they do not live under and enjoy the blessings of the Constitution which we live under. Yet even in this free country some have sought to deprive us of the free enjoyment of the privileges granted unto us in the Constitution of our country, and they will have to pay the penalty for so doing, for they trample under foot the Constitution that grants to them their own liberties, and thus subvert their own liberties, which it becomes them as well as us to preserve inviolate.

It becomes us to cleave to God and our holy religion, trusting in Him because in Him there is power—in Him there is strength; and if we remain faithful, we shall come off victorious, and walk under our feet every principle that is calculated to destroy, and rear the standard of truth and righteousness in the world in spite of hell and all the hosts thereof. Let us be encouraged, and go steadily on in the performance of our duties, cultivating the earth, and bringing from the elements all we need for our sustenance that we may be free and independent, so far as we can, by depending on our own resources with which the Lord has abundantly blessed us. We are greatly blessed in that the Lord has planted our feet in these quiet valleys from those who sought our destruction; while he has brought an overwhelming destruction on them, he has brought safety to us. We can see his wisdom, and his mighty hand manifested in this. Let us henceforth put our trust in that arm which has been so prominently made bare in saving the righteous.[329]

—*Daniel H. Wells*

THIS DAY IN AMERICAN HISTORY (1787)

The first of the Federalist Papers is published in New York newspapers.

America Is a Chosen Land, Preserved and Discovered Under Divine Inspiration

We believe in peace, patriotism, and loyalty, and the fact that America is a chosen land, preserved and discovered under diving inspiration, with a Constitution which we believe was inspired and which we must, under all circumstances, maintain.

Let us always remember that the planting of America in the strain that determined our country's character was a spiritual planting. The fathers who planted this nation were Christians. They came here as Christians. They came because they were Christians. They came on a specifically Christian venture. Get it fixed in your mind that the planting that determined the genius of America was a Church-not a town, not a colony, not a trading or exploring venture, not a gold rush, but a church, a little Pilgrim church crossed the sea for the sake of its church life.

We should understand that each of us has a duty to honor, support, and sustain our civil leaders and the law. The fact that everyone is entitled to his or her own opinion insofar as various matters of law and government are concerned does not relieve any of us of the personal responsibility to obey, honor and sustain the elected governmental officers and the law which it is their duty to administer.

America which surpasses all others is the jewel of the restored gospel of Jesus Christ, because through it men can come to know that their Father in Heaven is real, that He loves them, and that He has prepared a place for them. If they but follow the path that leads to the straight gate, the joy that transcends all other joy awaits them.[330]

—*Hugh B. Brown*

THIS DAY IN AMERICAN HISTORY (1776)

American forces retreat to New Jersey after the Battle of the White Plains.

God Raised Up George Washington, Thomas Jefferson, and Benjamin Franklin

They say we are traitors because we speak of the kingdom of God; that a kingdom cannot exist within a republic; that it is imperium in imperio; that there is no room in this broad land for the kingdom of our God. They might as well say there is no room in Christianity for the love of God. Why, this great government was established for the very purpose of introducing this work. Inspired men like Washington and Jefferson were raised up to frame a Constitution liberal in its provisions, extending the utmost freedom to all men, Christian or heathen, who desired to make this glorious land their home; that they might have the unrestricted right to worship God according to the dictates of their consciences.

We believe that God raised up George Washington, that He raised up Thomas Jefferson, that He raised up Benjamin Franklin and those other patriots who carved out with their swords and with their pens the character and stability of this great government which they hoped would stand forever, an asylum for the oppressed of all nations, where no man's religion would be questioned, no man would be limited in his honest service to his Maker, so long as he did not infringe upon the rights of his fellow men. We believe those men were inspired to do their work, as we do that Joseph Smith was inspired to begin this work; just as Galileo, Columbus, and other mighty men of old, whom I have no time to mention, were inspired to gradually pave the way leading to this dispensation; sentinels, standing at different periods down the centuries, playing their parts as they were inspired of God; gradually freeing the human mind from error, gradually dispelling the darkness as they were empowered by their Creator so to do, that in culmination of the grand scheme of schemes, this great nation, the Republic of the United States, might be established upon this land as an asylum for the oppressed; a resting place, it might be said, for the ark of the covenant, where the temple of our God might be built; where the plan of salvation might be introduced and practiced in freedom, and not a dog would wag his tongue in opposition to the purposes of the Almighty.[331]

—*Orson F. Whitney*

THIS DAY IN AMERICAN HISTORY (1929)

The Great Stock Market Crash occurs, which contributes to the Great Depression.

Our Fathers Were Inspired to Write the Constitution of the United States

It is true that the founders of this nation, as a preliminary step for the introduction of more correct principles and that liberty and the rights of man might be recognized, and that all men might become equal before the law of the land, had that great palladium of liberty, the Constitution of the United States, framed. This was the entering wedge for the introduction of a new era, and in it were introduced principles for the birth and organization of a new world.

The Prophet Joseph Smith said that the Constitution of the United States was given by the inspiration of God. But good, virtuous, and holy principles may be perverted by corrupt and wicked men. The Lord was opposed by Satan; Jesus had His sacred palladium of liberty and seek to trample it under foot. Joseph Smith said they would do so, and that when deserted by all, the elders of Israel would rally around its shattered fragments and save and preserve it inviolate. But even this, good as it was, was not a perfect instrument. It was one of those steppingstones to a future development and in the progress of man to the intelligence and light, the power and union that God alone can impart to the human family.

We believe that our fathers were inspired to write the Constitution of the United States, and that it is an instrument, full, lucid, and comprehensive; that it was dictated by a wise and foreseeing policy, and does honor to the heads and hearts of its framers; that it is the great bulwark of American liberty; and that the strict and implicit observance of which is the only safeguard of this mighty nation. We therefore rest ourselves under its ample folds.[332]

—John Taylor

THIS DAY IN AMERICAN HISTORY (1954)

The Department of Defense announces the end of racial segregation in the United States military.

OCTOBER 31

Self-Governance through Righteousness

Today mankind, as probably never before, needs the gifts of the gospel—wisdom, discernment, vision, and comfort. These precious tidings come only from good living and prayerful hearts. If, as a nation, we cannot maintain faith, there is little hope for us. We had a lecturer in our city a few weeks ago who held out the view that the world is fast approaching a gigantic competition—a competition that will eventually envelop all nations and peoples—a competition of ideologies which in essence resolves itself into an issue between the liberty of democracy and the power of the totalitarian state. He thought that America would inevitably be the supreme exponent of individual freedom, but he cautioned that in this great contest we should have a poor chance to win the favor and allegiance of the many nations who are expected in the future under the right of self-determination to choose their forms of government if we did not demonstrate more adequately than we have done in the immediate past the virtues and efficacy of democracy. He urged a speedy return to the faith of our fathers and to the restraint and disciplines which a righteous self-control imposes upon us.

When lawlessness is advertised as our national characteristic and the nudity of Hollywood is a pictorial representation of America in the battle camps of the world, it is not too likely that the serious-minded people of the earth will choose us as their prototype of good government and a sound society. God grant that the return to wisdom and righteousness through national repentance for which Lincoln and Washington so earnestly pleaded shall come quickly before it is too late, and God grant that the leadership which He has chosen may be prepared to show the way I humbly pray.[333]

—*Stephen L. Richards*

THIS DAY IN AMERICAN HISTORY (1864)

Nevada receives statehood as the 36th state.

The Spiritual Force behind Freedom and Prosperity

Democracy [is] a thing of the spirit. It does not consist in frameworks such as constitutions and presidents and legislatures and statutes and judicial bodies and enforcement officers. You may have all these [bureaucracies, legislative bodies, etc.] completely democratic in form and not have a democracy at all. But no one would argue from this that you could have a living democracy without them. The essence of democracy—its spirit—is by itself an intangible ideal, inert and unfruitful, even though it burn in the hearts of individual men.

Put that flaming spirit, that throbbing, pulsating ideal into a mechanical organization comprising a constitution which defines the limitations on the powers of government; write into it a bill of rights which protects the individual against invasion of his guaranteed privileges by governmental authority; let it provide for the making of laws to which all agree to render obedience; give it an executive authority to carry those laws into effect; set up a tribunal to interpret the laws and resolve disputes between man and man and between citizen and government, and it will carry a nation triumphant from a narrow fringe on the seashore across six thousand miles of continent, plant towns, and cities by the way, set up in them local governments by consent, establish schools, rear industries, subdue the earth and give to one hundred million people more of creature comfort, more of individual self-respect, more of the recognition of human dignity, more independence of action and consequent self-reliance, more liberty of thought and freedom of action than were ever before known to any people during the period of recorded history.[334]

—*Albert E. Bowen*

THIS DAY IN AMERICAN HISTORY (1765)

The Stamp Act goes into effect in Britain's American colonies.

Righteousness Is Fundamental to the Peace and Progress of the World

These are not ordinary days. We live in momentous times. A survey of conditions in the troubled world of today reveals the fact that we have made little if any progress toward that peace and good will which the Savior of mankind taught nineteen centuries ago. Civilized nations of the earth are marshalling their manpower and their material resources for war and for defense on a scale the world has never known before. Forces are abroad in the earth which threaten the overthrow of liberty, of democracy and of our way of life, if not of our very civilization. War, devastating, destructive and barbarous, is scourging the air, the sea and the land. These are anxious days for all of us. . . .

The ingenuity of man seems powerless to stay the dreadful ravages of modern war. The world is in distress; it is struggling in agony because men in their selfishness have forgotten God; they have forsaken the ways of truth, mercy, justice and righteousness. Somehow or other the fate of mankind hangs on faith in the Creator of the world.

The religion of the Latter-day Saints, which is the religion of our Lord and Master Jesus Christ, contains and presents the forces that make for righteousness and peace in the earth. Morality centers in religion. Without its saving power democracy cannot survive. Selfishness, greed, ambition, and lust for power always, if they go unbridled, manifest themselves in contention and bloodshed. Unless these tendencies are chastened and controlled by the spirit written in the Sermon on the Mount, unless the unselfish spirit of the gospel of Jesus Christ finds a place in the hearts of men and manifests itself in their relationship one to another, civilization is sure to decline. Righteousness is fundamental to the peace and progress of the world. How can this spirit be cultivated? What can be done to bring to the world that peace for which we pray? How can we cultivate and make effective the spirit of the Master? These are pertinent questions that should be asked these days.[335]

—*Richard R. Lyman*

THIS DAY IN AMERICAN HISTORY (1889)

North and South Dakota receive statehood
as the 39th and 40th states, respectively.

Communism Shall Have No Place in America

We call upon all Church members to completely eschew communism. The safety of our divinely inspired constitutional government and the welfare of our Church imperatively demand that communism shall have no place in America.

Communism is not a political party nor a political plan under the Constitution; it is a system of government that is the opposite of our constitutional government, and it would be necessary to destroy our government before communism could be set up in the United States.

Communists cannot establish the United Order, nor will communism bring it about. The United Order will be established by the Lord in His own due time and in accordance with the regular prescribed order of the Church.

Furthermore, it is charged by universal report, which is not successfully contradicted or disproved, that communism undertakes to control, if not indeed to proscribe the religious life of the people living within its jurisdiction, and that it even reaches its hand into the sanctity of the family circle itself, disrupting the normal relationship of parent and child, all in a manner unknown and unsanctioned under the constitutional guarantees under which we in America live. Such interference would be contrary to the fundamental precepts of the gospel and to the teachings and order of the Church. Communism being thus hostile to loyal American citizenship and incompatible with true Church membership, of necessity no loyal American citizen and no faithful Church member can be a communist.[336]

—George Albert Smith, J. Reuben Clark, David O. McKay

THIS DAY IN AMERICAN HISTORY (1791)

Vermont adopts the Bill of Rights.

All the Perils That Threaten This Country Shall Be from Within

The whole attention of the world is focused upon the great democracy of the world, America. Shall it stand; shall it survive? Yes, because the Lord God of Heaven has established it. I am not afraid of outside enemies. All the perils that threaten this country shall be from within. There shall never come any disaster nor distress that shall destroy America from the outside, if the peoples of this land shall rally to the standards established by our fathers, and maintain the stability of the Constitution and the law, and the order established in this land wherein our fathers long ago agreed that the will of the majority expressed in laws shall be obeyed by the minority.

Yes, I agree that there are troublesome times, days of sorrow and distress ahead of the world, and that the devil is in the world grasping to maintain his power, yet the Lord God of Heaven has established His kingdom, and He is in the world with it, and it shall be triumphant and victorious. The Lord help us to adhere to these glorious principles, and we shall fulfil the prophecies of old wherein they declare that the ends of the world, the east and the west and the north and the south shall say, "Come ye, and let us go up to the mountain of the Lord, to the house of the God of Jacob; and he will teach us of his ways, and we will walk in his paths." Zion arise and shine. Thy day hath come.

God help us to prove to a world that is doubtful and skeptical about the gospel of Jesus Christ, that in the real gospel, restored with its power and its authority, there is a virility and strength sufficient to meet and to solve human problems, and let us go gloriously toward our destiny, as the Lord hath pointed it out. God help us as Latter-day Saints to be found still standing by these standards and loyally supporting the law and order and the great democracy established here, that it may live for the blessing of all flesh, as the Lord has decreed it; for after days of sorrow and trial and dictatorships, the world will be prepared, by and by, for the fruits and the blessings of the democracy that shall survive in America.[337]

—*Melvin J. Ballard*

THIS DAY IN AMERICAN HISTORY (1979)

Iranian students loyal to Ayatollah Khomeini seize hostages at the U.S. embassy in Tehran, Iran; they are freed 444 days later.

Reminding the People of Our Duty as Members of the Church

We can very well afford to abide by the Constitution of the United States, and to sustain it, and we can afford to believe in the Bible and to obey its ordinances, and to practice them. . . . As I have said, we can afford to treat all men well, and to pray for those which despitefully use us and persecute us.

There are thousands in the world—I have spoken with hundreds I believe—who have made a similar confession—that faith, repentance, baptism, and the laying on of hands for the reception of the Holy Ghost were scriptural principles, that they could not be denied, that the same gospel was preached by Jesus Christ and His Apostles—but I have found among those hundreds very few who were willing to obey those principles. I am happy to say, however, that some few have obeyed them—that I have been the means, in the hands of God, of bringing some to a knowledge of the truth, and I am very thankful for this privilege.[338]

—*John Q. Cannon*

THIS DAY IN AMERICAN HISTORY (1940)

Franklin D. Roosevelt is re-elected U.S. president for an unprecedented third term.

NOVEMBER 6

Resist the Allurements of Sin and Walk in the Path of Righteousness

We cannot and will not lay aside our fealty to the nation at the bidding of political demagogues, religious fanatics, or intolerant despots.

If men and women would only profit by the experience of those who have fallen, they would resist the allurements of sin and walk in the path of righteousness.

Every faithful Latter-day Saint has rejoiced in the abundance of the gifts of the Spirit which He has bestowed; and no promise that was made to the ancient Saints, or that has been made to us, upon the condition of our faithfully obeying the gospel, has been withheld from us. We have been a people greatly blessed of the Lord, and our hearts should swell with gratitude and thanksgiving to our God for His abundant mercies.[339]

—John Taylor, George Q. Cannon, and Joseph F. Smith

THIS DAY IN AMERICAN HISTORY (1860)

Abraham Lincoln is elected as the sixteenth president of the United States.

We Have Been Blessed as a Nation

We consider that we have been blessed as a nation in possessing the freedom and privileges guaranteed by the Constitution of the United States. They have been a rich legacy from our fathers. We consider our form of government superior to any other on the earth.

This gospel makes us free. Was there ever a more free people than the Latter-day Saints are? No, there never was in any age of the world. There is not anything that will give a man joy or consolation, or any blessing temporal or spiritual, but what is within our reach as far as man in a mortal state has a right to receive. When we contemplate the gifts and blessings the gospel of Christ has given to us, we of all men should be the most cheerful, thankful, and faithful, and should honor our calling, and acknowledge the hand of our God in the mercies which we enjoy.

We consider that we have been blessed as a nation in possessing the freedom and privileges guaranteed by the Constitution of the United States. They have been a rich legacy from our fathers. We consider our form of government superior to any other on the earth. It guarantees to us "life, liberty and the pursuit of happiness."[340]

—Wilford Woodruff

THIS DAY IN AMERICAN HISTORY (1916)

Jannette Rankin (Montana) is elected as the first woman to serve in the U.S. House of Representatives.

The King of Kings Shall Reign Politically

The great struggle for religious liberty that is going on in Mexico is also going on in South America. Within the last five years two great nations have established absolute separation of Church and state, and others are struggling to that end. It will come. No power can stay it. The theory that the great dominant church there has, that its head has the right to rule over the Church and state, (and within the last year he has ascended unto that position, wherein he is now king and also the head of the church) is not the spirit of the democracy of South America, nor is it the spirit of the democracy of North America or Mexico. It may be a lingering symbol of that which was once in Europe, but that order of things cannot live in this land, for this is the age of the separation of the Church and the state. Yes, there will come a time when it shall be united again, but not under any earthly man.

I believe that the Lord God Almighty is working not only in this Church but in this nation. Yes, this is the beginning of the realization of Daniel's dream. But I firmly believe too that God, as our scriptures very clearly teach, both the Book of Mormon and the Doctrine and Covenants, raised up this mighty nation of the Gentiles, and that His hand has been in it. He was with the patriot fathers who laid its foundation. He sustained them in their struggles. He was with Lincoln. He has carried the work on by his power, and men have acknowledged God as the King of the land. And so I believe when He comes whose right it is to rule and reign He will come as King of kings, and that is politically, and that He will be Lord of lords, and that is in His Church. I believe that when he comes to rule and reign there will be a union of Church and state under Him whose right it is to rule and reign. But never has that right been given to a mortal man.[341]

—Melvin J. Ballard

THIS DAY IN AMERICAN HISTORY (1889)

Montana receives statehood as the 41st state.

Joseph Smith Was a Real and True American

A wonderful and startling change was wrought when men arose upon these Western shores who dared to say and maintain: We, the people, are the true sovereigns. We choose our rulers, and they are our servants, not our masters, and are accountable to us for the manner in which they govern the commonwealth and administer the laws enacted by our representatives for the general welfare.

That is the American idea, "government of the people, by the people, for the people," as Lincoln expressed it in his famous Gettysburg speech. And nothing proves more conclusively that Joseph Smith, God's prophet, was a real and true American, than his reply to one who inquired of him how he managed to govern a people made up of so many different nationalities, with all their varied languages, customs, and traditions. Said the Prophet: "I teach them correct principles, and they govern themselves." The United States is a republic, in which the people are recognized as the one source of power. The Church of Christ is a theo-democracy, in which God speaks and the people say "Amen." It is the Church of God and His people—The Church of Jesus Christ of Latter-day Saints.

Were I to say that the founders of this nation builded better than they knew, few if any would question the statement. But if, in addition to that, I should voice my conviction that this great government established purposely to favor the coming forth of the Church of Christ in this dispensation—the Dispensation of the Fulness of Times—many would deem my declaration presumptuous and even preposterous. Great movements are generally so regarded in the beginning.[342]

—*Orson F. Whitney*

THIS DAY IN AMERICAN HISTORY (1620)

The *Mayflower* lands at Plymouth, Massachusetts.

The American Republic and Ancient Israel

There has been no king in this country. Do you know that Washington was upon several occasions requested, almost demanded, to assume the role of king, for that was the form of government which was best known to those who established this one. He persistently declined, and the makers of our Constitution saw the wisdom of his action. They recognized too that kings and the so-called divine right of kings were not compatible with the great spirit of liberty and democracy which was to underly the structure of our government. Does it not seem somewhat significant that in the Israelitish form of government, for a period of four hundred and seventy years, there were no kings to rule in Israel, in spite of the repeated demands of the people for a king, that they might be like other nations. They were told that God was their king, and, that no king should rule them so long as they subscribed to the great principles of truth and righteousness which the Lord had laid down for them to follow. . . .

So might be pointed out, if time would permit, a large list and line of comparisons which establish a very close relation between the government which predominated during the time that the children of Israel were governed by their judges, and the government established here. I wonder how many know that in that form of government which prevailed in olden times, there were three departments which are comparable to our three departments of government, namely, the legislative, the executive, and the judicial. Perhaps it is not generally understood that the judiciary held supremacy in the old time as in reality it holds supremacy now. For while the three departments of government are usually said to be co-ordinate, every student of our institutions knows that it is the Supreme Court of the United States which has the last word to say with reference to the interpretation of law and its enforceability in this country. Time will not permit further detail, but there is abundant evidence to warrant the conclusion that the fathers drew liberally on their knowledge of, and training in, the Hebrew scripture, in building the democracy of the New World.[343]

—*Stephen L. Richards*

THIS DAY IN AMERICAN HISTORY (1775)

The Second Continental Congress organizes the Continental Marines, the predecessor of the United States Marine Corps.

Blessings and Privileges Guaranteed by the Constitution

We have been blessed as a nation in possessing the freedom and privileges guaranteed by the Constitution of the United States. . . . It has been a blessing to us as a people, and it is to the whole nation, as far as it is carried out. But in order to fully receive its blessings we have to honor its precepts.

This gospel has been revealed to us. We have received the light of it and rejoice in it. By it and its Author we have been sustained from the commencement until today. The gospel of Christ has never disappointed any man or woman that ever dwelt in the flesh. The God of heaven—the Author of this gospel—has never disappointed anybody who ever proved faithful to its precepts. And if the inhabitants of the earth expect salvation through any other medium they will be disappointed. Whatever salvation they may get, they will not be saved in the celestial kingdom of God. If they have another glory, it will be the glory of the law they keep in the flesh. If a man cannot abide a celestial law, he cannot receive a celestial glory. If a man cannot abide a terrestrial law, he cannot receive a terrestrial glory; and if he cannot abide a telestial law, he cannot receive a telestial glory, but will have to dwell in a kingdom which is not a kingdom of glory. This is according to the revelations of God to us.[344]

—Wilford Woodruff

THIS DAY IN AMERICAN HISTORY (1620)

Passengers on the *Mayflower* sign the Mayflower Compact.

NOVEMBER 12

If Religion Is to Be Saved

The youth who is led to an understanding of nature and of economics and left blind and deaf to the appeals of literature, of art, of morals, and of religion, has been shown but a part of that great environment which is his inheritance as a human being. The school and the college do much, but the school and the college cannot do all. Since Protestantism broke up the solidarity of the ecclesiastical organization in the western world, and since democracy made intermingling of state and church impossible, it has been necessary, if religion is to be saved for men, that the family and the church do their vital cooperative part in a national organization of educational effort.

The school, the family, and the Church are three cooperative educational agencies, each of which has its weight of responsibility to bear. If the family be weakened in respect to its moral and spiritual basis, or if the Church be neglectful of its obligation to offer systematic, continuous, and convincing religious instruction to the young who are within its sphere of influence, there can be no hope for a Christian education or for the powerful perpetuation of the Christian faith in the minds and lives of the next generation and those immediately to follow. We are trustees of a great inheritance. If we abuse or neglect that trust we are responsible before Almighty God for the infinite damage that will be done in the life of individuals and of nations.[345]

—George Albert Smith

THIS DAY IN AMERICAN HISTORY (1954)

Ellis Island closes as an emigration processing facility.

Lead Courageously in Promoting Religious Freedom on the World Stage

Virtually all Western democracies claim to believe in the *principle* of religious freedom. It is the application of the principle that can create controversy. Threats to religious freedom typically arise when religious people and institutions seek to say or do something—or refuse to say or do something—that runs counter to the philosophy or goals of those in power, including political majorities. Religion is often countercultural and thus unpopular. For this reason, religious freedom, even where it is generally supported in principle, is often vigorously opposed in practice.

I encourage you to hold fast to the freedoms you have forged at home and to lead courageously in promoting religious freedom on the world stage. The need to protect and preserve religious liberty—in a fair and balanced way that also protects others' fundamental rights—is acute.

The Church of Jesus Christ of Latter-day Saints is pleased to stand with you and others in this vital effort. Although we are optimistic that our efforts will make a difference, we must make these efforts collectively, since none of us can win this fight alone. . . . Our task will be difficult and require constant vigilance, but it is of utmost importance. . . . May we pursue peace by working together to preserve and protect the freedom of all people to hold and manifest a religion or belief of their choice, whether individually or in community with others, at home or abroad, in public or private, and in worship, observance, practice, and teaching.[346]

—*D. Todd Christofferson*

THIS DAY IN AMERICAN HISTORY (1775)

The Continental Army occupies Montreal, Canada.

Latter-day Saints Will Save the Constitution a Natural Way

We've heard that the Prophet Joseph said something about the time when the Constitution would be in. We don't know just what turn that will take. He also said something about the elders of Israel rising to the challenge and helping to save the Constitution of this land. It's entirely possible that that may come about in a rather natural way. To our young people, as they mature and develop and take their positions in industry and the professions in agriculture clear across this land, they might represent the balance of power in a time of crisis when they'll stand up and defend those eternal principles upon which this Constitution has been established. I've had many evidences of this fact, that the world is willing to pay for the services of young men and women who live the gospel, who maintain our standards. No, the world doesn't live our standards and probably will not, but they're willing to pay for the services of young men and women who do.

So if you're thinking only of getting ahead in the world materially, professionally, in your chosen field, it pays to maintain the standards. And so we want you to be successful in your chosen field, and the Lord also wants you to be successful. He'll do his part if you do your part. He can't help you very much if you don't live according to his plan. Thirdly, we'd like you to become good citizens of this great land in which we live, or any other free nation from which some of you may come. There's so much of a tendency for us to take our citizenship for granted, that all the blessings of freedom and liberty have come to us.[347]

—*Ezra Taft Benson*

THIS DAY IN AMERICAN HISTORY (1993)

Puerto Rico votes against becoming the 51st state.

We Honor the Man That God Honors

Every Latter-day Saint believes that Abraham Lincoln was raised up and inspired of God, and that he reached the Presidency of the United States under the favor of our Heavenly Father.

From my childhood days I have understood that we believe absolutely that the Constitution of our country is an inspired instrument, and that God directed those who created it and those who defended the independence of this nation. Concerning this matter it is my frequent pleasure to quote the statement by Joseph Smith, regarding the Constitution:

"The Constitution of the United States is a glorious standard; it is founded in the wisdom of God. It is a heavenly banner; it is, to all those who are privileged with the sweets of liberty, like the cooling shades and refreshing waters of a great rock in a weary and thirsty land. It is like a great tree under whose branches men from every clime can be shielded from the burning rays of the sun."

And such the Constitution of the United States must be to every faithful Latter-day Saint who lives under its protection.

We honor the man that God honors. We honor Abraham Lincoln because we believe absolutely that God honored him and raised him up to be the instrument in His hands of saving the Constitution and the Union.[348]

—*Heber J. Grant*

THIS DAY IN AMERICAN HISTORY (1777)

The Articles of Confederation are proposed.

In Condemning and Working Against Racism

One way our common ground with others can be undermined is if any contending party sows division and separates communities. In condemning and working against racism, we encourage our students, our teachers, and all our members to avoid extreme or polarizing positions and teachings that undermine the U.S. Constitution and other core institutions.

We know that the Constitution was inspired of God despite its birth defect of slavery. Its inspired principles, including the freedoms of speech and religion, and its authorized amendments have allowed subsequent generations to continue to improve and strengthen the rights of all of its citizens. That is part of our history, and it should not be distorted by trying to substitute other motivations for the Constitution of the United States, as some are doing in our time.

A gospel-centered approach to combating racism empowers all parties to support, apply, and teach the power and light of the gospel of Jesus Christ. The Church has made this positive approach in its efforts, both within its membership and with outside organizations.[349]

—*Dallin H. Oaks and Clark G. Gilbert*

THIS DAY IN AMERICAN HISTORY (1907)

Oklahoma receives statehood as the 46th state.

We Live in a Government Raised Up by the God of Heaven

I know as God lives that if this or any other government departs from the principles of truth, becomes ripened in iniquity, forsakes the Lord, forsakes the principles of life and liberty, the God of heaven will hold it responsible. Judgements will come upon the wicked. When men depart from the principles of truth and cleave unto darkness and wickedness, they reap the whirlwind; they lay the foundation for desolation (JD 25:11, January 6, 1884).

In all the history of the dealings of God with man this one principle, sooner or later, has manifested itself: that virtue exalteth a nation, well sin is a reproach to any people. You will see that this has been manifested in the history of all nations under heaven—in their rise and progress and prosperity, and in their fall and decline and in their final overthrow and destruction. You will find in every instance that sin, error, darkness, falsehood, wrongdoing, have laid the foundation of the overthrow of every nation and city under heaven from the foundation of the world until the present time. What men sow they will reap, and what measure they measure to others will be measured unto them (JD 25:6–7, January 6, 1884).

The American Constitution. I am an American citizen; a great many of this group, I hope, are. I was born in the state of Connecticut, and many of the New England forms and teachings in our childhood, sixty-five years ago, we're good to receive and live by. But what I want to say is: we live in a government raised up by the God of heaven.[350]

—Wilford Woodruff

THIS DAY IN AMERICAN HISTORY (1915)

A German submarine sinks the British ocean liner *Lusitania,* killing 128 Americans and influencing the U. S. declaration of World War I.

Many Will React to the Failures of Too Much Government by Calling for Even More Government

In any event, possessed of such insights, we Latter-day Saints are often responded to a little like John the Baptist. Minus such fundamental insights, I fear that, as conditions worsen, many will react to the failures of too much government by calling for even more government. Then there will be more and more lifeboats launched because fewer and fewer citizens know how to swim. Unlike some pendulums, political pendulums do not swing back automatically; they must be pushed. History is full of instances when people have waited in vain for pendulums to swing back.

A little experience with federal and state bureaucracies has taught me that such bureaucracies are inhabited by basically good civil servants, onto whom voters have pushed too much power for their good or ours. What we unwittingly court in such circumstances is learning again, painfully, that "almost all" men can't handle authority without abusing it. Whether or not the American people, regardless of party, can tame their governments is yet to be determined, but sunset laws alone will not do it. If citizen appetites, once aroused, merely look to a new agency to do what a disestablished agency once did, it won't be enough. Addicts can always find new pushers.[351]

—*Neal A. Maxwell*

THIS DAY IN AMERICAN HISTORY (1883)

American and Canadian Railroads standardize four standard time zones:
Eastern, Central, Mountain, and Pacific
(replacing over 100 hundred previous time zones).

The Lord Has Watched Over America with Jealous Care

No nation has been more greatly blessed than has the United States. We live in a land which has been called choice above all other lands by divine pronouncement. The Lord has watched over it with a jealous care and has commanded its people to serve Him lest His wrath be kindled against them and His blessings be withdrawn. Our government came into existence through divine guidance. The inspiration of the Lord rested upon the patriots who established it, and inspired them through the dark days of their struggle for independence and through the critical period which followed that struggle when they framed our glorious Constitution which guarantees to all the self-evident truth proclaimed in the Declaration of Independence, "that all men are created equal: that they are endowed by their Creator with certain inalienable rights: that among these are life, liberty, and the pursuit of happiness." That is to say, it is the right of every soul to have equal and unrestricted justice before the law, equal rights to worship according to the dictates of conscience and to labor according to the individual inclinations, independently of coercion or compulsion. That this might be, the Lord has said, "I established the Constitution of this land, by the hands of wise men whom I raised up unto this very purpose and redeemed the land by the shedding of blood" (D&C 101:80).

The founders of this nation were men of humble faith. Many of them saw in vision a glorious destiny for our government, provided we would faithfully continue in the path of justice and right with contrite spirits and humble hearts, accepting the divine truths which are found in the holy scriptures. The appeal of these men has echoed down the passing years with prophetic warning to the succeeding generations, pleading with them to be true to all these standards which lay at the foundation of our government. This country was founded as a Christian nation, with the acceptance of Jesus Christ as the Redeemer of the world. [352]

—*Joseph Fielding Smith*

THIS DAY IN AMERICAN HISTORY (1778)

New Jersey Ratifies the Articles of Confederation.

NOVEMBER 20

George Washington Was an Inspired Instrument of the Almighty

We can trace the providences of the Almighty in raising up certain individuals to establish religious organizations, and we see in these things the workings of the Spirit of God for the general interest of the human family. We look upon George Washington, the father of our country, as an inspired instrument of the Almighty; we can see the all-inspiring Spirit operating upon him. And upon his co-workers in resisting oppression, and in establishing the thirteen colonies as a confederacy; and then again the workings of the same Spirit upon those men who established the Constitution of the United States. In a revelation contained in the Book of Doctrine and Covenants the Lord says: "And for this purpose have I established the Constitution of this land by the hands of wise men, whom I raised up unto this very purpose." We see the hand of the Lord in these things.[353]

—*Lorenzo Snow*

THIS DAY IN AMERICAN HISTORY (1789)

New Jersey adopts the Bill of Rights.

There Is No Power beneath the Heavens That Can Remove Zion Out of Her Place

We have a constitution that was given by inspiration from God to man. . . . It is beyond the power of man to destroy the principles of the Constitution. . . . The God of heaven will maintain them until Jesus Christ comes in the clouds of heaven to set up His throne in Jerusalem, and to reign on the earth a thousand years. . . . There is no power beneath the heavens that can remove Zion out of her place, or destroy this Church and kingdom, as long as the people do the will of God, for He will sustain, them, and overrule the acts of their enemies for their good and for the final triumph of His truth in the earth.

We should be men and women of faith, valiant for the truth as it has been revealed and committed into our hand. We should be men and women of integrity to God, and to His holy priesthood, true to him and true to one another. We should not permit houses and land, gold and silver, nor any of this world's goods to draw us aside from pursuing the great object which God has sent us to perform. Our aim is high, our destiny is high, and we should never disappoint our Father, nor the heavenly hosts who are watching over us. We should not disappoint the millions in the spirit world, who too are watching over us with an interest and anxiety that have hardly entered into our hearts to conceive of. These are great and mighty things which God requires of us. We would not be worthy of salvation, we would not be worthy of eternal lives in the kingdom of our God, if anything could turn us away from the truth or from the love of it. The Lord told Joseph that He would prove him, whether he would abide in his covenant or not, even unto death. He did prove him; and although he had the whole world to contend against, and the treachery of false friends to withstand, although his whole life was a scene of trouble and anxiety and care, yet, in all his afflictions, his imprisonments, the mobbings and ill-treatment he passed through, he was ever true to his God, and true to his friends.[354]

—*Wilford Woodruff*

THIS DAY IN AMERICAN HISTORY (1789)

North Carolina ratifies the Constitution 194–77
and receives statehood as the 12th state.

Many of the Prophecies Referring to America's Preservation Are Conditional

Many of the prophecies referring to America's preservation are conditional. That is, if we do our duty we can be preserved, and if not, then we shall be destroyed. This means that a good deal of the responsibility lies with the priesthood of this Church as to what happens to America and as to how much tragedy can be avoided if we do act now.

And now as to the last neutralizer that the devil used most effectively—it is simply this: "Don't do anything in the fight for freedom until the Church sets up its own specific program to save the Constitution." This brings us right back to the scripture about the slothful servants who will not do anything until they are "compelled in all things." Maybe the Lord will never set up a specific Church program for the purpose of saving the Constitution. Perhaps if He set one up at this time it might split the Church asunder, and perhaps He does not want that to happen yet, for not all the wheat and tares are fully ripe.[355]

—*Ezra Taft Benson*

THIS DAY IN AMERICAN HISTORY (1889)

North and South Dakota receive statehood
as the 39th and 40th states, respectively.

We May Be Dissatisfied with the Decision of Judges

I hope with all my soul that the members of The Church of Jesus Christ of Latter-day Saints will be loyal in their very hearts and souls, to the principles of the Constitution of our country. From them we have derived the liberty that we enjoy. They have been the means of guaranteeing to the foreigner that has come within our gates, and to the native born, and to all the citizens of this country, the freedom and liberty that we possess. We cannot go back upon such principles as these. We may go back upon those who fail to execute the law as they should. We may be dissatisfied with the decision of judges, and may desire to have them removed out of their places. But the law provides ways and means for all these things to be done under the Constitution of our country, and it is better for us to abide the evils that we have than to fly to greater evils that we know not what the results will be.[356]

—*Joseph F. Smith*

THIS DAY IN AMERICAN HISTORY (1786)

New Jersey selects five delegates to the Constitutional Convention.

We Must Make Our Influence Felt by Our Vote, Our Letters, and Our Advice

We must be righteous and moral. We must live the gospel principles—all of them. We have no right to expect a higher degree of morality from those who represent us than what we ourselves are. To live a higher law means we will not seek to receive what we have not earned by our own labor. It means we will remember that government owes us nothing. It means we will keep the laws of the land. It means we will look to God as our Lawgiver and the source of our liberty.

We must learn the principles of the Constitution and then abide by its precepts. Have we read the Constitution and pondered it? Are we aware of its principles? Could we defend it? Can we recognize when a law is constitutionally unsound? The Church will not tell us how to do this, but we are admonished to do it.

We must become involved in civic affairs. As citizens of this republic, we cannot do our duty and be idle spectators. It is vital that we follow this counsel from the Lord: "Honest men and wise men should be sought for diligently, and good men and wise men ye should observe to uphold; otherwise whatsoever is less than these cometh of evil" (D&C 98:10). Note the qualities that the Lord demands in those who are to represent us. They must be good, wise, and honest. We must be concerted in our desires and efforts to see men and women represent us who possess all three of these qualities.

We must make our influence felt by our vote, our letters, and our advice. We must be wisely informed and let others know how we feel. We must take part in local precinct meetings and select delegates who will truly represent our feelings.[357]

—*Ezra Taft Benson*

THIS DAY IN AMERICAN HISTORY (1954)

The First Air Force One presidential airplane is christened.

Freedom of Religion Is Vital to Express Our Core Convictions

The other First Amendment right protecting religion forbids the government from enacting laws "prohibiting the free exercise" of religion. Notice the word *exercise*. It protects the right to "exercise" religion in our daily lives—not just to believe whatever we like or to worship privately in our homes and chapels, but to live openly and freely according to our faith as long as we respect the fundamental rights of others.

The First Amendment's protection against an established religion and its guarantee of the free exercise of religion are not the only freedoms that make religious liberty possible. The First Amendment's freedom of speech and press and assembly, plus the freedom to petition the government for redress of grievances, all ensure that religious people and institutions can function freely and openly in our society as equal citizens.

The right to exercise religion would be seriously diminished if we couldn't say what we believe. Fortunately, in common with all Americans, religious believers and organizations are entitled to the freedom of speech. Their right to speak on matters of public concern is beyond dispute. The Supreme Court has taught "that private religious speech, far from being a First Amendment orphan, is as fully protected under the Free Speech Clause as secular private expression."[358] Religious speech cannot be singled out for government suppression. Nor is there any question that churches and other religious organizations—not just individuals—hold the right of free speech too.

To be effective, the freedom to speak must also include the freedom to publish one's opinions. Whether communicated through traditional means, such as books, newspapers, and television, or through the global medium of the Internet, religious voices cannot be silenced any more than other points of view. All of these rights—including the freedom of peaceful assembly—are indispensable to what we mean by religious freedom.[359]

—D. Todd Christofferson

THIS DAY IN AMERICAN HISTORY (1783)

British troops leave New York City.

NOVEMBER 26

If the Constitution Be Saved At All

It is said that Brother Joseph in his lifetime declared that the elders of this Church should step forth at a particular time when the Constitution would be in danger, and rescue it, and save it. This may be so; but I do not recollect that he said exactly so. I believe he said something like this—that the time would come when the Constitution and the country would be in danger of an overthrow; and said he, "If the Constitution be saved at all, it will be by the elders of this church." I believe this is about the language as nearly as I can recollect.

The question is whether it will be saved at all, or not. I do not know that it matters to us whether it is or not; the Lord will provide for and take care of His people, if we do every duty, and fear and honour him, and keep His commandments; and He will not leave us without a constitution.[360]

—*Orson Hyde*

THIS DAY IN AMERICAN HISTORY (1791)

George Washington holds the first presidential cabinet meeting in his home in Philadelphia, Pennsylvania.

The Devil Knows That if the Elders of Israel Should Ever Wake Up, They Could Step Forth and Help Preserve Freedom

Now where do we stand in this struggle, and what are we doing about it? The devil knows that if the elders of Israel should ever wake up, they could step forth and help preserve freedom and extend the gospel. Therefore, the devil has concentrated, and to a large extent successfully, on neutralizing much of the priesthood. He has reduced them to sleeping giants. His arguments are clever. Here are a few samples.

First: "We really haven't received much instruction about freedom," the devil says. This is a lie, for we have been warned time and again. No prophet of the Lord has ever issued more solemn warning than President David O. McKay. . . . "You want to be loved by everyone," says the devil, "and this freedom battle is so controversial you might be accused of engaging in politics." Of course, the government has penetrated so much of our lives that one can hardly speak for freedom without being accused of being political. Some might even call the war in heaven a political struggle—certainly it was controversial. Yet the valiant entered it with Michael. Those who support only the popular principles of the gospel have their reward. And those who want to lead the quiet, retiring life but still expect to do their full duty can't have it both ways. . . .

"Wait until it becomes popular to do," says the devil, "or, at least, until everybody in the Church agrees on what should be done." But this fight for freedom might never become popular in our day. And if you wait until everybody agrees in this church, you will be waiting through the second coming of the Lord. Would you have hesitated to follow the inspired counsel of the Prophet Joseph Smith simply because some weak men disagreed with him? God's living mouthpiece has spoken to us—are we for him or against him? In spite of our prophets' opposition to increased federal aid and compulsory unionism, some Church members still champion these freedom-destroying programs. Where do you stand? [361]

—*Ezra Taft Benson*

THIS DAY IN AMERICAN HISTORY (1901)

The U.S. Army War College is established in Washington, D.C.

If You Want Changes, Go to the Polls on Election Day

Latter-day Saints should have nothing to do with secret combinations and groups antagonistic to the constitutional law of the land, which the Lord "suffered to be established," and which "should be maintained for the rights and protection of all flesh, according to just and holy principles."

Of course there are errors in government which some would correct. Certainly there are manifest injustices and inequalities, and there will always be such in any government in the management of which enter the frailties of human nature. If you want changes, go to the polls on election day, express yourself as an American citizen, and thank the Lord for the privilege that is your to have a say as to who shall serve you in public office.

Next to being one in worshiping God, there is nothing in this world upon which this Church should be more united than in upholding and defending the Constitution of the United States![362]

—David O. McKay

THIS DAY IN AMERICAN HISTORY (1943)

President Franklin D. Roosevelt, Winston Churchill, and Joseph Stalin hold a strategy conference.

God's Base of Operations Will Not Be Destroyed

God will not permit America, His base of operations, to be destroyed. He has promised protection to this land if we will but serve the God of the land. He has also promised protection to the righteous even, if necessary, to send fire from heaven to destroy their enemies (1 Nephi 22:2).

No, God's base of operations will not be destroyed. But it may be weakened and made less effective. One of the first rules of war strategy—and we are at war with the adversary and his agents—is to protect the base of operations. This we must do if we are to build up the kingdom throughout the world and safeguard our God-given freedom.

To protect this base we must protect the soul of America—we must return to a love and respect for the basic spiritual concepts upon which this nation has been established. We must study the Constitution and the writings of the Founding Fathers. Yes, we must protect the Lord's base of operations by moving from unsound economic policies which encourage creeping socialism and its companion, insidious, atheistic communism.

If we are to protect this American base, we must realize that all things, including information disseminated by our schools, churches, and government, should be judged according to the words of the prophets, especially the living prophet. This procedure coupled with the understanding which will come through the Spirit of the Lord, if we are living in compliance with the scriptures, is the only sure foundation and basis of judgment. Any other course of action leaves us muddled, despondent, wandering in shades of gray, easy targets for Satan.

The mission the Lord has proffered and outlined for America and for his divinely restored Church. Yes, this is a choice land—a nation with a prophetic history. God bless America and all the free world. And may God protect His latter-day base of operation that his glorious message of salvation may go forth to all the world.[363]

—*Ezra Taft Benson*

THIS DAY IN AMERICAN HISTORY (1887)

The U.S. receives naval rights to Pearl Harbor, Hawaii.

Because They Rejected the Words of Life

All you now know can scarcely be called a preface to the sermon that will be preached with fire and sword, tempests, earthquakes, hail, rain, thunders and lightnings, and fearful destruction. What matters the destruction of a few railway cars? You will hear of magnificent cities, now idolized by the people, sinking in the earth, entombing the inhabitants. The sea will heave itself beyond its bounds, engulfing mighty cities. Famine will spread over the nations, and nation will rise up against nation, kingdom against kingdom, and state against states, in our own country and in foreign lands; and they will destroy each other, caring not for the blood and lives of their neighbors, or their families, or for their own lives.

They will be like the Jaredites who preceded the Nephites upon this continent, and will destroy each other to the last man, through the anger that the devil will place in their hearts, because they rejected the words of life and are given over to Satan to do whatever he listeth to do with them. You may think that the little you hear of now is grievous; yet the faithful of God's people will see days that will cause them to close their eyes because of the sorrow that will come upon the wicked nations. The hearts of the faithful will be filled with pain and anguish for them.[364]

—*Brigham Young*

THIS DAY IN AMERICAN HISTORY (1782)

British and Americans sign preliminary Articles of Peace.

A Scene of Bloodshed That Had No Parallel

And now I am prepared to say by the authority of Jesus Christ, that not many years shall pass away before the United States shall present such a scene of bloodshed as has not a parallel in the history of our nation; pestilence, hail, famine, and earthquake will sweep the wicked of this generation from off the face of the land, to open and prepare the way for the return of the lost tribes of Israel from the north country.[365]

I saw men hunting the lives of their own sons, and brother murdering brother, women killing their own daughters, and daughters seeking the lives of their mothers. I saw armies arrayed against armies. I saw blood, desolation, fires. The Son of Man has said that the mother shall be against the daughter, and the daughter against the mother. These things are at our doors. They will follow the Saints of God from city to city. Satan will rage, and the spirit of the devil is now enraged. I know not how soon these things will take place; but with a view of them, shall I cry peace? No; I will lift up my voice and testify of them. How long you will have good crops, and the famine be kept off, I do not know; when the fig tree leaves, know then that summer is nigh at hand.[366]

—Joseph Smith, Jr.

THIS DAY IN AMERICAN HISTORY (1961)

The U.S. holds the first military draft since World War II.

America Is an Asylum for the Oppressed of All Nations

We find no fault with its institutions, neither do we particularly object to its form of government; but it is its administration, and the way its institutions and laws have been abused. The way it is now and has for years past been administered has founded the cause of complaint. It recognizes the principle of self-government, that the people have the right to control. Of that principle we have long been apprised, but it has never been extended to us as a people. Through the arts and plans of politicians, they have managed to deprive territories of that which is given to the states. This is contrary to the genius of the Constitution which gives the people the right to choose their own rulers: taxation should only be exacted where representation is allowed. These privileges have been withheld from this, as well as from other territories; and the pattern given for this territory in the organic act is not materially different from any other. Our offense has been that we have asked for those of our own choosing to rule us. It has been the case, it is true, that they have chosen persons from the states to hold offices in all the territories, and ostensibly they have made no difference; but this should be considered, that the appointing power has given others the opportunity of making known their preference, and such wishes have generally been considered, with the exception of the people of this territory.

I am now speaking of the past. Hitherto it has been as I have now mentioned. This government has been partial in this and in many other respects, and has no real claim upon our affections; but still we seek to preserve those institutions and to keep sacred those wise provisions which are embodied in the Constitution as it was formed by our fathers; and perhaps we are the only people that do seek the salvation of our country at the present time; and it will finally be shown that we are the only people that will stand by its principles, and make it what it was intended to be—an asylum for the oppressed of all nations.[367]

—*Daniel H. Wells*

THIS DAY IN AMERICAN HISTORY (1787)

Pennsylvania ratifying convention ends.

A Nation of Destiny and Divine Purpose

This nation did not come into being by chance. God declared that the gentiles who came here were to be brought out of captivity by His hand. The prophecies previously quoted concerning the establishment of this nation have been fulfilled to the letter. The people coming here in the beginning did so to find religious freedom. Nevertheless, they were subjected to tyrannical rule, unjust demands, and no representation. They had lost the opportunities, the privileges, the religious freedom and liberty which impelled them to settle in this new land.

The colonists became an aroused group because of oppression; therefore, the time had arrived in the economy of God for the people to break off the yoke of domination which subjected them to these unjust and intolerable conditions. The Lord, knowing beforehand the events which would set the pattern for independence, raised up strong and valiant men to meet this hour of crisis and challenge. The Declaration of Independence came from a determined people. The successful Revolutionary War which followed united the colonies; and the gentile nation of destiny and of divine purpose, as foretold by the prophets, was born. A Constitution was needed to set forth the purposes, obligations, and the guide lines for the new nation. God was prepared and ready and did not neglect this newborn nation which he had ordained to be established thousands of years previously.

God gave the men chosen to formulate the Constitution the inspiration of heaven to guide them. It becomes, therefore, an enduring document for this nation. It is not the prerogative of man to change its basic and fundamental principles and concepts.[368]

—*Delbert L. Stapley*

THIS DAY IN AMERICAN HISTORY (1818)

Illinois receives statehood as the 21st state.

We Should Continue to Come to the Aid of Patriots

We all should know by now what President McKay has said about liberty-loving people's greatest responsibility. We've heard him tell of our drift toward socialism and communism. We know of his feelings regarding recent tragic decisions of the Supreme Court. We know the Church's position supporting right to work laws and the Church's opposition to programs of federal aid to education. These and many more things has President McKay told us that involve the great struggle against state slavery and the anti-Christ. Now, inasmuch as all these warnings have come through the only mouthpiece of the Lord on the earth today there is one major question we should ask ourselves. Assuming we are living a life so we can know, then what does the Holy Spirit have to say about it?

We are under obligation to answer this question. God will hold us responsible. Let us not be deceived in the sifting days ahead. Let us rally together on principle behind the prophet as guided by the promptings of the Spirit.

We should continue to speak out for freedom and against socialism and communism as President McKay has consistently admonished us. We should continue to come to the aid of patriots, programs and organizations which are trying to save our Constitution, through every legal and moral means possible.

God has not left us in darkness regarding these matters. We have the scriptures ancient and modern. We have a living prophet, and we may obtain the Spirit.[369]

—Ezra Taft Benson

THIS DAY IN AMERICAN HISTORY (1945)

The U.S. Senate approves American participation in the United Nations.

Speak Optimistically and Enthusiastically about America

This church is one of the most powerful agencies for the progress of the world, and we should all bear our testimonies that we must all sound with one voice. We must tell the world how we feel about this land and this nation and should bear our testimonies about the great mission and destiny that it has. These are the subjects we should be talking about . . . and if we do this, we will help turn the tide of this great country and lessen the influence of the pessimists. We must be careful that we do not say or do anything that will further weaken the country. It is the negative pessimistic comments about the nation that do as much harm as anything to the country today. We who carry these sacred responsibilities must preach the gospel of peace, and peace can only come by overcoming the things of the world. Now, we must be the dynamic force that will help turn the tide of fear and pessimism.

I think our people are just waiting for somebody to tell them the way to go. Our people are like soldiers in the ranks. They are waiting for us as leaders to tell them which way to go, and brethren, we must tell them in a positive way what they should be doing. This is the Lord's way, as so we should not be concerned about finding out what is wrong with America, but we should be finding what is right about America and should be speaking optimistically and enthusiastically about America.[370]

—*Harold B. Lee*

THIS DAY IN AMERICAN HISTORY (1933)

The 21st Amendment repeals the 18th Amendment to the U.S. Constitution.

We Should Not Be Led Astray by Fallacies

It is pleasing to me as a member of the Church to know that our Heavenly Father is interested in us, and in our government. . . .

In these days of confusion, when the Constitution of our country is assailed, by those who have no understanding of the purpose of God regarding this great country, it behooves those who do understand to consider seriously and faithfully, the benefits that will flow to us by honoring and sustaining the government that was reared under the direction of our Heavenly Father.

We are a peculiar people in many ways, and in this particularly are we peculiar, in that we believe that the Constitution of the United States was inspired by our Heavenly Father, and He has told us that He raised up the very men who should frame the Constitution of the United States. Knowing that, we should not be led astray by the fallacies of individuals whose selfishness inclines them to attack that which our Heavenly Father has prepared for the people of this land.[371]

—*George Albert Smith*

THIS DAY IN AMERICAN HISTORY (1865)

The 13th Amendment, abolishing slavery, is ratified.

Let Us Awaken to Our Responsibilities—and to Our Opportunities

Now I know that Moscow has ordered that all anti-communists are to be attacked and discredited in every way possible. I know the Communist Party of the United States has issued a similar mandate. This does not disturb me at all. It should be expected. Meanwhile we should pursue a calm and steady course. We should expose to the light of public inquiry hose forces which would destroy our country and our way of life. We should pay no attention to the recommendations of men who call the Constitution an eighteenth-century agrarian document—who apologize for capitalism and free enterprise. . . .

My own political and economic creed is a simple one. I commend it to you: I am for freedom and against slavery. I am for social progress and against socialism. I am for a dynamic economy and against waste. I am for the private competitive market and against unnecessary government intervention. . . .

Let us awaken to our responsibilities—and to our opportunities. I love America. I know you do. God and our children will judge us for what we do with our land and our liberties. [372]

—Ezra Taft Benson

THIS DAY IN AMERICAN HISTORY (1787)

The Delaware ratifying convention ends; Delaware ratifies the Constitution 30–0 and receives Statehood as the first state.

DECEMBER 8

Only Wise Men and Women Can Maintain the Constitution

I believe that we should think seriously about the Constitution and rededicate ourselves to understanding and living by the principles it stands for. As the Savior raised up wise men to establish this tremendous ideal of government, only wise men and women can maintain it. If we do not practice the ideals of the Constitution, we can become anonymous and ineffective.

Our forefathers believed that we should always know what is going on in government and should do our best to keep it relatively small and dedicated to protecting each of us in the enjoyment of life, liberty, and property. We must insist that our government refrain from running our individual lives, so long as we are law-abiding. We must not permit government to take responsibilities that we should bear for ourselves.[373]

—*Joseph B. Wirthlin*

THIS DAY IN AMERICAN HISTORY (1941)

President Roosevelt delivers his famous "A Day Which Will Live in Infamy" speech.

Teach the Truth

In dedicated spaces, like temples, houses of worship, and our own homes, we should teach the truth and the commandments plainly and thoroughly as we understand them from the plan of salvation revealed in the restored gospel. Our right to do so is protected by constitutional guarantees of freedom of speech and religion, as well as by the privacy that is honored even in countries without formal constitutional guarantees.

In public, what religious persons say and do involves other considerations. The free exercise of religion covers most public actions, but it is subject to qualifications necessary to accommodate the beliefs and practices of others. Laws can prohibit behavior that is generally recognized as wrong or unacceptable, like sexual exploitation, violence, or terrorist behavior, even when done by extremists in the name of religion. Less grievous behaviors, even though unacceptable to some believers, may simply need to be endured if legalized by what a Book of Mormon prophet called "the voice of the people" (Mosiah 29:26).

On the subject of public discourse, we should all follow the gospel teachings to love our neighbor and avoid contention. Followers of Christ should be examples of civility. We should love all people, be good listeners, and show concern for their sincere beliefs. Though we may disagree, we should not be disagreeable. Our stands and communications on controversial topics should not be contentious. We should be wise in explaining and pursuing our positions and in exercising our influence. In doing so, we ask that others not be offended by our sincere religious beliefs and the free exercise of our religion. We encourage all of us to practice the Savior's Golden Rule: "Whatsoever ye would that men should do to you, do ye even so to them" (Matthew 7:12).

When our positions do not prevail, we should accept unfavorable results graciously and practice civility with our adversaries. In any event, we should be persons of goodwill toward all, rejecting persecution of any kind, including persecution based on race, ethnicity, religious belief or nonbelief, and differences in sexual orientation.[374]

—*Dallin H. Oaks*

THIS DAY IN AMERICAN HISTORY (1803)

The 12th Amendment to the U.S. Constitution
is proposed for Ratification.

DECEMBER 10

The Only Way to Enjoy Peace Is by Sustaining Constitutional Law

I felt that on this occasion, and at this time, when there is so much unrest in our land, that I would like to read to you what our people conceived to be their duty to the government under which they lived. We still believe that there is only one way whereby we may enjoy peace and happiness, and that is by observing the constitutional law of our land, and by sustaining that constitutional law that was inspired by our heavenly Father at the inception of this great government. There are those who are misguided in the belief that they may organize groups and take into their own hands the punishment of those who have differed from them in their ideas of religion or government. We may well understand that men who do that come in conflict with the orderly system that our heavenly Father has decreed should govern the children of men I am grateful that I belong to a Church that has been directed by our Heavenly Father to observe the constitutional law of the land.[375]

—*George Albert Smith*

THIS DAY IN AMERICAN HISTORY (1817)

Mississippi receives statehood as the 20th state.

We Trace the Hand of the Almighty

We see the providences of God in all things; we see them in raising up different communities and establishments in the world for the general and universal benefit of mankind. We see the providences of God in raising up a Luther and a John Wesley; we see the providences of God in all the Christian organizations and communities; we trace the hand of the Almighty in framing the constitution of our land, and believe that the Lord raised up men purposely for the accomplishment of this object, raised them up and inspired them to frame the constitution of the United States. We trace the hand of God, His Spirit, His workings upon and among all classes of people, whether Christian or heathen, that His providences may be carried out, and that His designs, formed before the morning stars sang together or the foundations of the earth were laid, may be ultimately fulfilled. He slackens not his hand, He gives not up His designs nor His purposes; but His work is one eternal round. We trace the hand of the Almighty and we see His Spirit moving in all communities for their good, restraining and encouraging, establishing governments and nations, inspiring men to take a course that shall most advance His purposes until the set time shall come when He shall work more fully and effectually for the accomplishment of His designs, and when sorrow, wickedness, evil, crime, bitter disappointments, vexation, distress and poverty shall cease and be no more known, and the salvation and happiness of His children be secured, when the earth shall be rolled back into its pristine purity and the inhabitants thereof dwell upon it in perfect peace and happiness.[376]

—*Lorenzo Snow*

THIS DAY IN AMERICAN HISTORY (1816)

Indiana receives statehood as the 19th state.

DECEMBER 12

Democracy Need Not Drive Men toward Despair

Today we have a plethora of Paul Reveres warning us about the coming of so many dangers, and it is difficult to sort out the crucial warnings from the false warnings. The very decibel level of multiple warnings has the consequence of turning many of us off

I am intrigued by the scriptures that describe a time when men's hearts shall fail them. Presumably, the despair level at that point in human history will be so great that many will doubt, and doubt deeply, man's capacity to cope with the challenges around him. But democracy need not drive men toward despair; in fact, it offers them an excellent way of avoiding the consequence. If the "voice of the people" chooses wisely.[377]

—*Neal A. Maxwell*

THIS DAY IN AMERICAN HISTORY (1787)

Pennsylvania ratifies the Constitution and receives statehood as the second state.

We Will Stand by the Constitution

We frequently hear, "You are not loyal." Who is it that talks of loyalty? Those who are stabbing the country to its very vitals. Are they the men that are loyal? Those who are sowing the seeds of discord; those who are perjuring themselves before high heaven and the country they profess to serve? Are these the loyal men? If so, God preserve me and this people from such loyalty from this time, henceforth, and forever. We look at these things from another standpoint, and view them in a different light entirely from most others.

We had a grand celebration yesterday. I was there, and much pleased to see the brethren turn out as they did. I was glad to hear the remarks of Judge Titus. They were very good; very patriotic. I wish the principles then advanced could always be carried out; that is the worst I wish. Sometimes people think we are acting almost hypocritically when we talk of loyalty to the constitution of the United States. We will stand by that constitution and uphold the flag of our country when everybody else forsakes it. We cannot shut our eyes to things transpiring around us. We have our reason, and God has revealed unto us many things; but never has he revealed anything in opposition to those institutions and that Constitution, no, never; and, another thing, he never will. [378]

—*John Taylor*

THIS DAY IN AMERICAN HISTORY (1774)

Paul Revere and Wentworth Cheswell ride to Portsmouth to warn of British warships.

DECEMBER 14

The Constitution Is Deserving of Our Prolonged Spiritual Applause

Illustrative of the interplay of man's agency and God's supremacy, the scriptures contain many glistening jewels over which we pass too lightly. The compressed truth in these doctrinal diamonds defies our present and full comprehension. . . . One such cluster has to do with the unique founding of this American nation, wherein the Lord revealed that He had established the Constitution of the United States "by the hands of wise men whom [He] raised into this very purpose" (D&C 101:80). No parallel declaration exists with regard to the constitution of any other nation, ours being the first written constitution. . . . If pondered—both as to its substance and the miraculous process of its coming forth—the Constitution is deserving of our prolonged spiritual applause.

Think of all the Lord oversaw, including the shaping events which of necessity occurred long before the Constitution was written, ratified, and implemented. First, it was necessary for God to cause a handful of highly talented and "wise" individuals to be "raised up" (D&C 101:80). Second, they needed to live on one geographic area on this planet. Third, this contiguity also had to occur within a short time frame! Fourth, a citizenry had to be prepared who wanted and would then implement self-governance. This incubation was as important as the later ratification. Thus, the words raised up involve multiple and concurrent conditions. Without similar incubation, establishing modern republics and democracies has not proven easy. Founders were required but also foundational building blocks. Otherwise, holding elections could have been cathartic but not, finally, consequential.[379]

—Neal A. Maxwell

THIS DAY IN AMERICAN HISTORY (1819)

Alabama receives statehood the 22nd state.

Maintain Its Principles and the Rights of All Men of Every Color

We will trust in the living God, who is the Savior of all men, especially of those that believe. We will do right, we will treat all men right and will maintain every institution of our country that is according to the Constitution of the United States, and the laws thereof, and we will sustain them. By and by, you will find they will tear the Constitution to shreds, as they have begun now; they won't have to begin; they have started long ago to rend the Constitution of our country in pieces; and in doing so they are letting loose and encouraging a principle which will re-act upon themselves with terrible consequences; for if law-makers and administrators can afford to trample upon justice, equity, and the Constitution of this country, they will find thousands and tens of thousands who are willing to follow in their wake in the demolition of the rights of man, and the destruction of all principles of justice, and the safeguards of the nation; but we will stand by and maintain its principles and the rights of all men of every color, and every clime; we will cleave to the truth, live our religion and keep the commandments of God, and God will bless us in time and throughout the eternities that are to come.[380]

—*John Taylor*

THIS DAY IN AMERICAN HISTORY (1791)

The Bill of Rights is added to the Constitution in the form of Ten Amendments.

Fundamental Principles Which Have Allowed the United States to Progress So Rapidly and Yet Remain Free

What are these fundamental principles which have allowed the United States to progress so rapidly and yet remain free? First, a written Constitution clearly defining the limits of government so that government will not become more powerful than the people.

Second, a sound economic system. Third, building an open society where each individual enjoys the greatest opportunity to improve himself, to travel, to become educated, to invent, to compete, to build, to speak, to worship, and to pursue happiness in whatever way the individual finds most satisfying and worthwhile.

Fourth, assigning government the role of referee rather than competitor—giving it enough power to provide peace, order and security but not enough power to rob the people of their liberty or take away their property "without due process of law."

Of course, it immediately becomes apparent that if certain people wanted to seize control of private property, if they wanted to nationalize the land, if they wanted to have the government take over all the industries, the schools, the transportation complex and communications network, the way to do it would be by "due process of law." Therefore, certain people have set out to do this very thing. [381]

—*Ezra Taft Benson*

THIS DAY IN AMERICAN HISTORY (1773)

Colonists stage the Boston Tea Party.

When Men Begin to Tear Away with Impunity One Plank after Another from Our Constitution

We see a policy being introduced to listen to the clamor of mobs and of unprincipled men who know not of what they speak, nor whereof they affirm, and when men begin to tear away with impunity one plank after another from our Constitution, by and by we shall find that we are struggling with the wreck and ruin of the system which the forefathers of this nation sought to establish in the interests of humanity. But it is for us still to sustain these glorious principles of liberty bequeathed by the founders of this nation, still to rally round the flag of the Union, still to maintain all correct principles, granting the utmost extent of liberty to all people of all grades and of all nations.

If other people see fit to violate these sacred principles, we must uphold them in their entirety, in their purity, and be patriotic and law-abiding and act honorably toward our nation and to its rulers. It is truly deplorable to see our President, the President of this great and mighty nation, one of the greatest rulers in the world stricken down by an assassin. Yet these things we have to mourn over. But in all cases, it is for us to be true to our God and to our religion, to obey the laws of God, cleaving to correct principles, letting purity, virtue, honor, truth and integrity characterize all our acts, that we may be the blessed of the Lord.[382]

—*John Taylor*

THIS DAY IN AMERICAN HISTORY (1957)

The U.S. successfully test-fires the Atlas intercontinental ballistic missile.

DECEMBER 18

Worshipping Freely under the Constitution

The Constitution was so framed that every one might worship according to the dictates of their own conscience, and we see the result of it in the wonderful blessing that has been poured out upon this most favored of all lands. . . .

When our Father in Heaven inspired men to write the Constitution, and give unto us the great charter that vouchsafed to us the liberty we enjoy, he did it in order that men might develop and be free, as the gospel of Jesus Christ intends that all men shall be. . . . They did not understand that underlying this apparent peacefulness, in this great land, there was a fixed determination that men should be free; that God Himself had written it, as it were by his own finger, in the Constitution of our great government, . . . and then, when the time came, he inspired his sons to rally around Old Glory and, if need be, give their lives that liberty might be perpetuated in the earth. . . .

On this day, so near the anniversary of the birth of that great document, the Constitution of the United States, it is fitting that we should assemble ourselves together in commemoration of it. It is proper that the governors of the several states of this nation, and the mayors of cities, should call attention to it. On next Tuesday, in the city of Salt Lake, here in the valleys of the mountains, and I presume in other cities, but in this city in our public schools and high schools there will be delivered addresses to the children explaining to them the birth of the Constitution, and it will be brought to their attention in a more forceful way, perhaps, than it has ever been before.[383]

—*George Albert Smith*

THIS DAY IN AMERICAN HISTORY (1917)

The 18th Amendment is passed.

There Is a Respectable Balance in Favor of Liberty and Freedom and Equal Rights

I will tell you what I think about the Constitution. I have just the same opinion of it that Joseph Smith had, and he said it was given by inspiration of God. The men did not know this who wrote it; the men did not know it who adopted it; nevertheless it is true. There is an embodiment of principles contained therein that are calculated to bless and benefit mankind. "What do you think about the government of the United States as a government? I think it is a good deal ahead of most governments, but I think the administrators are apostatizing very fast from the principles that the fathers of this nation instituted." It has become quite a question now-a-days, whether men can be preserved in their rights or not, whether men can worship God according to the dictates of their conscience or not, or whether we are living in a land of freedom or not. What is the matter? Why, they are like the religionist. How is it with them? They profess to believe in the Bible. They do believe it shut, but when you open it they deny it. The people of this nation profess to believe in the Constitution. They do until it comes to be applied to the people and then they do not. That is perhaps too broad a saying; but I will say there are many who feel like this—not all by a long way. There are thousands and tens of thousands who are imbued with the same principles as were the framers of the Constitution and who desire to see human freedom perpetuated. The principles of freedom and the love of human liberty have not quite died out of the hearts of all men in these United States. There is a respectable balance in favor of liberty and freedom and equal rights. . . . We would say to men who profess so much loyalty and patriotism to the government, be true to your institutions, be true to the Constitution of the United States, as we say to all our people to be true to the same. We expect the Latter-day Saints to be so, and to be subject to law, to avoid lawlessness of every kind and the interference with men's rights in any shape.[384]

—*John Taylor*

THIS DAY IN AMERICAN HISTORY (1777)

Washington's amy retires to Winter Quarters at Valley Forge.

It Is Better to Trust and Sometimes Be Disappointed

In addition to this yearning for identity and belonging, we see about us also a yearning for freedom taking its familiar forms—political and economic. But we also see more and more individuals who sense that the freedom they desire involves more than a new constitutional caress. Thoughtful souls see that something even deeper is involved. So many have erred, thinking that freedom, included both freedom to obey or not to obey eternal laws and, wrongly, that it included freedom to change those laws. Not so. Ultimately, freedom involves choice between eternal alternatives, but not the altering of the alternatives. We can choose wickedness or happiness, but not wickedness with happiness. A confused Cain, a vain Cain, not only murdered his brother while they conversed together in the field, but also gloried in the murder of Abel, when Cain said (probably shouted), "I am free." . . .

I have found, too, that it is better to trust and sometimes be disappointed than to be forever mistrusting and be right occasionally. This is to endorse empathy, not naivete. Neither is this to suggest that our fellowship be flaccid. The finest of friends must sometimes be stern sentinels, who will insist that we become what we have the power to become. The "no" of such stern sentinels is more to be prized than a "yes" of others. God's seeming sternness is actually a sweetness beyond our comprehension.[385]

—*Neal A. Maxwell*

THIS DAY IN AMERICAN HISTORY (1776)

The Third Continental Congress convenes.

Saving the Constitution from Destruction

Our friends wish to know our feelings towards the government. I answer, they are first-rate, and we will prove it too, as you will see if you only live long enough, for that we shall live to prove it is certain; and when the Constitution of the United States hangs, as it were, upon a single thread, they will have to call for the "Mormon" elders to save it from utter destruction; and they will step forth and do it.

We love the Constitution of our country; it is all we could ask; though in some few instances there might be some amendments made which would better it. We love the federal government and the laws of Congress. There is nothing in those laws that in the least militates against us, not even to our excluding common law from this territory. I can inform our lawyers who plead at the bar here, that the Congress of the United States have passed laws giving us the privilege of excluding common law at our pleasure, and that too without any violation of the Constitution, or general statutes. They have also given us privilege to stop drunkenness, swearing, and gambling, and to prevent horse racing, and to punish men for hurting and robbing each other. The Constitution of the United States, and the whole federal government, in their acts, have given us this privilege.[386]

—*Brigham Young*

THIS DAY IN AMERICAN HISTORY (1620)

Mayflower pilgrims come ashore in Plymouth Bay.

Zion: A Refuge in the Days of Constitutional Challenge

And then the day is not far distant when this nation will be shaken from center to circumference. And now, you may write it down, any of you, and I will prophesy it in the name of God. And then will be fulfilled that prediction to be found in one of the revelations given through the Prophet Joseph Smith. Those who will not take up their sword to fight against their neighbors must needs flee to Zion for safety. And they will come, saying, we do not know anything of the principles of your religion, but we perceive that you are an honest community; you administer justice and righteousness, and we want to live with you and receive the protection of your laws, but as for your religion we will talk about that some other time. Will we protect such people? Yes, all honorable men. When the people shall have torn to shreds the Constitution of the United States, the elders of Israel will be found holding it up to the nations of the earth and proclaiming liberty and equal rights to all men and extending the hand of fellowship to the oppressed of all nations. This is part of the program, and as long as we do what is right and fear God, he will help us and stand by us under all circumstances.[387]

—*John Taylor*

THIS DAY IN AMERICAN HISTORY (1789)

North Carolina adopts the Bill of Rights.

No People Can Be Bound to Acknowledge and Adore the Invisible Hand

The gentiles were to come forth upon this land of America. They were to be set up as a free people. They were to be thus established by the power of the Father, and the purpose of it all was that the gospel might come forth and be preached to the children of men in order that God could fulfill the covenant that he had made "with his people, O house of Israel." And why was freedom so necessary in connection with the restoration of the gospel and its promulgation among the children of men? In order that those to whom the gospel would be restored might have the freedom of speech to preach the gospel; the freedom of the press to publish the gospel; freedom of assembly so they could gather together in congregations and worship the Lord; and religious freedom so that they could worship God according to the dictates of their own conscience.

Did our American colonists feel that they were assisted by the Almighty in winning independence from their mother country? They certainly did and so expressed themselves. Among them was George Washington who, in the inaugural address he delivered on April 30, 1789, said this: "No people can be bound to acknowledge and adore the Invisible Hand which conducts the affairs of men more than those of the United States. Every step by which they have advanced to the character of an independent nation seems to have been distinguished by some token of Providential agency."

And, furthermore, not only did the Lord raise up these men and inspire them to write free agency into the government of this land, but he declared his intention that the elders of this Church should defend that Constitution and the freedoms and the rights allowed us in that great document. And so he said "that law of the land, which is constitutional," and I call your attention to the phraseology: ". . . that law of the land which is constitutional, supporting that principle of freedom in maintaining the rights and privileges, belongs to all mankind, and is justifiable before me. Therefore, I, the Lord, justify you, and your brethren of my church, in befriending that law which is the constitutional law of the land; And as pertaining to law of man, whatsoever is more or less than this, cometh of evil" (D&C 98:5–7).[388]

—*Mark E. Petersen*

THIS DAY IN AMERICAN HISTORY (1783)

George Washington resigns as commander of the Continental Army.

America's Religious Freedom Made the Book of Mormon Possible

Julia Ward Howe felt impressed to share her deep personal feelings for the need of divine direction in the struggle between the states in America. During the night, these eloquent words came into her mind and she quickly wrote them down:

> Mine eyes have seen the glory of the coming of the Lord;
> He is trampling out the vintage where the grapes of wrath are stored.
> He hath loosed the fateful lightning of his terrible, swift sword;
> His truth is marching on.
> He has sounded forth the trumpet that shall never call retreat;
> He is sifting out the hearts of men before his judgment seat.
> Oh, be swift, my soul, to answer him; be jubilant my feet!
> Our God is marching on.
> ["Battle Hymn of the Republic," *Hymns,* 1985, no. 60.]

The religious freedom established in America made possible the coming forth of the plain and precious truths of the Book of Mormon "to the convincing of the Jew and Gentile that Jesus is the Christ, the Eternal God, manifesting himself unto all nations" (preface to the Book of Mormon). These writings are to come unto the Gentiles that they may "know the decrees of God" and repent (Ether 2:11). It is incumbent upon the members of the Church who have had the gift of religious freedom to share this knowledge and testimony with the peoples of the world. Do not underestimate the profound influence—politically and socially—of the principles of the restored gospel upon all of mankind.[389]

—David B. Haight

THIS DAY IN AMERICAN HISTORY (1814)

The War of 1812 ends (Treaty of Ghent).

When Will the Nation Repent?

As soon as the Saints had found a shelter in the Rocky Mountains, this feeling of lawlessness went rampant throughout the Union. Men despised the statutes and the laws with which they were bound, and it was mob upon mob, army against army, until the whole country has been deluged in blood and creped in mourning. When will the nation repent of these follies and maintain those institutions God has introduced for the perfection of mankind? When will they hold the Constitution sacred and inviolable, and seek no longer to prostitute it for the destruction of the innocent? Until this is done they may expect to see sorrow and woe, which will increase upon their heads until they shall repent.

We should consider these things within ourselves. We commenced to make our settlements here under these circumstances, and here we have found a shelter. It has been a home for the oppressed, and a shelter to everybody that desired rest. The weary traveler has had a chance here to refresh himself and enjoy the blessings that are to be enjoyed in these valleys, and no man's rights have ever been trampled upon.[390]

—*George Albert Smith*

THIS DAY IN AMERICAN HISTORY (1787)

The Georgia ratifying convention begins.

DECEMBER 26

Obey Every Institution of Man so Far as We Can Without Violating Our Consciences

While other men are seeking to trample the Constitution under foot, we will try to maintain it. We have prophecies something like this somewhere; that the time would come when this nation would do as they are now doing—that is, they would trample under foot the constitution and institutions of the nation, and the elders of this Church would rally around the standard and maintain those principles which were introduced for the freedom and protection of men. We expect to do that, and to maintain all correct principle. I will tell you what you will see by and by. You will see trouble, trouble, trouble enough in these United States, but let us be on the side of human liberty and human rights, and the protection of all correct principles and laws and government, and maintain every principle that is upright and virtuous and honorable, and let the world take the balance if they want, we don't want it. We will cleave to the truth, God being our helper, and try to introduce principles whereby the will of God will be done on earth as it is in heaven. And we will obey every institution of man for the Lord's sake so far as we can without violating our consciences and doing things that are wrong and improper.[391]

—*John Taylor*

THIS DAY IN AMERICAN HISTORY (1776)

Washington crosses the Delaware and captures Trenton from Hessians.

Safety for Our Nation

America is choice land—choice above all others. Blessed by the Almighty, our forebears have made and kept it so. It will continue to be a land of freedom and liberty so long as we are able to advance in the light of sounds and enduring principles of right. To sacrifice such principles for momentary expediency—often selfishly motivated—is to endanger our noble heritage and is unworthy of our great American people.

With all my heart I love our great nation. I have lived and traveled abroad just enough to make me appreciate rather fully what we have in America. To me the U.S. is not just another nation. It is not just one of a family of nations. The U.S. is a nation with a great mission to perform for the benefit and blessing of liberty-loving people everywhere. It is my firm conviction that the Constitution of the U.S. was established by men whom the God of heaven raised up unto this very purpose. This is part of my religious faith.

The days ahead are sobering and challenging and will demand the faith, prayers, and loyalty of every American. Our challenge is to keep America strong and free—strong socially, strong economically, and above all, strong spiritually, if our way of life is to endure. There is no other way. Only in this course is there safety for our nation.[392]

—*Ezra Taft Benson*

THIS DAY IN AMERICAN HISTORY (1941)

The Constitution arrives at Fort Knox, Kentucky, for safekeeping during World War II.

An Act of God

Without the Constitution there would be no government such as the Lord had in mind. The Lord gave us that government by providing the Constitution written by the hands of wise men whom he raised up for this very purpose. It was an act of God. It was another step in establishing the free conditions under which the gospel could be restored and then taken by the believing Gentiles to all other nations.

As the Lord indicated so plainly through Nephi and likewise in His own declaration to the Nephites after His resurrection as quoted above, it was a giant step in the divine plan to fulfill the promise made to Abraham, that God would recover His scattered seed by the preaching of the gospel. (See 1 Nephi 22:7–11; 3 Nephi 21:4.) His sheep would know his voice.

This, then, is why there is a United States.[393]

—*Mark E. Peterson*

THIS DAY IN AMERICAN HISTORY (1846)

Iowa receives statehood as the 29th state.

Religious Liberty Is a Fundamental Right

The First Amendment to the Constitution declares: "Congress shall make no law respecting an establishment of religion, or prohibiting the free exercise thereof; or abridging the freedom of speech, or of the press; or the right of the people peaceably to assemble, and to petition the government for a redress of grievances."

Notice that religious liberty is the first freedom mentioned in the First Amendment. It consists, first, of protection from laws "respecting an establishment of religion." This is what we lawyers call the Establishment Clause. (Some of you didn't know I used to be a lawyer. I hope that doesn't lower your opinion of me!) Unlike England, for example, this country knows no national church, and government may not officially prefer one religious denomination over another. But some have misunderstood the ban on establishing an official religion to mean that government should treat religion with skepticism, even hostility. Not so. The Supreme Court has said:

"The Establishment Clause does not license government to treat religion and those who teach or practice it . . . as subversive of American ideals and therefore subject to unique disabilities." And, contrary to what some say, a law does not become unconstitutional when it coincides with religious principles. Otherwise we couldn't have laws punishing murder and theft.[394]

—*D. Todd Christofferson*

THIS DAY IN AMERICAN HISTORY (1845)

Texas receives statehood as the 29th state.

Democracy Leaves Terribly Important Things up to Ordinary People

It was G. K. Chesterton who first warned us about what can happen to a "tired democracy," a democracy in which the people are willing to leave their chores to a few "lonely sentinels." There are many who now believe that American democracy is, in fact, a "tired democracy," with "deliberate apathy" eating away at the vitals of our society. There are also those who argue that things are so complex now and the consequences of decisions so grave that democracy will falter simply because—by its very nature—democracy leaves, in the words of Chesterton again, terribly important things up to ordinary people.

Significantly, the American presidents whom we admire most are men who have, in one way or another, cracked the Constitution we venerate—whether it was Jefferson in making the unauthorized purchase of the Louisiana Territory, or Jackson defying the United States Supreme Court, or Lincoln suspending certain civil and constitutional rights in order to save the union, or Teddy Roosevelt digging an unfunded Panama Canal while Congress was still debating the merits of the project, or Franklin D. Roosevelt threatening to impose some economic controls whether or not Congress fashioned such a law. It should give us pause that our admiration flows to leaders who were decisive and who assumed great psychological size in American affairs; John Stuart Mill warned about laying our liberties at the feet of even great men. We must "want the consequences of what we want."

Yet in today's hurley-burly world, our democracy finds it difficult to get most of us even to participate in the periodic, formal decision making of elections, let alone in the careful, time-consuming assessment of various alternatives and consequences.

So much of what we have done in America is simply to equalize expectations without, at the same time, increasing our capacity to deal on those expectations. Thus, most of the rhetoric on the American scene today consists either of creating unrealistic expectations or of decrying our failures to deliver on those expectations![395]

—*Neal A. Maxwell*

THIS DAY IN AMERICAN HISTORY (1972)

President Richard M. Nixon halts the bombing of North Vietnam and announces peace talks.

Building Bridges of Understanding

Civility and decency seem to have disappeared during this era of polarization and passionate disagreements. Vulgarity, faultfinding, and evil speaking of others are all too common. Too many pundits, politicians, entertainers, and other influencers throw insults constantly. I am greatly concerned that so many people seem to believe that it is completely acceptable to condemn, malign, and vilify *anyone* who does not agree with them. Many seem eager to damage another's reputation with pathetic and pithy barbs! . . .

My dear brothers and sisters, this should not be. As disciples of Jesus Christ, we are to be examples of how to interact with others—*especially* when we have differences of opinion. One of the easiest ways to identify a *true follower* of Jesus Christ is how compassionately that person treats other people.

The Savior's Atonement made it possible for us to overcome *all* evil—including contention. Make no mistake about it: contention *is* evil! Jesus Christ declared that those who have "the spirit of contention" are not of Him but are "of the devil, who is the father of contention, and [the devil] stirreth up the hearts of men to contend with anger, one with another."[8] Those who foster contention are taking a page out of Satan's playbook, whether they realize it or not. "No man can serve two masters." We cannot support Satan with our verbal assaults and then think that we can still serve God. . . .

If a friend on social media has strong political or social views that violate everything you believe in, an angry, cutting retort by you will not help. Building bridges of understanding will require much more of you, but that is exactly what your friend needs. . . . Brothers and sisters, we can literally change the world—one person and one interaction at a time.

How? By modeling how to manage honest differences of opinion with mutual respect and dignified dialogue.[396]

—Russell M. Nelson

THIS DAY IN AMERICAN HISTORY (1946)

President Harry S. Truman officially declares the end of the Second World War.

Endnotes

1. Journal, December 1842–June 1844; Book 2, 10 March 1843–14 July 1843,193, *The Joseph Smith Papers,* https://www.josephsmithpapers.org/paper-summary/journal-december-1842-june-1844-book-2-10-march-1843-14-july-1843/201?highlight=Constitution%20hanging%20by%20a%20thread.
2. Donald Q. Cannon, *Latter-Day Prophets and the United States Constitution* (Provo: Religious Studies Center, Brigham Young University, 1991), xii–xiii.
3. Ezra Taft Benson, "Our Divine Constitution," *Ensign,* Nov. 1987, 7.
4. Thomas V. Griffith, "Discussion on President Oaks Address 'Defending Our Divinely Inspired Constitution,'" *The 2021 Religious Freedom Annual Review,* June 16, 2021. https://jrcls.org/articles/the-2021-religious-freedom-annual-review-an-overview.
5. Ezra Taft Benson, "Our Immediate Responsibility" (BYU Devotional, October 25, 1966), speeches.byu.edu.
6. Russell M. Nelson, "Peacemakers Needed," *Liahona,* May 2023.
7. Discourse, circa 19 July 1840, as Reported by Martha Jane Knowlton Coray–A[a],13[a], *The Joseph Smith Papers,* https://www.josephsmithpapers.org/paper-summary/discourse-circa-19-july-1840-as-reported-by-martha-jane-knowlton-coray).
8. Neal A. Maxwell, "Our Need for True Patriotism," Provo Freedom Festival Fireside, July 4, 1993, BYU Speeches, https://speeches.byu.edu/talks/neal-a-maxwell/our-need-for-true-patriotism/.
9. Russell M. Nelson, "Confidence in the Presence of God," *Liahona,* May 2025.
10. Dallin H. Oaks, "Divine Love in the Father's Plan," *Liahona,* May 2022, 102.
11. J. Reuben Clark, Jr. "Religion and the Constitution," Conference Report, April 1935, 94.
12. Mark E. Peterson, *The Way to Peace* (Salt Lake City: Deseret Book, 1969), 62.
13. Heber J. Grant, in *Latter-day Prophets and the United States Constitution,* ed. Donald Q. Cannon (Provo, UT: Religious Studies Center, Brigham Young University, 1991), 99.
14. Hinckley, Standing for *Something,*57–58, 60.
15. Harold B. Lee, *Ye Are the Light of the World* (Salt Lake City: Deseret Book, 1974), 174–75.
16. Gerald N. Lund, *The Second Coming of the Lord* (Salt Lake City: Deseret Book, 2020), 183–84.
17. Boyd K. Packer, *Let Not Your Heart Be Troubled* (Salt Lake City: Bookcraft, 1991), 68.
18. Harold B. Lee, *Decisions for Successful Living* (Salt Lake City: Deseret Book, 1973), 209.
19. Martin B. Hickman, "J. Reuben Clark, Jr.: The Constitution and The Great Fundamentals," *BYU Studies Quarterly* 13, no. 3 (1973).
20. James E. Talmage, Conference Report, October 1918, 60.
21. Parley P. Pratt, *Journal of Discourses* (London: Latter-day Saints' Book Depot, 1853), 1:137.
22. Ezra Taft Benson, *Title of Liberty* (Salt Lake City: Deseret Book, 1964), 89.
23. Orson F. Whitney, Conference Report, October 1917, 55.
24. Harold B. Lee, "True Patriotism—An Expression of Faith," in *Ye Are the Light of the World* (Salt Lake City: Deseret Book, 1974), 180–82.
25. Thorpe B. Isaacson, "Address," Conference Report, April 1964, 52–56.

26. B. H. Roberts, "An American Prophet," in *Joseph Smith the Prophet-Teacher* (Salt Lake City: Deseret Book, 1908), 69.
27. George Q. Cannon, *Journal of Discourses*, November 20, 1881, 23:102.
28. Ezra Taft Benson, "Our Duty as Citizens," October 1954 general conference.
29. David B. Haight, "Filling the Whole Earth," *Ensign*, May 1990, 24.
30. Ronald A. Rasband. "To Heal the World," *Liahona*, May 2022, 91.
31. Gerald N. Lund, *The Second Coming of the Lord* (Salt Lake City: Deseret Book, 2020), 169–70.
32. Tad Walch, "Elder Oaks Leads Special Mormon Regional Conference on 'Defining Issue' of Religious Freedom," *Deseret News*, September 11, 2016.
33. Orson F. Whitney, "The Perfect Government Yet to Come," Conference Report, April 1909, 73.
34. Mark E. Peterson, "Washington and Franklin," *Way to Peace* (Salt Lake City: Deseret Book, 1969), 102.
35. Neal A. Maxwell, "The Lonely Sentinels of Democracy," *New Era*, July 1972.
36. Joseph Fielding Smith, *Gospel Doctrine: Selections from the Sermons and Writings of Joseph F. Smith* (Salt Lake City: Deseret Book Company, 1920), 513–15.
37. Roberts, "An American Prophet," 70–1.
38. Joseph F. Smith, in *Latter-day Prophets and the United States Constitution*, ed. Donald Q. Cannon (Provo, UT: Religious Studies Center, Brigham Young University, 1991), 88–89.
39. Dallin H. Oaks, "The Divinely Inspired Constitution," *Ensign*, February 1992, 6.
40. Orson Pratt, "The Kingdom of God," *Journal of Discourses*, 3:70.
41. Lund, *The Second Coming of the Lord*, 173–4.
42. Ezra Taft Benson, *Title of Liberty* (Salt Lake City: Bookcraft, 1964), 112–13.
43. Albert Carrington, *Journal of Discourses*, 17:165–68.
44. George Q. Cannon and Jerreld L. Newquist, "Constitutional Government and Politics," in *Gospel Truth: Discourse and Writings of President George Q. Cannon* (Salt Lake City: Deseret Book, 1957), 347–48.
45. Harold B. Lee, *Ye Are the Light of the World* (Salt Lake City: Deseret Book, 1974), 164.
46. Antoine R. Ivins, Conference Report, October 1959, 116–17.
47. John Taylor, *Journal of Discourses*, July 3, 1881, 22:141.
48. Ezra Taft Benson, *Title of Liberty* (Salt Lake City: Bookcraft, 1964), 30–31.
49. George Albert Smith, "Perpetuating Liberty," *Improvement Era*, February 1950, 94.
50. "First Presidency Urges Observance of Bicentennial of Constitution," *Church News*, January 31, 1987.
51. Harold B. Lee, N. Eldon Tanner, ad Marion G. Romney, "The First Presidency Statement on the Constitution," *Ensign*, November 1973, 90.
52. E Benson, *An Enemy Hath Done This*, 53.
53. Joseph F Smith, John R. Winder, and Anthon H. Lund, Conference Report, April 1907.
54. Hinckley, *Standing for Something*, 115–17.
55. George Q. Cannon and Jerreld L. Newquist, "Constitutional Government and Politics," in *Gospel Truth: Discourse and Writings of President George Q. Cannon* (Salt Lake City: Deseret Book, 1957), 335–36.
56. Benson, *An Enemy Hath Done This*, 118.
57. 19 July 1840, as recorded by Martha Jane Knowlton Coray; ms. in Church Historian's Office, Salt Lake City; Joseph Smith Papers, LDS Church Historical

Archives, Box 1, March 10, 1844, Also, D. Michael Stewart, "I Have a Question," *Ensign,* June 1976, 64–65.

58. James R. Clark, comp., *Messages of the First Presidency* (Salt Lake City: Deseret Book, 2009), 3:185.
59. Tad R. Callister, *America's Choice: A Nation Under God or Without God* (Meadville, PA: Fulton Books, 2021), 143–44.
60. Dallin H. Oaks, "Fundamentals of Our Constitutions," Utah Constitution Day Celebration, September 17, 2010, Salt Lake City, Utah.
61. *Improvement Era,* December 1937, 735.
62. John Wesley Hill, *Abraham Lincoln—Man of God,* 4th ed. (New York: G. P. Putnam's Sons, 1927), 334.
63. Mark E. Petersen, "The Savor of Men," *Ensign,* November 1976.
64. Neal A Maxwell, "The Lonely Sentinels of Democracy," *New Era,* July 1972.
65. J. Reuben Clark, Jr., Conference Report, April 1957, 50–51.
66. Ezra Taft Benson, "Paramount Issue Today- Liberty Against Creeping Socialism," *Church News,* September 2, 1961.
67. Tad R. Callister, *America's Choice: A Nation Under God or Without God* (Meadville, PA: Fulton Books, 2021), 131–32.
68. Brigham Young, *Discourses of Brigham Young,* comp. John A, Widtsoe (Salt Lake City: Deseret Book, 1925), 359.
69. Norman Cousins, ed., *In God We Trust,* (New York, Harper and Brothers, 1958), 1.
70. L. Tom Perry, "For the Time Will Come When They Will Not Endure Sound Doctrine," *Ensign,* November 1975.
71. Ezra Taft Benson, *The Constitution: A Heavenly Banner* (Salt Lake City: Deseret Book Company, 1986), 28–31.
72. Neal A. Maxwell, *By the Hands of Wise Men: Essays on the Constitution,* in Ray Cole Hillam, ed. (Provo: Brigham Young University Press, 1979), 114.
73. Dallin H. Oaks. "Going Forward with Religious Freedom and Nondiscrimination," Joseph Smith Lecture, November 12, 2021, https://newsroom.churchofjesuschrist.org/article/president-dallin-h-oaks-speech-university-of-virginia.
74. Joseph Smith, Liberty, MO, to Isaac Galland, [Commerce, IL], 22 March 1839, in *Times and Seasons,* February 1840, 1:53, 55–6, *Joseph Smith Papers.*
75. J. Reuben Clark, Jr. "Religion and the Constitution," Conference Report, April 1935, 94.
76. Dallin H. Oaks. "Going Forward with Religious Freedom and Nondiscrimination" (Joseph Smith Lecture, November 12, 2021), https://newsroom.churchofjesuschrist.org/article/president-dallin-h-oaks-speech-university-of-virginia.
77. Ezra Taft Benson, *Title of Liberty* (Salt Lake City: Bookcraft, 1964), 84–85.
78. Bruce R. McConkie, *A New Witness for the Articles of Faith* (Salt Lake City, Utah: Deseret Book Co, 1985), 690.
79. Neal A. Maxwell, "Our Need for True Patriotism," Provo Freedom Festival Fireside, July 4, 1993, https://speeches.byu.edu/talks/neal-a-maxwell/our-need-for-true-patriotism/.
80. David O. McKay. "A Philosophy of Happiness," in *Gospel Ideals: Selections from the Discourses of David O. McKay* (Salt Lake City: Deseret Book Company, 1953), 498.
81. Hinckley, *Standing for Something,* 123.
82. Benson, *An Enemy Hath Done This,* 143.
83. Joseph B. Wirthlin, "Earning Our Heritage," in *Finding Peace in Our Lives* (Salt Lake City, Deseret Book Company, 1995), 137–46.

84. Heber J. Grant, "Admonition and Blessing," Conference Report, October 1944, 11.
85. Ezra Taft Benson, Title of Liberty (Salt Lake City: Bookcraft, 1964), 15.
86. Brigham Young, *Journal of Discourses,* 5:232.
87. D. Todd Christofferson, "Religious Freedom—A Cherished Heritage to Defend," BYU Speeches, June 26, 2016.
88. George Q. Cannon, *Journal of Discourses,* 18:9–10.
89. George Albert Smith, "From a Prophet to His People," Conference Report, April 1949, 169.
90. Hinckley, *Standing for Something,* 115–17.
91. Ezra Taft Benson, "The Constitution-A Heavenly Banner," BYU Speeches, September 16, 1986, 27.
92. Callister, *America's Choice,* 143–44.
93. L. Tom Perry, "For the Time Will Come When They Will Not Endure Sound Doctrine," *Ensign,* November 1975.
94. John Taylor, Journal of Discourses (London: Latter-day Saints' Book Depot, 1857), August 23, 1857, 5:148.
95. Joseph F. Smith, "Opening Address," Conference Report, October 1912, 8.
96. Dallin H. Oaks, "Fundamentals of Our Constitutions," Utah Constitution Day Celebration, September 17, 2010, Salt Lake City, Utah.
97. Hinckley, *Standing for Something,* 120–21.
98. David O. McKay, "Education," in *Pathways to Happiness* (Salt Lake City: Deseret Book, 1957), 70–71.
99. Ezra Taft Benson, "Our Duty As Citizens," October 1954 general conference.
100. Callister, *America's Choice,* 139–40.
101. Hinckley, *Standing for Something,* 61–62.
102. Lund, *The Coming of the Lord* (Salt Lake City: Bookcraft, 2005), 67–68.
103. Dallin H. Oaks, "Fundamentals of Our Constitutions" (Utah Constitution Day Celebration, September 17, 2010, Salt Lake City, Utah).
104. L. Tom Perry, "Truth and Liberty"(Brigham Young University devotional, September 17, 1987), speeches.byu.edu.
105. Neal A Maxwell, "My Testimony," in *Moving in His Majesty and Power* (Salt Lake City: Deseret Book, 2004), 93–94.
106. Robert D. Hales, "Freedom and Personal Liberty" (Brigham Young University devotional, July 6, 1975), speeches.byu.edu.
107. Loren C. Dunn, "Freedom of the Press in Our Bicentennial Year" (Brigham Young University devotional, January 20, 1976), speeches.byu.edu.
108. George Albert Smith, Conference Report, April 1947, 163.
109. L. Tom Perry, "The Church and the American Bicentennial" (Brigham Young University devotional, February 24, 1976), speeches.byu.edu.
110. George Albert Smith, *Sharing the Gospel with Others* (Salt Lake City: Deseret Book, 1948), 19.
111. "Manuscript History of the Church, vol. E-1, 1838–1856 [1 July 1843–30 April 1844]," *The Joseph Smith Papers,* 1886. History, 1838–1856, volume E-1 [1 July 1843–30 April 1844], 1886.
112. Parley P. Pratt, *Journal of Discourses,* 1:137.
113. Parley P. Pratt, *Journal of Discourses,* 1:138.
114. George Albert Smith, *Church News,* February 16, 1946, 8.
115. Jeffrey R. Holland, "Prologue: A Promised Land," in *Just and Holy Principles: Latter-Day Saint Readings on America and the Constitution,* ed. Ralph C. Hancock

(New York: Simon and Schuster Custom Publishing, 1998), xv–xx.
116. Joseph B. Wirthlin, "Earning Our Heritage," *Finding Peace in Our Lives* (Salt Lake City, Deseret Book Company, 1995), 203–204.
117. Ezra Taft Benson, Conference Report, April 1965.
118. George Q. Cannon, *Journal of Discourses*, 26:5.
119. Harold B. Lee, "A Time of Decision," Conference Report, April 1972.
120. Lee, "A Time of Decision."
121. Ezra Taft Benson, "A Four-Fold Hope" (Brigham Young University devotional, May 24, 1961).
122. Gerald N. Lund, *The Second Coming of the Lord* (Salt Lake City: Deseret Book, 2020), 169–70.
123. Martin B. Hickman, "J. Reuben Clark, Jr.: The Constitution and The Great Fundamentals," *BYU Studies Quarterly* 13, no. 3, 272.
124. Hinckley, *Standing for Something*, 169.
125. George Albert Smith, Conference Reports, October 1924,45–46.
126. Orson F. Whitney, "Pre-Existence of Man," *Journal of Discourses*, 26:194–204.
127. Hinckley, *Standing for Something*,197–8, 200.
128. George Q. Cannon, *Journal of Discourses*, 26:142–43.
129. *The Discourses of Wilford Woodruff*, ed. G. Homer Durham (Salt Lake City: Deseret Book, 1946), 270–1.
130. John Taylor, *Journal of Discourses*, 23:36.
131. Tad R. Callister, *America's Destiny, Choosing God's Will or Ours* (Springville, UT: Cedar Fort, Inc., 2023), 47–48.
132. David O. McKay, "Essentials of a Better World," Conference Report, October 1940, 104.
133. Neal A. Maxwell, "The Lonely Sentinels of Democracy," *New Era*, July 1972.
134. Marion G. Romney, America's Destiny," October 1975 general conference.
135. Ezra Taft Benson, "Our Duty as Citizens," October 1954 general conference.
136. Mark E. Peterson, *The Great Prologue* (Salt Lake City: Deseret Book, 1975), 74–75.
137. L. Tom Perry, "The Church and the U.S. Bicentennial: A Conversation with Elder L. Tom Perry of the Council of the Twelve," *Ensign*, June 1976.
138. Tad R. Callister, *America's Choice: A Nation Under God or Without God* (Meadville, PA: Fulton Books, 2021), 52–3.
139. J. Reuben Clark, "Constitutional Government: In Which America Is Founded Upon the Scriptures," in Ray C. Hillam, ed., *By the Hands of Wise Men: Essays on the U.S. Constitution* (Provo, UT: Brigham Young University Press, 1979), 178.
140. Brigham Young, *Discourses of Brigham Young*, comp. John A, Widtsoe (Salt Lake City: Deseret Book, 1925), 360.
141. Bruce R. McConkie, *A New Witness for the Articles of Faith* (Salt Lake City, Utah: Deseret Book Co, 1985), 655–56.
142. J. Reuben Clark, Jr., *Stand Fast by Our Constitution* (Salt Lake City: Deseret Book Company, 1973), 1–3.
143. Abraham Lincoln, letter to J. M. Cutts, October 26, 1863, quoted in Ralph B. Winn, *Concise Lincoln Dictionary of Thoughts and Statements* (New York: New York Philosophical Library, 1959), 107.
144. Russell M. Nelson, "The Canker of Contention," April 1989 general conference.
145. Gordon B. Hinckley, "The Times in Which We Live," *Ensign*, November 2001.
146. Samuel W. Taylor and Raymond W. Taylor, *The John Taylor Papers: Records of the Last Utah Pioneer* (Redwood City, CA: Taylor Trust, 1984), 1:282.

147. Dallin H. Oaks, Facebook post, March 21, 2017.
148. James R. Clark, comp., *Messages of the First Presidency* (Salt Lake City: Deseret Book, 2009), 6:17–8.
149. Mark E. Petersen, *The Great Prologue* (Salt Lake City: Deseret Book Co., 1975), 95.
150. Petersen, *The Great Prologue,* 75.
151. N. Eldon Tanner, "If They Will But Serve the God of the Land," *Ensign,* May 1976,
152. Ezra Taft Benson, "The Ten Commandments," *New Era,* July 1978.
153. David O. McKay, *Church News,* May 29, 1954.
154. Moses Thatcher, *Journal of Discourses,* 23:213–4.
155. Ezra Taft Benson, *A Plea for America* (Salt Lake City: Deseret Book Company, 1975), 26.
156. J. Reuben Clark, Jr., *Stand Fast by Our Constitution* (Salt Lake City: Deseret Book, 1973), 189.
157. Orson Pratt, *Journal of Discourses,* 3:72.
158. Harold B. Lee, *Ye Are The Light of the World* (Salt Lake City: Deseret Book, 1974), 120.
159. J. Reuben Clark, Jr., "Private Ownership . . . under the United Order," October 1942 general conference.
160. Harold B. Lee, *Ye Are the Light of the World* (Salt Lake City: Deseret Book, 1974), 350–51.
161. Mark E. Peterson, *The Great Prologue* (Salt Lake City: Deseret Book, 1975), 4.
162. Bruce R. McConkie, *A New Witness for the Articles of Faith* (Salt Lake City, Utah: Deseret Book Co, 1985), 678–79.
163. David B Haight. "Ethics and Honesty," in *Light unto the World* (Salt Lake City: Deseret Book, 1997), 160–61.
164. Bruce R. McConkie, *A New Witness for the Articles of Faith* (Salt Lake City, Utah: Deseret Book Co, 1985), 683–84.
165. Harold B. Lee, *Ye Are the Light of the World* (Salt Lake City: Deseret Book, 1974), 232–33.
166. John Taylor, *Journal of Discourses,* 20:318.
167. Tad R. Callister, *America's Choice: A Nation Under God or Without God* (Meadville, PA: Fulton Books, 2021), 43–44.
168. Ezra Taft Benson, "The Heritage of Freedom," October 1958 general conference.
169. Joseph F. Smith, *Journal of Discourses,* 23:70.
170. George Albert Smith, "Liberty Under the Constitution," Conference Report, October 1950, 7.
171. Mark E. Peterson, *The Great Prologue* (Salt Lake City: Deseret Book, 1975), 2.
172. Jeffrey R. Holland, "'Mirror, Mirror, on the Wall': A Look at the 'Me Decade'" (Brigham Young University devotional, February 20, 1979), speeches.byu.edu.
173. Bruce R. McConkie, *A New Witness for the Articles of Faith* (Salt Lake City, Utah: Deseret Book Company, 1985), 690.
174. Dallin H. Oaks and Clark G. Gilbert, "Stand Fast with Love in Proclaiming Truth" (Ensign College devotional, 17 May 2022), ensign.edu/devotionals.
175. Gordon B. Hinckley, "Let Not Your Heart Be Troubled" (Brigham Young University devotional, September 17, 1974), speeches.byu.edu.
176. Ezra Taft Benson, *So Shall Ye Reap: Selected Addresses* (Salt Lake City: Deseret Book Company, 1960), 151.
177. Dallin H. Oaks, "Racism and Other Challenges" (Brigham Young University devotional, October 27, 2020), speeches.byu.edu.

178. D. Todd Christofferson, "Lord God of Hosts, Be with Us Yet" (Brigham Young University devotional, September 19, 2023), speeches.byu.edu.
179. Alma Sonne. "Religious Foundations," Conference Report, October 1969, 15.
180. Holland, "'Mirror, Mirror, on the Wall."
181. Wilford Woodruff, *Journal of Discourses,* 22:176.
182. Dallin H. Oaks, "Truth and Tolerance" (Brigham Young University devotional, September 11, 2011), speeches.byu.edu.
183. Discourse, 8 February 1844, as reported by Wilford Woodruff, *The Joseph Smith Papers,* 192, accessed August 12, 2025, https://www.josephsmithpapers.org/paper-summary/discourse-8-february-1844-as-reported-by-wilford-woodruff/1.
184. History, 1838–1856, volume E-1 (1 July 1843–30 April 1844), *The Joseph Smith Papers,* 1666, accessed August 12, 2025, https://www.josephsmithpapers.org/paper-summary/history-1838-1856-volume-e-1-1-july-1843-30-april-1844/36?highlight=I%20am%20just%20as%20ready%20to%20die%20in%20defending%20the%20rights%2.
185. Gerald N. Lund, *The Coming of the Lord* (Salt Lake City: Bookcraft, 2005), 60–61.
186. George Albert Smith, Conference Report, April 1948, 182.
187. Martin B. Hickman, "J. Reuben Clark, Jr.: The Constitution and The Great Fundamentals," *BYU Studies Quarterly* 13, no. 3, 270.
188. Dallin H. Oaks, "The Divinely Inspired Constitution," *Ensign,* February 1992, 6.
189. Joseph Smith. "Editorial, 16–17 February 1844, as published in Times and Seasons: Pacific Innuendo," *The Joseph Smith Papers,* 15 February 1844.
190. Noelle Baldwin, "Elder Christofferson Defends Religious Freedom at Patriotic Service," *Church News,* July 1, 2016.
191. Neal A Maxwell, "Unto This Very Purpose," *Moving in His Majesty and Power* (Salt Lake City: Deseret Book, 2004), 32–33.
192. John Taylor, *Journal of Discourses,* 21:69.
193. Dallin H. Oaks, "The Divinely Inspired Constitution," *Ensign,* February 1992, 6.
194. Lund, *The Coming of the Lord,* 56–7.
195. John Taylor, *Journal of Discourses,* 22:229.
196. David O. McKay, *Pathways to Happiness* (Salt Lake City: Bookcraft, 1957), 70–71.
197. George Albert Smith, "Idaho Falls Idaho Temple, Dedicatory Prayer."
198. J. Reuben Clark, *Improvement Era,* May 1944, 337.
199. Neal A. Maxwell, "Our Need for True Patriotism" (Provo Freedom Festival Fireside, July 4, 1993), speeches.byu.edu. speeches.byu.edu.
200. Wilford Woodruff, *Journal of Discourses,* 12:275.
201. Callister, *America's Choice,*134.
202. *Church News,* September 7, 1968.
203. "Government, Laws, War, and Peace," *Teachings of Harold B. Lee* (Salt Lake City: Deseret Book, 1996), 360.
204. David O. McKay, "Closing Address," Conference Report, October 1952, 130.
205. Ezra Taft Benson, *God, Family, Country: Our Three Great Loyalties* (Salt Lake City: Deseret Book Company, 1974), 87.
206. David O. McKay. "What Is Man that Thou Art Mindful . . ." Conference Report, October 1962, 6–7.
207. Joseph F. Smith, *Journal of Discourses,* 22:45.
208. Robert D. Hales. "Preserving Agency, Protecting Religious Freedom," *Ensign,* May 2015, 111–12.

209. Neal A. Maxwell, *Moving in His Majesty & Power* (Salt Lake City: Deseret Book, 2004), 36–37.
210. Brigham Young, *Journal of Discourses*, 6:344.
211. Bruce R. McConkie."Constitution of the United States," *Mormon Doctrine* (Salt Lake City: Deseret Book, 1966), 159.
212. John Q. Cannon, *Journal of Discourses*, 25:211.
213. Ezra Taft Benson,"Our Immediate Responsibility" (Brigham Young University devotional, October 25, 1966), speeches.byu.edu.
214. History, 1838–1856, volume C-1 [2 November 1838–31 July 1842],911, The Joseph Smith Papers, https://www.josephsmithpapers.org/paper-summary/history-1838-1856-volume-c-1-2-november-1838-31-july-1842/93.
215. George Albert Smith, Conference Report, April 1947, 163.
216. George Q. Cannon, *Journal of Discourses*, 18:6.
217. James E. Faust,"He Restoreth My Soul," in *To Reach Even unto You* (Salt Lake City, Deseret Book, 1990), 33.
218. "Political Liberty," in *Gospel Ideals: Selections from the Discourses of David O. McKay* (Salt Lake City: Deseret Book, 1953), 315.
219. David O. McKay,"Political Liberty," in *Gospel Ideals: Selections from the Discourses of David O. McKay* (Salt Lake City: Deseret Book, 1953), 315.
220. Dallin H. Oaks,"Defending Our Divinely Inspired Constitution," *Liahona*, April 2021, 107.
221. Oaks and Gilbert,"Stand Fast with Love Proclaiming Truth."
222. "The Constitution," in *Teachings of Ezra Taft Benson* (Salt Lake City: Deseret Book, 1988), 593.
223. Dallin H. Oaks,"The Divinely Inspired Constitution" *Ensign*, February 1992, 9.
224. Orson Pratt, *Journal of Discourses*, 20:151.
225. Ibid., December 27, 1868, 12:344.
226. Dallin H. Oaks,"Love Your Enemies," *Ensign*, November 2020, 26–29.
227. Russell M. Nelson,"Thou Shalt Have No Other Gods," *Ensign*, May 1996, 14–16.
228. Heber J. Grant,"Lincoln and Law," *Improvement Era*, February 1940, 127.
229. John Taylor, *Journal of Discourses*, 21:32.
230. Dallin H. Oaks,"Responsibilities of Citizenship"(Freedom Festival, July 3, 1994, Provo, Utah), speeches.byu.edu.
231. J. Reuben Clark, Jr.,"Constitution and Its Signers" (Brigham Young University devotional, May 21, 1957), speeches.byu.edu.
232. M. Russell Ballard,"Provo 1992 Freedom Festival Fireside"(Brigham Young University devotional, July 2, 1992)," Devotional Address, Brigham Young University, speeches.byu.edu.
233. Marion G. Romney,"America's Fate and Ultimate Destiny" (Brigham Young University devotional, May 2, 1976), speeches.byu.edu.
234. N. Eldon Tanner,"If They Will But Serve the God of the Land," *Ensign*, May 1976, 49–51.
235. Ronald A. Rasband,"To Heal the World," *Liahona*, May 2022, 92–93.
236. Church Newsroom,"The LDS Church Believes in Political Neutrality," June 1, 2023, https://newsroom.churchofjesuschrist.org/official-statement/political-neutrality.
237. Robert S. Wood,"Instruments of the Lord's Peace," *Ensign*, May 2006, 93–95.
238. Wilford Woodruff, *Journal of Discourses*, 22:346.
239. Levi Edgar Young, Conference Report, April 1937, 115.
240. Lund, *The Coming of the Lord*, 47–48.

241. Ezra Taft Benson, "The Heritage of Freedom," General Conference, October 1958.
242. Antoine R. Ivins, Conference Report, April 1938, 47.
243. James R. Clark, comp., *Messages of the First Presidency* (Salt Lake City: Deseret Book, 2009), 3:185–6.
244. Wilford Woodruff, *Journal of Discourses,* 7:100.
245. J. Reuben Clark, Jr. "A Nation With Christian Standards," Conference Report, October 1939, 10–11.
246. Ezra Taft Benson, *A Plea for America* (Salt Lake City: Deseret Book Company, 1975), 2.
247. Church Newsroom, "Part 2 of 3: Civil Society: Engaging the Differences among Us," newsroom.churchofjesuschrist.org, June 1, 2016.
248. Ezra Taft Benson, "America-A Man and an Event" Conference Report, October 1965, 122.
249. Levi Edgar Young, Conference Report, October 1934, 114–15.
250. "Washington's Letter to the Hebrew Congregation of Newport, Rhode Island," George Washington Institute for Religious Freedom, https://www.gwirf.org/washingtons-letter-to-the-hebrew-congregation-of-newport-rhode-island/.
251. D. Todd Christofferson, "Religious Freedom: A Cherished Heritage to Defend" (Brigham Young University devotional, June 26, 2016), speeches.byu.edu.
252. *The Teachings of Spencer W. Kimball,* ed. Edward L. Kimball (Salt Lake City: Bookcraft, 1982), 405.
253. Joseph F. Smith, Conference Report, October 1912, 8.
254. Richard R. Lyman. "The Spirit of America," Conference Report, April 1929, 77–79.
255. Alvin R. Dyer, Conference Report, October 1968, 106.
256. D. Todd Christofferson, "Religious Freedom: A Cherished Heritage to Defend" (Brigham Young University devotional, June 26, 2016), speeches.byu.edu.
257. Benson, *An Enemy Hath Done This,* 55.
258. Orson Pratt, "Progress of the Work of God, Etc.," *Journal of Discourses,* 20:326–27.
259. Maxwell, Neal A. "The Lonely Sentinels of Democracy." *New Era,* July 1972.
260. Orson Hyde, "Unity Required Among the People," Conference Report, October 1873, 231.
261. Joseph L. Wirthlin, Conference Report, October 1946, 31.
262. Ronald A. Rasband, "To Heal the World," *Liahona,* April 2022, 91.
263. Dallin H. Oaks, "The Divinely Inspired Constitution," *Ensign,* February 1992, 6.
264. David O. McKay, Conference Report, April 1935, 110.
265. Milton R. Hunter, Conference Report, October 1959, 31.
266. Bruce R. McConkie, Conference Report, April 1974, 102.
267. John Taylor, *Journal of Discourses,* 14:267.
268. David O. McKay, *Teachings of President David O. McKay,* ed. Claire Middlemiss (Salt Lake City: Deseret Book, 1902), 345.
269. George Albert Smith, Conference Report, October 1922, 94.
270. George Q. Cannon, *Journal of Discourses,* 26:5–6.
271. Ezra Taft Benson, *God, Family, Country: Our Three Great Loyalties* (Salt Lake City: Desert Book Co., 1974), 385.
272. Dallin H. Oaks, "Opposition in All Things," *Ensign,* May 2016, 116.
273. Orson Hyde, *Journal of Discourses,* 6:151.
274. Mark E. Petersen, "America—World Leader"(Brigham Young University devotional, July 1976), speeches.byu.edu.

275. D. Todd Christofferson, "Religious Freedom: A Cherished Heritage to Defend," BYU Speeches, June 26, 2016), https://speeches.byu.edu/talks/d-todd-christofferson/religious-freedom-cherished-heritage-defend/.
276. Brigham Young, *Journal of Discourses,* 10:106.
277. "First Presidency Urges Support of Constitution Week," *Church News,* September 18, 1982, 4.
278. Benson, *An Enemy Hath Done This,* 91.
279. Neal A. Maxwell "The Lonely Sentinels of Democracy," *New Era,* July 1972.
280. George Q. Cannon, *Journal of Discourses,* 23:102.
281. David O. McKay, "War," *Pathways to Happiness* (Salt Lake City: Deseret Book, 1957), 368.
282. Joseph Smith, Letter to Noah C. Saxton, January 4, 1833,16, *The Joseph Smith Papers,* https://www.josephsmithpapers.org/paper-summary/letter-to-noah-c-saxton-4-january-1833/3.
283. Harold B. Lee, *Ye Are the Light of the World* (Salt Lake City: Deseret Book, 1974), 232.
284. David Ramsay, *The History of the American Revolution in Two Volumes* (Indianapolis: Liberty Fund, 1990), 1:199.
285. Harry S. Stout, *The New England Soul: Preaching and Religious Culture in Colonial New England* (Oxford: Oxford University Press, 2012), 7.
286. John Witherspoon, "The Dominion of Providence over the Passions of Men" (1776), reprinted in *Political Sermons of the American Founding Era: 1730–1805,* vol. 1, ed. Ellis Sandoz, 2nd ed. (Indianapolis: Liberty Fund, 1998), 549.
287. D. Todd Christofferson, "Religious Freedom: A Cherished Heritage to Defend," (Brigham Young University devotional, June 26, 2016), speeches.byu.edu.
288. George Albert Smith, Conference Report, October 1928, 92.
289. John Taylor, *Journal of Discourses,* 20:357.
290. Joseph F, Merrill, "The Golden Rule," Conference Report, April 1950, 59.
291. Lund, *The Coming of the Lord,* 48.
292. Dallin H. Oaks, "The Divinely Inspired Constitution," *Ensign,* February 1992, 6.
293. Albert E. Bowen, Conference Report, October 1946, 52.
294. George Albert Smith, Conference Report, October 1922, 96.
295. Franklin D. Richards, *Journal of Discourses,* 26:171.
296. Delbert L. Stapley, Conference Report, October 1963, 101.
297. George Albert Smith, *Latter-Day Prophets Testify of the Savior* (Salt Lake City: Deseret Book, 1990), 113.
298. Brigham Young, *Journal of Discourses,* 9:5.
299. Antoine R. Ivins, Conference Report, October 1918, 49.
300. "Virginia Bill of Rights, §16 (12 June 1776)," in Samuel Eliot Morison, ed., *Sources and Documents Illustrating the American Revolution, 1764–1788, and the Formation of the Federal Constitution,* 2nd ed. (London: Oxford University Press, 1965), 151; emphasis added.
301. Alexis de Tocqueville, *The Old Regime and the Revolution,* vol. 1, ed. François Furet and Françoise Mélonio, trans. Alan S. Kahan (Chicago: University of Chicago Press, 1998), 206.
302. D. Todd Christofferson, "Religious Freedom: A Cherished Heritage to Defend," BYU Speeches, June 26, 2016, https://speeches.byu.edu/talks/d-todd-christofferson/religious-freedom-cherished-heritage-defend/.
303. Harold B. Lee, *Ye Are the Light of the World* (Salt Lake City: Deseret Book, 1974), 174–75.

304. Wilford Woodruff, Conference Report, April 1898, 89–90.
305. Ezra Taft Benson, *God, Family, Country: Our Three Great Loyalties* (Salt Lake City: Deseret Book Company, 1974), 405.
306. Lee, *Ye Are the Light of the World*, 176–77.
307. *Discourses of Brigham Young*, ed. John A. Widtsoe (Salt Lake City: Deseret Book, 1954), 2:175.
308. John Taylor, *Journal of Discourses*, 23:62.
309. Joseph Smith, History Draft, 1 January–31 December 1840,5, *The Joseph Smith Papers*, https://www.josephsmithpapers.org/paper-summary/history-draft-1-january-31-december-1840/5.
310. Joseph Smith, History, 1838–1856, volume D-1 [1 August 1842–1 July 1843],1553, The Joseph Smith Papers, https://www.josephsmithpapers.org/paper-summary/history-1838-1856-volume-d-1-1-august-1842-1-july-1843/196.
311. Joseph Smith, History, 1838–1856, volume E-1 [1 July 1843–30 April 1844], 1805, The Joseph Smith Papers, https://www.josephsmithpapers.org/paper-summary/history-1838-1856-volume-e-1-1-july-1843-30-april-1844/177.
312. John Taylor, *Journal of Discourses*, October 6, 1879, 20:318.
313. Ibid., June 8, 1883, 24:200.
314. Orson Pratt, *Deseret Evening News*, October 2, 1875, 8:265.
315. Martin Luther King Jr., "Letter from Birmingham City Jail," 16 April 1963, in *A Testament of Hope: The Essential Writings and Speeches of Martin Luther King Jr.*, ed. James M. Washington (New York: HarperCollins Publishers, 1986), 296.
316. United States Constitution, preamble.
317. Mark DeWolfe Howe, *The Garden and the Wilderness: Religion and Government in American Constitutional History* (Chicago: University of Chicago Press, 1965), 62.
318. Christofferson, "Religious Freedom."
319. Dallin H. Oaks, "The Divinely Inspired Constitution," *Ensign*, February 1992, 6.
320. Wilford Woodruff, Wilford Woodruff's Journal, July 5, 1877, 7:359.
321. Wilford Woodruff, *Journal of Discourses*, 21:301.
322. Harold B, Lee, N. Eldon Tanner, Marion G. Romney, "The First Presidency Statement on the Constitution," *Ensign*, November 1973, 90.
323. George Albert Smith, Conference Report, October 1992, 9.
324. Oaks and Gilbert, "Stand Fast with Love in Proclaiming Truth."
325. J. Reuben Clark, "Message of the First Presidency," Conference Report, April 1942, 90.
326. John Q. Cannon, *Journal of Discourses*, 25:211.
327. Mark E. Petersen, "The Savor of Men," *Ensign*, November 1976.
328. D. Todd Christofferson, "A Celebration of Religious Freedom," Church Newsroom, April 29, 2015, https://newsroom.churchofjesuschrist.org/article/a-celebration-of-religious-freedom.
329. Daniel H. Wells, *Journal of Discourses*, 10:7.
330. Hugh B. Brown, *Loyalty to our Country the Abundant Life* (Salt Lake City, Deseret Book), 347.
331. Orson F. Whitney, *Journal of Discourses*, 26:200.
332. John Taylor, *The Gospel Kingdom* (Salt Lake City: Deseret Book, 1943), 309.
333. Stephen L Richards. "The Gospel of Jesus Christ the Need of the World," Conference Report, April 1944, 75–77.
334. Albert E, Bowen, Conference Report, April 1943, 112.
335. Richard R. Lyman, "Faith the Only Remedy," Conference Report, April 1941, 66.

336. George Albert Smith, J. Reuben Clark, David O. McKay, "Warning on Communism, July 3, 1936," in Messages of the First Presidency, Vol. 6, ed. James R. Clark (Salt Lake City: Deseret Book, 1953), 17.
337. Melvin J, Ballard, Conference Report, April 1937, 93.
338. John Q. Cannon, *Journal of Discourses,* 25:216.
339. "Epistle to the Saints in General Conference, March 1886," in *Messages of the First Presidency,* vol. 3, edited by James R. Clark (Salt Lake City: Deseret Book Company, 1966), 46–71.
340. Wilford Woodruff, *Journal of Discourses,* 12:275.
341. Melvin J, Ballard, Conference Report, April 1930, 156–57.
342. Orson F. Whitney, "Lincoln and Joseph Smith," Conference Report, October 1926, 94.
343. Stephen L. Richards, Conference Report, October 1923, 46–47.
344. Wilford Woodruff, *Journal of Discourses,* 12:275.
345. George Albert Smith, Conference Report, April 1922, 48–49.
346. D. Todd Christofferson, "A Celebration of Religious Freedom," Church Newsroom, April 29, 2015, https://newsroom.churchofjesuschrist.org/article/a-celebration-of-religious-freedom.
347. Ezra Taft Benson, "A Four-Fold Hope" (Brigham Young University devotional, 24 May 1961), speeches.byu.edu.
348. Heber J. Grant, "Lincoln and Law," *Improvement Era,* February 1940, 127.
349. Oaks and Gilbert, "Stand Fast with Love in Proclaiming Truth."
350. *The Discourses of Wilford Woodruff,* ed. G. Homer Durham (Salt Lake City: Deseret Book, 1946), 269–70.
351. Neal A. Maxwell, "Insights from My Life" (Brigham Young University devotional, October 1976), speeches.byu.edu.
352. Joseph Fielding Smith, "Blessed is the Nation Whose God is the Lord," Conference Report, April 1943, 11.
353. Lorenzo Snow, *Journal of Discourses,* 14:304.
354. Wilford Woodruff, *Journal of Discourses,* 22:236.
355. Ezra Taft Benson, Conference Report, April 1965.
356. Joseph F. Smith, Conference Report, October 1912, 8.
357. Ezra Taft Benson, "The Constitution: A Heavenly Banner" (Brigham Young University devotional, September 16, 1986), speeches.byu.edu.
358. *Capitol Square Review and Advisory Board v. Pinette,* 515 U.S. 753, 760 (1995).
359. Christofferson, "Religious Freedom."
360. Orson Hyde, *Journal of Discourses,* January 3, 1858, 6:152.
361. Ezra Taft Benson, *God, Family, Country: Our Three Great Loyalties* (Salt Lake City: Desert Book Co., 1974), 385.
362. David O. McKay, *The Instructor,* February 1956, 34.
363. Ezra Taft Benson, *Title of Liberty* (Salt Lake City: Bookcraft, 1964), 91.
364. Brigham Young, *Journal of Discourses,* July 15, 1860, 8:123.
365. Joseph Smith, Letter to Noah C. Saxton, January 4, 1833,18, *The Joseph Smith Papers,* https://www.josephsmithpapers.org/paper-summary/letter-to-noah-c-saxton-4-january-1833/5.
366. Joseph Smith, Discourse, between circa 26 June and circa 4 August 1839–A, as Reported by Willard Richards,71, *The Joseph Smith Papers,* https://www.josephsmithpapers.org/paper-summary/discourse-between-circa-26-june-and-circa-4-august-1839-a-as-reported-by-willard-richards/9.

367. Daniel H. Wells, "Kingdom of God and the Governments of Men," *Journal of Discourses,* 8:371.
368. Delbert L. Stapley, "The Glorious Standard," October 1963, 101.
369. Ezra Taft Benson, "Be Not Deceived," Conference Report, October 1963.
370. Harold B. Lee, *Ye Are The Light of the World* (Salt Lake City: Deseret Book, 1974), 341–42.
371. George Albert Smith, "Obedience to Law," Conference Report, October 1924, 45–46.
372. Ezra Taft Benson, *Title of Liberty* (Salt Lake City: Bookcraft, 1964), 176.
373. Joseph B. Wirthlin, "Earning Our Heritage," *Finding Peace in Our Lives* (Salt Lake City: Deseret Book, 1995), 138.
374. Dallin H. Oaks, "Loving Others and Living with Differences," *Ensign,* November 2014.
375. George Albert Smith, *Church News,* February 16, 1946, 8.
376. Lorenzo Snow, *Journal of Discourses,* 14:301.
377. Neal A. Maxwell, "Insights from My Life" (Brigham Young University devotional, October 1976), speeches.byu.edu.
378. John Taylor, *Journal of Discourses,* 11:92.
379. Maxwell, *Moving in His Majesty & Power,* 31–33.
380. John Taylor, *Journal of Discourses,* 26:39.
381. Benson, *Title of Liberty,* 168.
382. John Taylor, *Journal of Discourses,* 22:144.
383. George Albert Smith, Conference Report, October 1924, 45.
384. John Taylor, *Journal of Discourses,* 22:295–96.
385. Maxwell, "Insights from My Life."
386. Brigham Young, *Journal of Discourses,* 2:32.
387. John Taylor, *Journal of Discourses,* August 31, 1879, 21:8.
388. Mark E. Petersen. "Freedom Essential for Restoration of the Gospel," Conference Report, April 1946, 169.
389. David B. Haight, "Filling the Whole Earth," *Ensign,* May 1990, 24.
390. George A. Smith, *Journal of Discourses,* 11:180.
391. John Taylor, *Journal of Discourses,* 26:156.
392. Ezra Taft Benson, *An Enemy Hath Done This* (Salt Lake City: Parliament Publishers, 1969), 28.
393. Mark E. Peterson, *The Great Prologue* (Salt Lake City: Deseret Book, 1975), 74.
394. Christofferson, "Religious Freedom."
395. Neal A. Maxwell, "The Lonely Sentinels of Democracy," *New Era,* July 1972.
396. Russell M. Nelson, "Peacemakers Needed," *Liahona,* April 2023, 98–100.

About the Author

Mary Jane Woodger, Ed.D., is a professor of Church history and doctrine at Brigham Young University. Born and raised in American Fork and Salt Lake City, Utah, Mary Jane has always had a great love for teaching. After obtaining a bachelor's degree in home economics education, she taught home economics and American history in Salt Lake City. She then completed her master of education degree at Utah State University, and received from Brigham Young University a doctor of education degree in educational leadership, with a minor in Church history and doctrine.

Since then, Dr. Woodger has written and published over twenty books including three books about the life and teachings of David O. McKay. She has also authored numerous articles on doctrinal, historical, and educational subjects. These articles have appeared in various academic journals, as well as the Journal of Mormon History, Mormon Historical Studies, the Ensign, and The Religious Educator. Awards Dr. Woodger has received include the Richard Lloyd Anderson Research Award, Best Article of the Year Award from the Utah Historical Society, the Brigham Young University Faculty Women's Association Teaching Award, The Harvey B. Black and Susan Easton Black Outstanding Publication Award and the Alice Louise Reynolds Women-in-Scholarship Honor. Dr. Woodger's current research interests include twentieth-century Church history, Latter-day Saint women's history, and Church education.